Zsuzsa Kaló, Julie Tieberghien & Dirk J. Korf (Eds.)

Why?
Explanations for drug use
and drug dealing in social drug
research

PABST SCIENCE PUBLISHERS
Lengerich

Bibliographic information published by Die Deutsche Nationalbibliothek
Die Deutsche Nationalbibliothek lists this publication in the Deutsche Nationalbibliografie; detailed bibliographic data is available in the Internet at <http://dnb.ddb.de>.

European Society for Social Drugs Research Board

© 2019 PABST SCIENCE PUBLISHERS · D-49525 Lengerich
        Internet: www.pabst-publishers.com, www.pabst-science-publishers.com
        E-mail: pabst@pabst-publishers.com

Print: ISBN 978-3-95853-537-4
eBook: ISBN 978-3-95853-538-1

Cover picture: © flipfine – Fotolia.com
Formatting: μ

Printed in Germany by KM-Druck, 64823 Groß-Umstadt

This book is dedicated to Michael Agar.

From the early years, Michael H. Agar was a valuable member of the European Society for Social Drug Research (ESSD). He was a brilliant scholar, a truly nice and very generous person, a wonderful speaker at our conferences, and a passionate teacher at our summer schools. Sadly, after a courageous struggle with ALS (amyotrophic lateral sclerosis), he passed away in Santa Fe, New Mexico (USA), in May 2017.

Michael (Mike) was born in Chicago around the time of the German surrender at the end of the Second World War in 1945. At the age of 11, he moved with his parents to a town in California that he always considered his hometown – in his own words – 'a strange mix of cowboys and science'. He graduated in anthropology at Stanford University in 1967, and received a PhD in linguistics at Berkeley (University of California, USA) in 1971. Mike defined himself as an 'internationalist'. During high school, he was an exchange student in Austria and many decades later, he still spoke German fluently, with a great Austrian accent. As a bachelor student, was a fieldworker in a small village in South India and then 'returned to enjoy the shift from beer to marijuana' that had occurred in his absence. Instead of becoming a South Asianist, he turned into a lifelong drug expert. He taught at several universities in the US and abroad, and ended his academic career as emeritus professor of Anthropology at the University of Maryland.

Mike wrote a lot. He was the son of a journalist and a photographer and considered himself a craftsman who worked with ideas rather than materials. His first book, Ripping and Running, was an ground-breaking study into the daily lives of drug users that opened new directions in ethnography. *The Professional Stranger* served as a resource for many students embarking on their first fieldwork.

The editors of this book and the ESSD members mourn the loss of our esteemed colleague and friend. He leaves us with his happy memories of inspiring conversations. And with his latest book, *Culture: How to make it work in a world of hybrids,* that was published 2019.

Contents

Acknowledgements

The European Society for Social Drug Research (ESSD) was established in 1990. Its principal aim is to promote social science approaches to drug research, with special reference to the situation in Europe. Organising annual conferences and producing an annual book are core activities of the ESSD. For this year's book, participants who presented their research at the 29th annual conference at the ELTE Eötvös Loránd University in Budapest in October 2018, and other members of the ESSD, were invited to submit a chapter outline on the theme of evidence, research and policy. After a first review of these outlines by the editorial team, a selection of authors were invited to submit papers which were then peer reviewed by distinguished scholars in the field. This book contains only the chapters that were approved during this process.

We would like very much to thank the authors for their diverse and original contributions to this book, their responses to queries and comments from the editors and peer reviewers, and their adherence to deadlines. We are especially grateful to the peer reviewers for their time and scholarly contribution to the review process. Without them this book would not have been possible: Caroline Chatwin (University of Kent, UK); Claudia Costa-Storti (EMCDDA, Portugal); Marcel de Kort (Ministry of Health, the Netherlands); Peter Degkwitz (Universitätsklinikum Hamburg-Eppendorf, Germany); Oskar Enghoff (University of Manchester, UK); Pekka Hakkarainen (Finnish National Institute for Health and Welfare, Finland); Gerrit Kamphausen (Goethe-Universität, Germany); Susanne MacGregor (London School of Hygiene and Tropical Medicine, UK); Karenza Moore (University of Salford, UK); Levente Móró (University of Turku, Finland); Leah Moyle (Royal Holloway University of London, UK); Alastair Roy (University of Central Lancashire, UK); Moritz Rosenkranz (Universitätsklinikum Hamburg-Eppendorf, Germany); Kostas Skliamis (University of Amsterdam, the Netherlands); Rebecca Stone (Suffolk University, US); Sharon R. Sznitman (University of Haifa, Israel); Meropi Tzanetakis (University of Vienna, Austria); Jaime Waters (Sheffield Hallam University, UK); Chris Wilkins (Massey University, New Zealand); Damian Zaitch (Utrecht University, the Netherlands); and Heike Zurhold (Universitätsklinikum Hamburg-Eppendorf, Germany).

We would like to offer a special thank you to our fellow members of the ESSD board Jane Fountain, Tom Decorte, Aileen O'Gorman Gary R. Potter and Bernd Werse for their work to prepare this book for publication, and for their ongoing support, advice and encouragement.

Editors

Zsuzsa Kaló is a Senior Lecturer in Psychology at the Institute of Psychology, ELTE Eötvös Loránd University, Budapest, Hungary. She is a linguist and a psychologist. Her primary research interests are NPS, female drug use and interdisciplinary qualitative research methods. Zsuzsa participated on the summer school for PhD students by the European Society for Social Drug Research (ESSD) in 2009 and became an active member of the society. She organised the annual conference in Budapest in 2018.

Julie Tieberghien is a Lecturer and a Researcher at the Centre for Research and Expertise in Social Innovation (CRESI) of VIVES University College, Belgium. Her main areas of research are the media framings of (il)legal drugs, drug use among young people, drug policy analysis, newsmaking criminology, qualitative research methodology, and risk management and applied security issues. Her most recent book is Change or continuity in drug policy: the roles of science, media, and interest groups (published by Routledge). Julie Tieberghien has been an active member of the ESSD since 2007 and she became a member of the ESSD Board in 2017.

Dirk J. Korf is a Professor of Criminology and director of the Bonger Institute of Criminology at the University of Amsterdam, Netherlands. He has been a member of the ESSD since its first conference in 1990 and has served as the chair of the society for over 20 years. Dirk is also member of the Scientific Committee of the EMCDDA. His main fields of research are patterns and trends in drug use and drug trafficking, drug policy, and crime and crime prevention. He has published numerous papers, reports and books on these issues.

1
Why?
Explanations for drug use and drug dealing in social drug research

Dirk J. Korf, Julie Tieberghien & Zsuzsa Kaló

1 What drives humans to use drugs?

For thousands of years, humans have been using substances that today are called 'drugs', to, for example, relieve pain, to relax, to gain energy, or in the course of cultural and religious rituals (Völger, von Welck & Legnaro, 1981). Furthermore, psychopharmacologist Siegel (1989) has argued that the pursuit of drugs is not only to be found across time and among humans, but across species. He even defined the desire for drugs as a fourth drive, alongside hunger, thirst, and sex.

'In a sense, intoxication allows animals to be in a different state, to act differently and to feel different. After sampling the numbing nectar of certain orchids, bees drop to the ground in temporary stupor, then weave back for more. Birds gorge themselves on inebriating berries, then fly with reckless abandon. Cats eagerly sniff aromatic "pleasure" plants, then play with imaginary objects. Cows that browse special range weeds will twitch, shake and stumble back to the plants for more' (Siegel, 1989, p. 11).

On the other hand, again from a biological angle, the contemporary discourse on drugs has become more and more framed in terms of actions of the brain, with a strong focus on the role of genetic aspects of drug use and addiction. Whilst not ignoring that genetic and biological variations make some individuals more susceptible to drug use and addiction, sociologists Granfield and Reinarman (2015) argue that defining addiction as a brain disease is an expression of a narrow disease ideology leads to biological reductionism. Instead, they plea for a more balanced contextual approach to addiction – and, more broadly, substance use.

In his classic study *Drug, Set, and Setting,* Norman Zinberg (1984) argued that drug use can only be understood in terms of the interaction between the drug (including the ways, doses and frequency in which the substance is taken), the person who takes it (the set) and the social and physical environment in which use takes place (the setting).

The blanket term 'drugs' is shorthand for a variety of psychoactive, intoxicating substances. The contemporary assortment is much larger than plant-based intoxicants such as marihuana and hashish, opium, coca leaves, or ayahuasca, and includes chemical transformations (e.g. cocaine, heroin) and hundreds of synthetic drugs (e.g. LSD, amphetamines, MDMA). Different drugs are associated with different effects or 'highs'. Yet even the use of the same drug can have divergent meanings (Fountain & Korf, 2007). A typical example is cocaine, a drug that unlike many other illicit drugs, is taken both recreationally (and could thus be considered a party drug) and by 'hard' drug users, who either inject it after dissolving powder cocaine in water or smoke it in the form of crack. It is particularly the latter group of users that have helped foster the image of cocaine as a strongly addictive drug. In terms of set, the sniffing of cocaine has long been associated with socially successful, prosperous individuals and luxury self-indulgence, while injecting the same substance dissolved in water or smoking it in a crack pipe are sure signs of social marginalisation (cf. Decorte & Slock, 2005). In other words, cocaine may symbolise either affluence or poverty and social exclusion (Wouters, Fountain & Korf, 2012).

To explain differences in substance use at individual level (set), research on alcohol and cannabis use has distinguished between 'coping motives' and 'enhancement motives'. In the case of alcohol, when used for coping, it serves as a means to deal with problems: coping motives are therefore negative motives. If people are driven by coping motives, drinking alcohol heightens their risk of misuse and dependency and of exacerbating other problems. If they are guided by enhancement motives, they have positive reasons to drink, such as pleasure and conviviality. A comparable differential approach has been applied to marijuana in recent years, yielding results strikingly similar to earlier empirical findings on alcohol (Simons, Gaher, Correia, Hansen & Christopher, 2005; Lee, Neighbors & Woods, 2007; Benschop et al., 2015).

Reasons or motives for drug use may change within the same individual over time, such as during the transition from adolescence into adulthood. The preference of young cannabis users may be for the 'strongest high' (high dose, deep inhalation, potent weed); the desires of more veteran users seem to shift to the 'consistent high' (lower dose, milder cannabis, shallower inhalation or smaller amounts of potent varieties); and, for those still smoking at an older age, to a 'steady quantity', whereby cannabis is smoked mostly alone at home and users are less inclined to adjust inhalation depth to cannabis potency (Korf, Benschop & Wouters, 2007).

For Zinberg (1984), the setting was a strong influence – maybe even the strongest one – on how drug users perceive and experience the effects of a particular drug. For example, the media labelling of MDMA as a 'love drug' and as 'ecstasy' almost certainly gave a boost to its explosive spread in the late 1980s and 1990s. The use of MDMA became typically associated with electronic dance music clubs, raves and festivals. Yet, Measham and Moore (2009) also showed that prevalence rates in the use of MDMA – as well as other substances – can strongly differ between clubs, even within the same city. Probably the strongest evidence for the importance of setting in understanding drug use in humans was found by Robbins, Davis & Goodwin (1974), who, in their classic study of US veterans who used heroin in Vietnam, found that the vast majority did not continue to use the drug once they were removed from the war zone and had returned to their home town. However, people do not simply have a free choice in where they grow up, live, and in whether or not they encounter or are exposed to drugs:

> 'Take as an example the career of a stereotypical "street addict." Before he [sic] could become addicted to, say, heroin or crack cocaine, those drugs had to be available – geographically and culturally – in the neighborhoods and the social circles in which he moved. He had to learn from others that such drug use was acceptable and desirable [...]. Not just anyone in any peer group is likely to regularly smoke crack cocaine or inject heroin into their vein' (Granfield & Reinarman, 2015, p. 8).

In search for explanations as to why so many people in the 21st century use drugs, and why in such a wide variety, several macro level factors or drivers need to be addressed.

A first and obvious factor appears to be scientific advancement and technological innovation. Already in the course of the 19th century, the upcoming pharmaceutical industry transformed opium into morphine, and later into heroin (Courtwright, 1982). This pharmaceutical evolution had a strong impact on another influential factor: military and war. During the US Civil War and the First and Second World Wars, morphine was abundantly prescribed to injured soldiers to relieve pain, and morphine addiction became known as 'soldiers' disease'. Morphine – and to some extent heroin, too, in the US in the early 1900s – was also clandestinely taken away from military drug depots, and became an attractive market for drug dealers (Kaplan, 1986). The same phenomenon occurred with synthetic drugs. According to Rasmussen (2008), the German Blitzkrieg at the start of the Second World War was powered by speed – i.e. pervitin (methamphetamine) and benzedrine (amphetamine) – as much as it was powered by machine. While the German military soon adopted a cautious approach, the British and US military sanctioned amphetamine use. Allied military dispensed speed for its subjective mood-altering effects, and Japanese soldiers used the drug to inspire the fighting spirit. Benzedrine was even more often used in the Vietnam War, with '30–40 tablets per service man per year consumption rate' (Rasmussen, 2008, p. 84).

The Vietnam War also fueled heroin use among US soldiers – not on medical prescription or from military drug depots, but from clandestine laboratories along the Vietnamese border. From the late 1960s/early 1970s onwards, when the Vietnam War was coming to an end, the illicit heroin market moved to Europe, where the drug found its way into segments of the new youth culture that had evolved, not least the protest against the war and the advocation of the use of cannabis and psychedelic drugs such as LSD.

The evolution of drug use in the past decades cannot be adequately understood without taking the illegal status of those substances into account. The swift subcultural spread of drug use and drug trade took place within the context of global prohibition that started in the early 20th century, and that increasingly became the dominant approach to restricting the consumption of drugs (McAllister, 2000). As a consequence, many known psychoactive drugs are outlawed by international conventions and national statutes, with their possession and supply considered criminal offences subject to potentially severe sanctions (Potter, 2018). This has led to a drugs market that works as a magnet for criminals – and, in recent years, online suppliers.

With criminalisation as a core characteristic of global drug policy, scholars, in particular those in the tradition of cultural studies, have underlined the importance of stigma in understanding drug use (e.g. Becker, 1953; Young, 1971), including its role as driver for resistance against stigma (Willis, 1993). Alternatively, in the course of the 1990s, social drug research increasingly shifted from a focus on stigma, deviance and marginalised drug users to an emphasis on interpreting young people's drug use, cannabis use in the general population in particular, in terms of normalisation, whereby the drug has largely been stripped of its subcultural connotations. Scholars argue cannabis use among adolescents and young adults has normalised, i.e. has moved from the margins to the mainstream (Parker, Aldridge & Measham, 1998; Parker, 2005) and can be seen as an unremarkable facet of an otherwise conventional way of life (Asbridge, Valleriani, Kwok & Erickson, 2016). More recently, cannabis use among older people has been examined (Lau et al., 2015; Moxon & Waters, 2016). However, frequent cannabis users may still fear stigma (Liebregts et al., 2015), and it is therefore questionable whether frequent cannabis use is normalised, or if normalisation is to be understood as a differential process and only applies to non-frequent use (e.g. Sandberg, 2012).

2 Why?

Chapters in this volume contribute to the understanding of drug use, drug users, drug markets and drug policy in Europe. All the authors work in this field, and are involved in local, national or international research on drug use, drug users or drug dealers. Their research is not carried out in laboratories nor treatment centres. Some of it is predominantly conducted in libraries and archives, but most takes place elsewhere – on the streets, in nightclubs, in private drug-dealing settings. The authors are social scientists from different disciplines – anthropology, criminology, geography, economics, linguistics, psychology, sociology, social psychiatry – and many of them have an interest in, or are specifically oriented to qualitative research methods, including participant observation, informal conversations and in-depth interviews. In the search for explanations as to why particular groups turn to, or continue to use certain substances over others, why some people use drugs, why users prefer particular methods of supply, or why current drug policies exist, each of the chapters underline the utmost importance of this book, which captures many of the complexities of how drug use and drug dealing is explained, experienced and often problematised today.

Why and when? Framing and shaping European drug policy

Drug policy has always been a theme for critical reflection and discussion at ESSD conferences, especially in recent years. In the light of a growing sense that global drug policy is at a crossroads, gaining a better understanding of the contours of drug policy developments – decriminalisation or legalisation, medical or recreational use, policy success or failure, the role of evidence and experts – is as important as ever.

Rafaela de Quadros Rigoni takes up a historical lens and puts forward the questions 'Why, when and how did European countries decide to develop joint policy to tackle drug use and trade?' By applying a frame analysis to historical data, this chapter discusses how European drug policy was established during the 1970s. The author rightly points out that the focus in drug research has often been, and still is, on the establishment of international drug control, mainly ignoring the evolution of European policies on drugs. To fill this gap, Rigoni thoroughly describes the creation and first steps of the Pompidou Group and outlines the different factors triggering the regulatory interventions in the early days of European drug policy. As such, this chapter provides us with new, interesting insights into how the broader political contexts, including the role of commercial and political interests and power disputes, may explain how drug control in Europe came about and, in particular, the reasons why countries frame drug issues in different ways.

While Rigoni's chapter explores how drugs came to be framed in European drug policy, *Zsuzsa Kaló, Zsolt Demetrovics and Katalin Felvinczi* approached the framing debate from a different perspective. As drugs is one of the most polarised subjects, the often inaccurate construction in policy and public discourses has been a recurrent concern, not at least in relation to New Psychoactive Substances (NPS). In their chapter, they explore how the NPS users' motivations substantially deviate from what experts believe they are. The background of the study is provided by a transnational project on NPS in six European countries (Germany, Hungary, Ireland, Poland, Portugal, and the Netherlands), including a survey among current NPS users and semi-structured interviews with European experts (health and social professionals, academics, and policy experts). A secondary analysis of the qualitative data set was conducted to explore and interrelate the perspective of users and experts about motivations of use. The study supports the notion that experts' opinions and attributions are of the utmost importance, as they may have an impact on formulating treatment, policy options, legislative directions. They also may influence the public discourse around drug-related issues.

Why and where? Role of place and space in drug use

Following the discussions in last year's ESSD book about place, space and time (Potter, 2018), some social drug researchers have deepened the questions of where and how drug use can be explained by social space and place, theoretically as well as methodologically. Two of the chapters in the current book focus on the role of place among traditional problem users in similar setting (the streets), using both new and old research methods.

Luise Klaus and Melina Germes address the relevant question of how we, drug researchers, are challenged to develop new research methodologies. Taking a unique perspective employed in social geography, they propose in their chapter a new method to study urban lived spaces of drug users in cities. Emotional mapping aims to obtain maps and narratives about how drug users inhabit public and private spaces, their everyday interactions, and the emotions they associate with these spaces. Overall, Klaus and Germes provide social drug researchers with innovative insights on how to study inner-city neighbourhoods drug scenes from the perspective of the users. Luise Klaus was honoured with the Early Career Researcher Award for her presentation on this issue at the 2018 annual ESSD conference in Budapest (Klaus, 2018).

Taken with other recent contributions – particularly last year's book chapter (Werse & Egger, 2018) – *Bernd Werse and Lukas Sarvari* add to an ever-increasing understanding of the Frankfurt open drug scene. At the same time, both authors contribute to an important understanding of the fluidity and dynamism of drug-using scenes in a city. Their study involves the qualitative content analysis of 30 semi-structured interviews. They skilfully describe the strong connection between patterns of crack cocaine use and the social space of the well-known Bahnhofsviertel in Frankfurt. Their study gives an insight to why and where users are living by putting forward the important trigger effect of the geographical setting. The chapter definitely improves the understanding of why people take drugs and/or why drug scenes differ in different places.

Why and in which direction? Normalisation versus stigma

The normalisation thesis is one of the most significant theoretical developments to have emerged in drug literature (e.g. Sznitman & Taubman, 2016), proposing that drug use becomes less stigmatised and more accepted as normative behaviour. The processes of normalisation and the (often) internalised stigma by the users are still highly relevant topics as outlined by two chapters in this volume. How the normalisation process influences the external and internal moral regulations and how it may affect the motivations for drug use are important questions raised by two chapters in this volume.

The chapter by *Marco Rossi* adds to the literature by identifying the typical evolution of cannabis consumers' careers through a process of normalisation within a theoretical framework of economics. In particular, Rossi focuses on the place of cannabis in the lives of aging cannabis users. Interestingly, he illustrates that adult users go through a process of social integration and normalisation, during which they change their patterns of use and socio-economic status over the years. The result is a unique economic look at the social benefit of market restrictions and the optimal tolerable quantity of cannabis consumption. Furthermore, Rossi argues that current policy responses are not likely to be grounded in the reality of the aging of cannabis users. He advocates an age-based regulation for cannabis – as applied in cases such as tobacco, alcohol, gambling, etc.

Michelle Van Impe aims to critically explore existing qualitative work on illegal drug use in relation to narrative identity and boundary work, thus contributing to the understanding of (internalised) stigma by users. In particular, her starting point is the question of how to develop a richer and fuller understanding of narrative struggles and empathy in (re)negotiating intra-group stigma. The conceptual understanding of stigma is absolutely relevant and important, although the role of stigma cannot be overstated. By means of a qualitative meta-synthesis (QMS), the study concludes that personal and social narrative identities are fluid and interactional and that drug research could benefit from further insights into how both these identities jointly (re)construct narrative struggles, identities and boundaries. From this perspective, Van Impe emphasises the need for more participatory and interactive research with heterogeneous groups of drug users.

Why and how to get drugs? Drug markets

Two of our chapters focus on drug markets and, particularly, address why some types of drugs are more present in some markets than others and why users turn to, or prefer certain types of online or offline dealing. Both chapters reflect how the market dynamics and the users' behaviours (and motivations) have changed because of the recent cultural-technological changes. Both studies observed and explored the experiences of the users.

The chapter by *Thomas Friis Søgaard* focuses on users' motives for sourcing drugs through delivery services. His research on drop-off delivery – including interviews with drug users in Denmark and an analysis of dealer-user communications – provides in-depth views on buyers' experiences of sourcing drugs from delivery dealers. Interestingly, he observes that the business of drop-off delivery entails benefits such as speed and convenience with which particular types of drugs – mostly cannabis and cocaine – can be obtained and, at the same time, involves new risks and concerns. Against the background that this supply model is likely to become more common in the coming years, this chapter engages further investigations on how drug policies influence the proliferation, organisation and buyer experiences of the drop-off supply model.

The role of trust in drug user communities has been critically assessed by *Ximene Rego, Jakub Greń and Olga S. Cruz*. Their chapter reflects the changes in the drug use and motivations caused by the social, economic and cultural transformation in globalisation and the recent innovations in the 'digital era'. Rego and colleagues explore how the role of trust is shaping online and offline Portuguese drug user communities. They invited 34 participants to four focus groups and, among several topics, participants discussed the role of trust in the online and offline communities. The authors' findings show that distrust may play an important role in participating or avoiding online business transactions. Their chapter also provides thoughtful considerations about online harm reduction opportunities.

Why and how to understand? Different meanings attached to drug use

The use or non-use of psychoactive substances, and the type, frequency and history of use have carried strong symbolic meaning. While pleasure is considered a typical experience of recreational drug use, it is absent in discourses on medical treatments. At the same time, governments around the world have developed a variety of policies intended to influence whether or not individuals decide to use drugs and to affect the meanings of use for the individual and the society. Meaning is socially fabricated: in short, symbolic. Two chapters of this volume address this significant issue.

Based on her study about the self-reported medicinal cannabis use in Flanders, *Frédérique Bawin* unravels the meaning of the concept of medicinal versus recreational cannabis use. Both concepts are often intertwined in users' narratives which demonstrate the complexity and the blurred boundaries between them. She highlights the need to critically rethink public and policy discourses as a way to break through existing, often stereotypical categorisations of cannabis use and users. Her chapter shows that the symbolic dimension remains important in the politics of drug use today.

This critical note is also echoed in the contribution by *Alfred Springer*. The chapter serves as a theory-driven elaboration of Bawin's empirical analysis. Springer makes some important points about the particular features of contemporary drug policies. In particular, in outlining the blurring of the boundaries between medical and non-medical use over the years, he critically debates the existing prohibitive drug policies which go beyond considering what drugs mean to those who use them. Currently, in our society where the non-medical use of psychoactive substances is illegal and generally rejected, users still run the risk of being paradoxically stigmatised and marginalised. Therefore, he urges better understanding of the search for pleasure and of the meanings that are attached to drug use in diverse cultural settings.

3   Final note

Overall, this book illustrates the unique contribution social science research can make to understanding the 'why?' of drug use, dealing and policies. For the contributions, data has been collected from archives and scientific literature, as well as from drug users, experts, dealers, by means of surveys, semi-structured interviews, focus group discussions, observations, maps, and text messages. The researchers analysed data using frame analysis, content analysis, emotional mapping and qualitative meta-synthesis (QMS). The chapters represent the European perspective, providing insight into hidden places, secret practices and understanding of the phenomena within the broad theoretical context of social drug research. Most of all they add new knowledge and new perspectives to understanding motivations as well as explanations for drug use and drug dealing. The book clearly illustrates innovative thinking in methodological and theoretical approaches in social drug research.

References

Asbridge, M., Valleriani, J., Kwok, J., & Erickson, P.G. (2016). Normalization and denormalization in different legal contexts: comparing cannabis and tobacco. *Drugs: Education, Prevention and Policy, 23 (3),* 1–12.

Becker, H.S. (1953). Becoming a marihuana user. *American Journal of Sociology, 59 (3),* 235–242.

Benschop, A., Liebregts, N., van der Pol, P., Schaap, R., Buisman, R., van Laar, M., van den Brink, W., de Graaf, R., & Korf, D.J. (2015). Reliability and validity of the Marijuana Motives Measure among young adult frequent cannabis users and associations with cannabis dependence. *Addictive Behaviors, 40,* 91–95.

Courtwright, D.T. (1982). *Dark paradise. Opiate addiction in America before 1940s.* Cambridge (Mass.): Harvard University Press.

Decorte, T., & Fountain, J. (Eds.) (2010). *Pleasure, pain and profit. European perspectives on drugs.* Lengerich: Pabst Science Publishers.

Decorte, T., & Slock, S. (2005). *The taming of cocaine III: a 6-year follow-up study of 77 cocaine and crack users.* Brussels: VUB.

Fountain, J., & Korf, D.J. (Eds.) (2007). *Drugs in society. European perspectives.* Oxford: Radcliffe.

Granfield, R., & Reinarman, C. (Eds.) (2015). *Expanding addiction. Critical essays.* New York: Routledge.

Hathaway, A.D., Comeau, N.C., & Erickson, P.G. (2011). Cannabis normalization and stigma: contemporary practices of moral regulation. *Criminology & Criminal Justice, 11 (5),* 415–469.

Kaplan, C.D. (1986). Droge und Militär [Drugs and military]. In D. Korczak (Ed.), *Die betäubte Gesellschaft* [The intoxicated society] (pp. 155–165). Frankfurt a. M.: Fischer.

Klaus, L. (2018). *Sketch mapping – an innovative method of researching drug users.* European Society for Social Drug Research 29th Annual Conference, Budapest, 4–6 October, 2018, Book of Abstracts.

Korf, D.J., Benschop, A., & Wouters, M. (2007). Differential responses to cannabis potency: a typology of users based on self-reported consumption behaviour. *International Journal of Drug Policy, 18,* 168–176.

Lau, N., Sales, P., Averill, S., Murphy, F., Sato, S.O., & Murphy, S. (2015). Responsible and controlled use: older cannabis users and harm reduction. *International Journal of Drug Policy, 26 (8),* 709–718.

Lee, C.M., Neighbors, C., & Woods, B.A. (2007). Marijuana motives: young adult's reasons for using marijuana. *Addictive Behaviors, 31 (10),* 1384–1394.

Liebregts, N. van der Pol, P., van Laar, M., de Graaf, R., van den Brink, W., & Korf. D.J. (2015). The role of leisure and delinquency in frequent cannabis use and dependence trajectories among young adults. *International Journal of Drug Policy, 26 (2),* 143–152.

McAllister, W.B. (2000). *Drug diplomacy in the twentieth century: An international history.* London: Routledge.

Measham, F., & Moore, K. (2009). Repertoires of distinction: exploring patterns of weekend polydrug use within leisure scenes across the English night time economy. *Criminology and Criminal Justice, 9 (4),* 437–464.

Moxon, D., & Waters, J. (2016). *Illegal drug use through the lifecourse: A study of 'hidden' older drug users.* London: Routledge.

Parker, H. (2005). Normalization as a barometer: recreational drug use and the consumption of leisure by younger Britons. *Addiction Research & Theory, 13 (3),* 205–215.

Parker, H., Aldridge, J. & Measham, F. (1998). *Illegal leisure. The normalization of adolescent recreational drug use.* London: Routledge.

Potter, G.R. (2018). Introduction. Drugs, space and time. In G.R. Potter, J. Fountain, & D.J. Korf, (Eds.), *Place, space and time in European drug use, markets and policy* (pp. 11–25). Lengerich: Pabst Science Publishers.

Rasmussen, N. (2008). *On speed. The many lives of amphetamine.* New York: New York University Press.

Robbins, L., Davis, D.H., & Goodwin, D.W. (1974). Drug use in U.S. army enlisted men in Vietnam: a follow-up on their return home. *American Journal of Epidemiology, 99,* 235–249.

Sandberg, S. (2012). Is cannabis use normalized, celebrated or neutralized? Analysing talk as action. *Addiction Research & Theory, 20 (5),* 372–381.

Siegel, R.K. (1989). *Intoxication. Life in pursuit of artificial paradise.* New York: Dutton.

Simons, J.S., Gaher, R.M., Correia, C.J., Hansen, C.L., & Christopher, M.S. (2005). An affective-motivational model of marijuana and alcohol problems among college students. *Psychology of Addictive Behaviors, 19 (5),* 326–334.

Sznitman, S.R., & Taubman, D.S. (2016). Drug use normalization: a systematic and critical mixed-methods review. *J Stud Alcohol Drugs, 77 (5),* 700–709.

Völger, G., von Welck, K., & Legnaro, A. (Eds.) (1981). *Rausch und Realität. Drogen im Kulturvergleich* [Intoxication and reality. Drugs in cross-cultural perspective.] Cologne: Rautenstrauch-Joest-Museum für Völkerkunde.

Werse, B., & Egger, D. (2018). 'I don't do this to get rich'. Dynamics of private low-key and street drug dealing careers. In G.R. Potter, J. Fountain, & D.J. Korf (Eds.), *Place, space and time in European drug use, markets and policy* (pp. 27–43). Lengerich: Pabst Science Publishers.

Willis, P.E. (1993). The cultural meaning of drug use. In S. Hall, & T. Jefferson (Eds.), *Resistance through rituals: Youth subcultures in post-war Britain* (pp. 106–118). London: Routledge. (Original work published in 1975).

Wouters, M., Fountain, J., & Korf, D.J. (Eds.) (2012). *The meaning of high. Variations according to drug, set, setting and time.* Lengerich: Pabst Science Publishers.

Young, J. (1971). *The drugtakers.* London: Paladin.

Zinberg, N.E. (1984). *Drug, set, and setting: the basis for controlled intoxicant use.* New Haven: Yale University Press.

2
Controlling drugs in Europe: the first collaboration attempts

Rafaela de Quadros Rigoni

While robust literature discusses the establishment of an international drug control regime, not much has been written on how drug control in Europe was created. Why, when and how did European countries decide to develop joint policy to tackle drug use and trade? This historical chapter describes the context of the first European collaboration around drug policies in the 1970s, with the creation of the Pompidou Group. The analysis focuses on the factors triggering regulatory interventions in the early days of European drug policy. The chapter combines the concept of 'mentalities of government' with frame analysis to investigate the discourses of country representatives during the Pompidou Group debates, based on archival material and literature. The study shows that curbing youth protests, protecting commercial agreements and national policies, and managing international pressure were all important factors shaping the first steps of a European drug control. Concerns other than drug use, dependence or related criminality can trigger regulatory interventions in the drug field. The study thus calls attention to the need to consider the broader political context when analysing drug policies, in order to arrive to more nuanced explanations of what shapes drug policy decisions.

Keywords: drug policy, history, Europe, Pompidou Group, EEC

1 European drug control

The worldwide growth in the movement of people and goods has increasingly influenced drug use and trade. Attempts to control cross-border flows have led to the creation and development of an international drug control regime that started in the 1900s. An extensive literature has reported on the history and the (unintended) consequences of this regime. This includes the fierce influence of countries like the US in the regulation process (Bruun, Pan, & Rexed, 1975; Musto, 2010), as well as the disastrous consequences in terms of human rights violations and questionable political-economic influences over other countries

(Room & Reuter, 2012). These studies have shown that the imposition of drug regulation regimes can be triggered not so much by the effects of the drugs on people, but rather by factors such as commercial and political interests and power disputes between professional groups.

The free movement of goods and people resulting from the creation of a European common market also led to discussions about the regulation of drugs. Yet, while solid literature on the establishment of international drug control exists, not much has been written on how drug control in Europe came about. Why, when and how did European countries decide on joint action to tackle drug use and trade? A historical perspective in understanding the evolution of European policies on drugs is (still) needed (Berridge, 1996).

This historical chapter contributes to filling this gap by describing the context of the first European collaborations around drug policies in the 1970s, with the creation of the Pompidou Group – Co-operation Group to Combat Drug Abuse and Illicit Trafficking in Drugs (hereafter PG). The group was founded as a European co-operation body at government level. Experts met regularly to debate health, prevention, law enforcement and legislation harmonisation regarding drug use and trade in the European Economic Community (EEC). Recommendations on planning coordinated actions were discussed and approved at ministerial meetings of the European Council. Set as an advisory body, the PG could only influence drug decision-making indirectly through its guidelines and recommendations. Nevertheless, as the only European discussion platform on the subject of drugs in the 1970s, the group played an important role in setting the framework for the establishment of a European drug control regime (Brule, 1983; Pompidou Group, 2017). Despite its importance, the PG workings during the 1970s are a largely unknown chapter of European drug policy history. Historical studies in the drug field only briefly mention the group (e.g de Kort, 1995; Boekhout van Solinge, 2002), and more recent studies on drug policies within the European Union (EU) do not mention it at all (e.g. Chatwin, 2011; Ysa, 2014). The few academic studies on the PG focus either on the group's structure and functioning (Brule, 1983; Nagler, 1987), or on specific actions it has taken (Hartnoll, Avico, Ingold, et al., 1989; Hartnoll, 1994; Simon, Donmall, Hartnoll, et al., 1999). The PG might have been neglected by researchers due to its advisory-only role, along with the emergence of more influential groups on EU drug policies in the last decades. Not addressing its role, however, is a mistake. The PG was the first – and only in the 1970s – to collectively debate and advise on EEC drug policies. As such, it has set the fundamentals of a drug regulation regime in Europe. Understanding its history can bring valuable insights into the factors and actors triggering drug regulations in Europe.

This chapter contributes to uncovering these first collaborations. Based on archival material and literature, it analyses how countries have framed a drug problem and regulatory interventions for it while trying to reach common grounds for European drug policy. Special attention is given to how and why definitions of a 'drug problem' have shifted in the debates over the course of the 1970s. Five different periods are described, each one representing specific timeframes of drug problems as discussed in the PG: an invitation to form a group to combat drugs (1971); finding a common drug problem definition (1971–1972); fighting the heroin epidemic (1973–1976); responding to the International Convention's framing (1973–1974); and fighting against production in drug-producing countries (1977–1980). A new phase of the Pompidou Group that started in 1980s is also briefly described.

2   Theoretical framework and methodology

While choosing a drug policy direction, different perspectives on what is desirable must be negotiated among a variety of actors. In this battlefield of definitions, perceptions about drugs and the problems they might bring are at stake, along with ideas on desirable regulations to avoid or resolve the problems. Policy positions rest 'on underlying structures of belief, perception, and appreciation, which we [can] call frames' (Schön & Rein, 1995, p. 23). They shape the way we view a subject such as drug use or trade as a specific type of problem in need of certain regulatory interventions.

Dean (2010) coined the term 'mentalities of governance' to explain how we understand and construct the need for regulating behaviours and activities, and how we organise regulation. He proposed looking at four aspects to investigate different mentalities of governance: what we seek to act upon; how we govern; who we are when we are governed in such a way; and which aims we want to achieve with it. The present chapter combines the concept of mentalities of government with frame analysis to identify underlying structures of belief and perceptions in the discourses of country representatives during the PG debates. This combination helps in identifying for this start of a drug control regime in Europe:
a) what was defined by representatives as a problem concerning drugs;
b) what their proposed solutions, or regulatory interventions were; and
c) what the aim of the regulation was.
By mapping how the framings shift over the decade and contextualising them, the chapter offers interpretations for why such a regime to control drugs was developed in the PG.

This chapter draws its analysis from archival data and literature. The Dutch National Archives, the archives for the Dutch Parliament (Staten Generaal Digitaal), the Nederlandse Staatscourant, and the online archives of the Pompidou Group of the Council of Europe were consulted. Archival material and literature were analysed and coded in NVivo software. The focus on Dutch archives as a primary source imposes limitations on the findings of this chapter, but does not invalidate its contribution. Ideally, a historical research on the emergence of

European drug control would require the analysis of archives from all countries partaking in the collaboration. Such endeavour, nevertheless, is beyond the scope of this chapter. To minimise the restrictions of a Dutch perspective only, for most of its analysis, the chapter draws on the official reports of the PG that were available in the Dutch archives, rather than on Dutch-specific summaries and preparatory documents which contain more country-based interpretations. The use of literature also helped to decrease bias by bringing the broader historical context into perspective. Words in italics in the text come from the archival records consulted and where they were in languages other than English, they have been translated. The original language is acknowledged in the references.

3   A French invitation to combat drugs (1971)

On the 6th of August 1971, the French president George Pompidou addressed a letter to the five members of the EEC – the Netherlands, Germany, Belgium, Luxemburg and Italy – and the United Kingdom, which was on the verge of becoming a member. Pompidou's letter invited the governments to participate in a joint effort to combat drugs:

> *'The spectacular development of addiction is very worrying. [...] There is a danger of incalculable consequences for our society and its future. Leaders must grasp the problem and organize the defence of the youth against a temptation of which they do not measure the dangers, and which the traffickers shamelessly arise, maintain and exploit, often with impunity'* (Pompidou, 1971, p. 1).

Three months later, delegations of all invited countries met Pompidou and the French delegation in Paris for a first meeting. The hosts framed the drug problem as alarming and requiring urgent and strict measures. The European youth using heroin and cannabis were framed as the victims of evil drug dealers. Users needed medical treatment for abstinence, while dealers were enemies to be targeted with strong repression. The French widely used words like *combat, force, victory* and *scourge* to strengthen the frame of fighting drugs as a necessity (French Delegation, 1971). If the French framed the drug problem as a rise in drug addiction (therefore, at the user end), the regulation they proposed was to intervene in the drug trade instead.

The reason behind this twist, and the very invitation to form a joint European front to combat drugs, lay beyond drug problems in Europe. US president Nixon was under pressure due to the increasing number of American soldiers who were becoming dependent on heroin and supply was largely coming via Europe. According to US narcotics experts, Marseille had become the centre for heroin processing. From the poppy fields in Turkey to the heroin refineries in Marseille, drug routes were passing through Italy and Germany, and sometimes Belgium and the Netherlands, before reaching the US (Matthew, 1971). The American government proposed to solve the heroin addiction problem by fighting heroin trafficking, and that implied interventions in the EEC countries.

President Pompidou was already helping president Nixon in organising secret meetings in Paris to negotiate the end of the war in Vietnam (Nixon, 1972). Leading the development of a European front to combat drugs could only help in alleviating US pressure related to heroin trafficking. As president Pompidou explained to other EEC members at the first meeting of the PG, this joint action could both protect European youth and rupture the illegal heroin supply to the US:

> 'Our action, if it succeeds, would reach two objectives: the protection of our own countries against a scourge which threatens our youth; [and] the rupture of supply to the American clandestine market through Europe. That's why president Nixon publicly congratulated the French initiative of uniting the efforts of the Common Market countries and Great-Britain in a European front against drugs' (Pompidou Group, 1971a, p. 1).

4   Finding a common problem (1971–1972)

In December 1971 the newly created PG commissions – law enforcement, public health, education and legislation harmonisation – held a four-day meeting to start the shared debate on drugs. Despite the previous French framing of an alarming situation, other countries did not perceive heroin nor rising *addiction* as urgent national problems. The German delegation, for instance, reported an increase in national drug offences along with an emerging illicit market, but affirmed that drug use remained mostly restricted to cannabis. Belgium and Luxemburg representatives mentioned that drug dependency among youth existed but was not alarming. In Italy too, drug problems were framed as being restricted to a few students using cannabis in big cities and there was no heroin addiction nor trafficking network. The Dutch delegation also perceived cannabis to be the most used drug nationally, with heroin being rarely seen (Pompidou Group, 1971b).

PG participants framed the drug problem, instead, as a rise in cannabis use by youth, attached to a growing countercultural movement. Drug use was framed as an *adaptation problem*, leading to contestation of the mainstream culture and norms, protests, and the search for new experiences, which included drug use (Pompidou Group, 1971b). The rise of youth drug use was a new phenomenon in 1970s Europe. Up to the late 1950s, use was low and mostly related to a middle-aged population using alcohol, or health professionals and war veterans using opioids. In the 1960s, however, this situation changed. The use of drugs such as cannabis and LSD became deeply embedded in youth countercultural movements (Snelders, 1999). Youth became a metaphor of change as young people united in favour of cultural transformation and political activism, fuelled by the rise of capitalism and its mass consumption, the controversial Vietnam War, and the events of May 1968 in Paris (Weinhauer, 2006). Drug use represented a revolt in lifestyle, characterised by hedonism and the search for self-realisation instead of competition and materialism.

In the PG, members framed the rebellious drug-using youth as in need of reintegration into society and help to either resist the scourge of drugs or to completely quit their use (Pompidou Group, 1972a). At least in cities such as Berlin, London and Amsterdam, most drug-using-youth were white, western, middle-upper class and educated (Weinhauer, 2006). This might have helped following the non-criminalising framing of seeing drug-using youth as victims more than criminals.

The PG approved its first recommendations, targeting a drug-free EEC, in October 1972. Abstinence was framed as the goal of drug treatment and prevention, but no specific common regulation was recommended in this sense. Instead, the PG proposed exchanging experiences on different methods, through expert meetings, joint research, and study visits to different EEC countries. Recommendations on curbing drug trafficking, however, were stronger and more concrete. They included constraining freedom of movement to those condemned for international trafficking; strengthening partnerships through Interpol; and increasing border control (Pompidou Group, 1972b).

Therefore, surprisingly, although the PG members did not agree with the urgent framing of the French, they did engage in combating drugs. Presumably, they joined the PG to demonstrate their willingness to collaborate with other EEC members, and to prevent further problems with drugs in their own territories. The free movement of labour established in the Rome Treaty (1957) could be endangered by drug trafficking and the spread of drug use in Europe, and a concerted effort by the countries involved could help prevent that. In addition, framing the problem as an increase of drug use by rebellious youth may also have facilitated justifying national government interventions on undesirable political manifestations. Framed as a drug problem, youth protests could be targeted as dangerous and irrational, and regulated in the name of the safety of the demonstrators themselves and society at large. Further research on national contexts, however, would be necessary to confirm this hypothesis.

5   Fighting a heroin epidemic (1973–1976)

The scene of the hippie-rebel cannabis user type would soon change, as heroin became an established social problem in many big European cities. While both drug use and related offences were on the rise, the figure of the heroin junkie hit the headlines, spreading a moral panic and creating the idea of a heroin epidemic (Weinhauer, 2006). In the PG too, heroin was at the centre of concerns between 1973 and 1976. Ten countries participated in the group, as Denmark, Ireland and Sweden had joined the founding members following their integration into the EEC. Different countries had distinct responses to the new drug problem. In Berlin, for instance, the lack of an organised drug policy response meant that heroin use was mostly handled by the police, prisons, psychiatric clinics and self-help groups, whose main aim was for people to abstain from drugs. In London, on the contrary, a well-coordinated drug treatment system was in place and about half of the opioid users were frequenting clinics where heroin was available on prescription (Weinhauer, 2006). Also, in Amsterdam regulatory interventions were framed not in terms of abstinence, but rather of providing care through methadone maintenance therapy (MMT) and low-threshold facilities (Blok, 2008). At that time, MMT was only being used on a larger scale in three countries: the Netherlands, Ireland and the UK (Berridge, 2009).

The PG framed regulatory interventions on two fronts: fighting heroin addiction and fighting drug trafficking. In terms of therapeutic solutions, PG members supported a multidisciplinary drug treatment, including therapeutic communities, outreach work, low-threshold walk-in centres and rehabilitation centres. The main goal of treatment, however, was abstinence (Health Commission, 1973b).

Many PG members were suspicious of substitution therapy and thought that methadone should be provided only temporarily. Some delegations did not even want to institutionalise methadone, as they feared its availability would discourage abstinence (Health Commission, 1973b). The different national reactions led foreign heroin users to seek out services offering heroin prescription and/or MMT in other cities (such as Amsterdam and London), causing regional distress and local challenges (Korf, 1995; Weinhauer, 2006). As a solution, the PG health committee advised that either eligibility for treatment in the host country should exist, or travel should be restricted (Health Commission, 1973a). Moreover, treatment services should arrange for solutions to avoid people being arrested for carrying their treatment drugs when crossing borders (Geerlings, 1973).

As before, and perhaps due to the complexity and variety of country care responses, the final PG recommendations on prevention and health were limited to exchanging information, visits and joint research. Again, more attention and concrete efforts went into fighting drug trafficking. Interpol set up coordinated anti-drugs actions at the EEC frontiers (Interpol, 1973a). The PG recommended that each country should have permanent representatives within Interpol to coordinate actions and exchange information. Officials should receive training to specialise in drugs (Law Enforcement Commission, 1973a) and the PG budget would support the costs (Interpol, 1973b). Harmonisation of customs legislation and agreements on the extradition of people who committed drug-related crimes were also recommended (Legislation Harmonization Commission, 1973b).

6 International conventions' framing (1973–1974)

While PG members were framing heroin as a regional drug problem, a broader and stricter frame was being set by the 1961 Single Convention on Narcotic Drugs and its 1972 amendments, and by the 1971 Convention on Psychotropic Substances (United Nations, 1962, 1972). These conventions framed as problematic the non-medical and non-scientific use of a whole array of controlled substances. They criminalised their use and trade outside these purposes, and strictly forbade those substances considered worthless for either medicine or science. Countries were pressed to join this international drug control strategy. Most PG members had not ratified the conventions yet and wanted to harmonise their decision with that of other EEC countries. PG members framed as problematic the conventions' strict control over substances used for therapeutic purposes – such as appetite suppressants (amphetamines), antidepressants and sedatives (benzodiazepines and barbiturates). The need to collect vast amounts of information on the volume of production and the destination of these drugs was also framed as an enormous bureaucratic burden on EEC commercial efforts (Legislation Harmonization Commission, 1973e).

PG members, however, were seeing a growing group of middle-aged users who were becoming dependent on amphetamines and barbiturates (Legislation Harmonization Commission, 1973b). Having common regulations for these substances, they framed, could help in fighting their illegal trade and in avoiding their non-medical use (Vonhögen, 1973). The free movement of medicines within the EEC ultimately asked for common regulations to protect trade.

The PG set itself to think of possible alternatives to the International Conventions that could benefit the EEC without added burdens. Countries' different regulatory systems, however, hampered the task. The possibility of using substances such as cannabis and heroin for medical purposes, for instance, was a point of disagreement in the group. While the Netherlands and UK advocated for it, other country members framed it as problematic, as they did not see any added value for these substances in medical practice (Vonhögen, 1973). France, Luxemburg and Germany were positive about measures such as the adoption of a special prescription receipt, or a double red tag on the packaging of controlled substances. Other countries, however, framed that as an unnecessary hassle that would raise the resistance from the medical professions and the pharmaceutical industry (Legislation Harmonization Commission, 1973c). Even so, PG members shared a common framing: common regulations were needed but should not hinder their commercial agreements. PG countries should prevent a situation where

> *'On the international scene there would be an impossible number of control measures that would endanger the trade in medicines between the different states'* (Legislation Harmonization Commission, 1973d, p. 4).

Unable to draw up alternative regional regulations, the PG recommended its members to adopt the Conventions. Exceptions were made for phencyclidine ('angel dust') and some hallucinogens, which were understood not to offer a concrete danger of abuse (Vonhögen, 1973). Stronger control over precursors of hallucinogens and amphetamines, and substances with similar workings to amphetamines was also recommended (Legislation Harmonization Commission, 1973e).

The International Conventions' framing triggered the need to control the use and the trade of medical substances. Regulations were seen as problematic by PG members, given their potential for hindering the production and the commercial flow of these substances within the EEC. The process of framing regulatory interventions stressed the difficult balance between compromising international agreements, securing national policy preferences, and assuring a profitable commercial context for controlled substances in the EEC.

7   The problem lies outside Europe (1977–1980)

By 1977, the drug problem was still framed by the PG as heroin, as the group perceived consumption and seizures of the drug to be on the rise (Samson, 1977). Fighting drug trafficking continued to be framed as the main regulatory intervention, but the target of interventions changed. Previously, regulations were planned for EEC countries, but now they targeted countries producing opium. In the 1950s and 1960s, Europe was producing and manufacturing most of the heroin consumed in the region and in the US. With the phasing out of Turkey's opium production, South-East Asian countries gradually became the major heroin suppliers. South-East Asia was growing over 70 percent of the world's illicit opium in the 1970s, and Chinese laboratories were producing some of the finest heroin in the world. The region had already established drug trafficking routes and networks to Europe and the US (McCoy, 1972) and such features made South-East Asia the perfect candidate to become a world leader of heroin supply.

In 1977, the Dutch delegation, echoed by others, confirmed to the PG that heroin was entering national territories through South-East Asian and Middle-East countries (Samson, 1977). PG members framed the illicit trafficking of heroin as *threatening the public health and welfare interests of [PG] countries,* and drafted interventions around fighting poppy production in the Middle East and South-East Asia (Pompidou Group, 1977). Approved in 1977, the PG's new *plan to combat heroin use and traffic* recommended coordinated diplomatic action to address opium-producing countries to control illicit trade by partnering with Interpol, customs and UN organisations. A ban on poppy cultivation was proposed, and the PG disussed that a condition for its implementation would be offering external financial aid to contribute to the substitution of other crops. Nevertheless, UN funds were found to be limited, and the PG member countries lacked the political will to increase their contributions. The framed solution, thus, ended up being that producing countries should finance crop substitution projects themselves through cooperation with other countries and international organisations (Pompidou Group, 1978).

Agreements in terms of health and prevention were once more limited to the exchange of information and experiences between countries. The PG *plan to combat heroin use and traffic* was almost exclusively about combating the latter. Focusing on trade was perhaps a way of manoeuvring through the different political situations of PG members. Organised crime had the most obvious appeal for international collaboration, and no country seemed to be against curbing illicit drug trade. The shift in the international drug market was probably a trigger to reframe the target of regulations to outside Europe. However, combatting the situation in drug-producing countries also allowed PG country members to alleviate regional European differences by having a common enemy outside European borders.

8   A new phase for the Pompidou Group

Until 1979, the PG operated without a formal status, being supported by the country occupying its chair: France from 1971–1977 and Sweden from 1977–1979 (Nagler, 1987). By 1980, the group became an organ of the Council of Europe (CoE) with a *partial agreement* status, where participation of member states is on a voluntary basis (Pompidou Group, 1979). After the attachment to the CoE, the number of group members rapidly expanded, especially in the 1980s and 1990s. Later, this expansion slowed down, particularly among EU members (Brule, 1983). To date, the group has 38 member states, comprising both EU and non-EU countries. The PG lost its *unique* position from the mid-1990s, when other groups and committees debating drug policies arose across Europe (Brule, 1983; Pompidou Group, 2017). The European Monitoring Centre for Drugs and Drug Addiction (EMCDDA), established in 1995, and the Horizontal Working Party on Drugs (HDG), established in 1997, assumed important political roles in EU debates on drugs. Since its establishment, the HDG coordinates all drug-related matters in the EU, including the European drug strategies and action plans. HDG members sometimes sit as representatives in the PG, either on a voluntary basis or following a request. Potentially, therefore, debates in one group might influence the workings of other through these delegates.

In 2010, Germany, UK and the Netherlands left the PG. Possible reasons for that include the number of more influential groups debating drug policies in the EU, coupled with limited (human) resources, and the fee paid for PG membership (Kattau, 2018). In addition, according to an ex-representative, the inclusion into the PG of countries with more restrictive drug policies has triggered stricter directions in the group's debates (Anonymous, 2018).

Although affected by the departure of important members, the PG remains active and with a much-expanded number of working groups and a much more liberal view on drug policies when compared to the 1970s. For its principal administrator, Tomas Kattau, the group still adds important value to the drug policy debate in Europe. Its less formalised setting potentially offers more fertile ground for innovation, as discussions are less restricted by official political positions. Moreover, given its attachment to the CoE, the group has a unique focus on human rights as a transversal issue in all its activities (Kattau, 2018).

If the future role of the PG is still under debate, its past has, without doubt, been of importance. The PG's workings have set the fundaments of European drug control in the 1970s, and further attention to its history can only benefit the understanding of drug policy development in Europe.

9   The first decade of European drug control: conclusion

The PG was the only group debating drug policies at the EEC level in the 1970s. Surprisingly, this European group to combat drugs was established when (and despite that) most participating countries considered that they did not have a national drug problem. The establishment of the group was initiated by the French and backed by the US to curb heroin trafficking flows from France to the US. Presumably, countries joined the PG to demonstrate their willingness to collaborate with other EEC members, and to prevent further problems with drugs. For smooth progress of EEC commercial agreements, the PG considered that the flow of goods and people should be protected from illegal activities.

Despite defining the drug problem on two fronts – drug use/dependency and drug trafficking – regulatory interventions were always framed to focus on curbing drug trafficking. While at first, this might have been triggered by external pressure, it also served regional purposes. Focusing on trade was perhaps a way of manoeuvring through the different political situations of PG members. Tackling organised crime had the most obvious appeal for international collaboration, and countries did not present any relevant restrictions to curb illicit drug trade.

Law enforcement and legislation harmonisation occupied a significant part of the debates and most of the concrete agreements of the PG during the 1970s. In health and prevention debates, a drug-free, productive and adjusted individual was usually framed as the goal. Here too, the objective of a strong and successful EEC might have influenced the framing of regulations. Agreements on health and prevention were limited to the exchange of information, study visits and research collaborations among members. On the one hand, this confirmed the group's target of fighting drug trafficking through a strict drug policy approach. On the other, it can be speculated, such loose agreements may have had the unintended consequence of opening the doors for a more liberal framing of drug policies in the PG in the following years. Despite the PG focus on combating drugs in the 1970s, some of its country members offered, for instance, opioid substitution treatment services instead of enforcing abstinence. Study visits, information exchange and research may have helped countries to gain insights into new ways of framing drugs, building the basis for spreading a public health approach towards drugs in the EEC in the following years. Such conclusions need, still, to be confirmed by further research.

This chapter is a starting point for further research, rather than a definite study of the PG. Its primary focus on Dutch sources has limitations and leaves the door open for future investigations. New research endeavours should look at the development of different national policies and cultures of drug use within Europe, considering sources from all countries involved as well as at the roles of various stakeholders. This nuanced approach has been achieved by studies focusing on the development of drug policies in specific countries (Boekhout van Solinge, 2004; Weinhauer, 2006; de Quadros Rigoni, 2019). Applying a similar standard to the European drug control development, in a multi-site research study, would be of much value to European drug policy history.

Finally, the concepts of frame analysis and 'mentalities of government' allowed an analysis of how European countries first justified the need for regulatory interventions for drug use and trade. Countries often framed drug issues in ways that contrasted with their own experience with drugs. Curbing youth protests, protecting commercial agreements and national policies, and managing international pressure were all important factors shaping the first steps of a European drug control. This chapter therefore echoes studies investigating the origins of an international drug control, and calls attention to the need of consideration of the broader political context also when analysing European drug control. Reasons other than concerns with the (national) rates of drug use, dependence or drug-related criminality might be important factors in triggering regulatory interventions in the drug field and must be considered for a more nuanced analysis of what shapes drug policy decisions, and why.

References

Anonymous (2018). *Interview with an ex-representative from the Pompidou Group.* Netherlands.

Berridge, V. (1996). European drug policy: the need for historical perspectives. *European Addiction Research, 2 (4),* 219–225.

Berridge, V. (2009). Heroin prescription and history. *The New England Journal of Medicine, 361 (8),* 820.

Blok, G. (2008). Pampering 'needle freaks' or caring for chronic addicts? Early debates on harm reduction in Amsterdam, 1972–1982. *The Social History of Alcohol and Drugs, 22 (2),* 243–261.

Boekhout van Solinge, T. (2002). *Drugs and decision-making in the European Union.* Amsterdam: CEDRO, University of Amsterdam.

Boekhout van Solinge, T. (2004). *Dealing with drugs in Europe: an investigation of European drug control experiences: France, the Netherlands and Sweden.* Amsterdam: CEDRO, University of Amsterdam.

Brule, C. (1983). The role of the Pompidou Group of the Council of Europe in combating drug abuse and illicit drug trafficking. *Bulletin on Narcotics, 35 (4),* 73–77.

Bruun, K., Pan, L., & Rexed, I. (1975). *Gentleman's club: international control of drugs and alcohol.* Chicago: University of Chicago Press.

Chatwin, C. (2011). *Drug policy harmonization and the European Union.* Basingstoke: Palgrave Macmillan.

de Kort, M. (1995). *Tussen patiënt en delinquent: geschiedenis van het Nederlandse drugsbeleid* [Between patient and criminal: history of Dutch drug policy]. Rotterdam: Erasmus University of Rotterdam.

de Quadros Rigoni, R. (2019). 'Drugs paradise': Dutch stereotypes and substance regulation in European collaborations on drug policies in the 1970s. *Contemporary Drug Problems.* doi.org/10.1177/0091450919847846

French Delegation (1971). Première Réunion des Experts Européens en matière de lutte contre la toxicomanie et le trafic des stupéfiants. Compte Rendu de séance [First Meeting of European experts on drug abuse and drug trafficking. Meeting report]. *DG Volksgezondheid, 2.15.65, Inv.Nr. 3284.* Den Haag: Nationaal Archief.

Geerlings, P. J. (1973). Correspondence from Geerlings to Samsom. Report on the sub-commission on treatment. Meeting 29–30 May, London. *NL-HaNA, DG Volksgezondheid, 2.15.65, Inv.Nr. 3286.* Den Haag: Nationaal Archief.

Hartnoll, R., Avico, U., Ingold, F. R., Lange, K., et al. (1989). A multi-city study of drug misuse in Europe. *Bulletin on Narcotics, 41 (1-2),* 3–27.

Hartnoll, R. (1994). *Multi-city study, drug misuse trends in thirteen European cities: Amsterdam, Barcelona, Copenhagen, Dublin, Geneva, Hamburg, Helsinki, Lisbon, London, Oslo, Paris, Rome, Stockholm.* Strasbourg: Council of Europe Press.

Health Commission (1973a). Second meeting of the health technical commitee. *NL-HaNA, DG Volksgezondheid, 2.15.65, Inv.Nr. 3286.* Den Haag: Nationaal Archief.

Health Commission (1973b). Report from Comission I: 'Health Action' to the Coordinating Committee of the Pompidou group. *NL-HaNA, DG Volksgezondheid, 2.15.65, Inv.Nr. 3286.* Den Haag: Nationaal Archief.

Interpol (1973a). Sepat plan, operation 'Narcontrol 1973'. *NL-HaNA, DG Volksgezondheid, 2.15.65, Inv.Nr 3285.* Interpol n. 3625/Stupe/1440/Sepat. Den Haag: Nationaal Archief.

Interpol (1973b). Evolution du plan SEPAt – Reinforcement de la cooperation contre le traffic illicite des stupefiants. [Evolution of the SEPAt-Reinforcement of cooperation against the illicit traffic in narcotic drugs]. *NL-HaNA, DG Volksgezondheid, 2.15.65, Inv.Nr 3285*. Telex Interpol 27.268. Den Haag: Nationaal Archief.

Kattau, T. (2018). *Interview with Tomas Kattau, principal administrator of the Pompidou Group*. Strasbourg.

Korf, D. J. (1995). *Dutch treat: formal control and illicit drug use in the Netherlands*. Amsterdam: Thesis.

Law Enforcement Commission (1973a). Cooperation Europeene dans la Lutte Contre L'usge et le trafic illicites des stupefiants [European cooperation in the fight against the use and illicit trafficking of narcotics]. *NL-HaNA, DG Volksgezondheid, 2.15.65, Inv.Nr 3285*. Den Haag: Nationaal Archief.

Legislation Harmonization Commission (1973b). Coperation Europeene en Matiere de Lutte contre les estupefiants. Commission "harmonisation des legislations". Session du 25 fevrier au ier mars 1973 [European co-operation in the fight against drugs. Commission "legislation harmonization". Session from 25 February to 1 March 1973]. *NL-HaNA, DG Volksgezondheid, 2.15.65, Inv.Nr. 3286*. Den Haag: Nationaal Archief.

Legislation Harmonization Commission (1973c). Notulen van de 1e vergadering gehouden in het Egmontpaleis te Brussel op 26 February en 1 maart 1973 [Minutes of the 1st meeting held at the Egmont Palace in Brussels on 26 February and 1 March 1973]. *NL-HaNA, DG Volksgezondheid, 2.15.65, Inv.Nr. 3286*. Den Haag: Nationaal Archief.

Legislation Harmonization Commission (1973d). Zitting van het subcomite pharmaceutische produkten van 25 en 26 juni 1973. [Session of the Pharmaceutical Products Subcommittee of 25 and 26 June 1973]. *NL-HaNA, DG Volksgezondheid, 2.15.65, Inv.Nr. 3286*. Den Haag: Nationaal Archief.

Legislation Harmonization Commission (1973e). Verslag van de Commissie voor harmonisering van wetgeving in het kader van de Europese samenwerking in de strijd tegen de verdovende middelen. [Report from the Commission legislation harmonization in the context of European cooperation in the fight against drugs]. *NL-HaNA, DG Volksgezondheid, 2.15.65, Inv.Nr. 3285*. Den Haag: Nationaal Archief.

Matthew, C. (1971). Joint drive against drug abuse. *European Community, 151, 20–22*.

McCoy, A.W. (1972). *The politics of heroin in Southeast Asia*. New York: Harper & Row.

Mitchell, D. (2010). *Governmentality: power and rule in modern society*. Thousand Oaks, CA: Sage.

Musto, D.F. (2010). *The American disease: origins of narcotic control*. New York: Oxford University Press.

Nagler, N.A. (1987). The Council of Europe Co-operation Group to Combat Drug Abuse and Illicit Trafficking in Drugs (the Pompidou Group). *Bulletin on narcotics, 39 (1)*, 31–40.

Nixon, R. (1972). *Address to the nation on Vietnam, April 26, 1972*. Online by Gerhard Peters and John T. Woolley, The American Presidency Project. http://www.presidency.ucsb.edu/ws/?pid=3384.

Pompidou, G. (1971). Correpondence from Georges Pompidou to Prime Minister of the Netherlands. *Ministerie van Sociale Zaken: Directoraat-Generaal Volksgezondheid, Nummer Toegang 2.15.65, Inventarisnummer 3284*. Den Haag: Nationaal Archief.

Pompidou Group (1971a). Première réunion des experts européens en matiére de lutte contre la toxicomanie et le trafic des stupéfiants. Compte Rendu de séance [First meeting of

European experts in the fight against drug addiction and drug trafficking. Meeting report]. *NL-HaNA, DG Volksgezondheid, 2.15.65, Inv.Nr. 3284.* Den Haag: Nationaal Archief.

Pompidou Group (1971b). Première session des comissions d'experts européens en matière de lutte contre la toxicomanie et le trafic des stupéfiants. Saint-Could 14 au 17 Décembre 1971. Compte Rendu de séance [First session of the European expert committees on drug abuse and drug trafficking. Saint-Could 14 to 17 December 1971. Meeting report]. *NL-HaNA, DG Volksgezondheid, 2.15.65, Inv.Nr. 3284.* Den Haag: Nationaal Archief.

Pompidou Group (1972a). Comissions des Experts Européens en matière de lutte contre la toxicomanie et le trafic des stupéfiants. Minutes [Committees of European experts in the fight against drug addiction and drug trafficking. Minutes]. *NL-HaNA, DG Volksgezond-heid, 2.15.65, Inv.Nr 3284 – 31 Janvier 1972.* Den Haag: Nationaal Archief.

Pompidou Group (1972b). Declaration. *NL-HaNA, DG CRM 2.27.19, Inv. Nr. 6568.* Den Haag: Nationaal Archief.

Pompidou Group (1977). Vergadering coordinatie commissie, Pompidou overleg [Meeting coordination committee, Pompidou consultation]. *NA. 2.15.65 DG Volksgezondheid. 3287.* Den Haag: Nationaal Archief.

Pompidou Group (1978). First meeting of the committee of experts on legislation and regulation. *NA. 2.15.65 DG Volksgezondheid. 3288.* Den Haag: Nationaal Archief.

Pompidou Group (1979). Fifth ministerial conference of the European cooperation in the struggle againts drug abuse and illicit traffic. Stockholm, November 12-13. *NA. 2.152.15.65 DG Volksgezondheid. 3289.* Den Haag: Nationaal Archief.

Pompidou Group (2017). Pompidou Group of the Council of Europe. http://www.coe.int/T/DG3/Pompidou/default_en.asp.

Room, R., & Reuter, P. (2012). How well do international drug conventions protect public health? *The Lancet, 379 (9810),* 84–91.

Samson, R. J. (1977, April 12). Vergadering coordinatie-commissie Pompidou-overleg dd 25 maart 1977 [Meeting of the Pompidou coordination committee meeting of 25 March 1977]. *NA. 2.15.65 DG Volksgezondheid. 3287.* Den Haag: Nationaal Archief.

Schön, D., & Rein, M. (1995). *Frame reflection: toward the resolution of intractable policy controversies.* New York: Basic.

Simon, R., Donmall, M., Hartnoll, R., Kokkevi, A., Ouwehand, A. W., Stauffacher, M., & Vicente, J. (1999). The EMCDDA/Pompidou Group treatment demand indicator protocol: a European core item set for treatment monitoring and reporting. *European Addiction Research, 5 (4),* 197–207.

Snelders, S. (1999). *LSD en de psychiatrie in Nederland* [LSD and psychiatry in the Netherlands]. Amsterdam: Vrije Universiteit Amsterdam.

United Nations (1962). Single convention on narcotic drugs, 1961. In *United Nations conference for the adoption of a single convention on narcotic drugs.* London: H.M. Stationery Off.

United Nations (1972). *Protocol amending the single convention on narcotic drugs, 1961.* Concluded at Geneva on 25 March 1972. treaties.un.org/doc/Publication/UNTS/Volume%20976/v976.pdf.

Vonhögen, H. P. (1973). Verslag van de op 25 t/m 29 juni 1973 te Brussel gehouden vergadering van Commissie IV [Report of the meeting of Commission IV held in Brussels from 25 to 29 June 1973]. *NL-HaNA, DG Volksgezondheid, 2.15.65, Inv.Nr. 3285.* Den Haag: Nationaal Archief.

Weinhauer, K. (2006). Drug consumption in London and Western Berlin during the 1960s and 1970s: Local and transnational perspectives. *The Social History of Alcohol and Drugs, 20 (2),* 187–224.

Ysa, T. (2014). *Governance of addictions: European public policies.* Oxford: Oxford University Press.

3
NPS use motivations
from the perspective of users
and experts

Zsuzsa Kaló, Zsolt Demetrovics & Katalin Felvinczi

The aim of this chapter is to explore how the NPS users' motivations substantially deviate from what experts believe. The background of this chapter is provided by a transnational project on New Psychoactive Substances (NPS). By means of data collection in six European countries (Hungary, Poland, the Netherlands, Germany, Portugal, Ireland), including a survey among current NPS users (n = 3,023) and 55 semi-structured interviews with health and social professionals, academics, and policy experts, the project explored the different NPS user groups, NPS user characteristics, extent and patterns of NPS use, market dynamics and best practices in prevention related to NPS. A secondary analysis of the qualitative data set was conducted to explore and interrelate the motivations from the perspective of users and experts. According to the results, the experts perceived that the reasons for NPS use were general availability, affordability, legality, and psychological motivational factors. The users found external factors less important: in particular, the (real and perceived) legal status of these substances were rated lower than it was supposed by the experts. The study, whilst small scale, is unique in terms of simultaneously studying of expert and user perspectives around the motivations for NPS use in six European countries.

Keywords: NPS, experts, users, motivation, motivational factors, secondary analysis, European

1 Introduction

New or Novel Psychoactive Substances (hereafter NPS) are defined as drugs that, due to their chemical structure, mimic the effects and are marketed globally as legal alternatives to conventional/classical drugs. Since the emergence of NPS, over 500 have been identified by the European Early Warning System (hereafter EWS) (EMCDDA, 2016). The EWS is designed to detect and spot the emerging trends in drug use (Griffiths, Vingoe, Hunt, Mounteney & Hartnoll, 2009; EMCDDA, 2016), including NPS-using use trends (Mounteney, Fry, McKeganey & Haugland, 2010). The EWS multi-indicator approach includes experts' observations and opinions and notes that these might be influenced by how experts perceive the specific motivations for using NPS. However, little knowledge is available about how the motivations for the use of NPS perceived by the experts are interrelated with the motivations for use expressed by NPS users themselves (Korf, Benschop, Werse et al., 2019). This chapter focuses on the different perspectives on why people use NPS, and gives an insight into how experts perceive reasons and motivations for NPS use.

Understanding why people are using different substances is challenging even for Old Psychoactive Substances (hereafter OPS) let alone for NPS. Studies that assessed the motivational background of different substances are based on Cooper's (1994) motivational scale model (alcohol, Cooper, 1994; cannabis, Simons, Correia, Carey & Borsari, et al., 1998; amphetamine-type stimulants, Thurn, Kuntsche, Weber & Wolstein, 2017; marijuana, Benschop, Liebregts, van der Pol, et al., 2015; NPS, Benschop, Urbán, Kapitány-Fövény, et al., unpublished). Cooper distinguished two types: individual/intrapersonal and external/internal motivations. Cooper's (1994) measuring tool Drinking Motives Questionnaire includes four scales: coping (avoidance of unwanted inner states); enhancement (enhancement of positive inner states); conformity (avoidance of external aversive consequences); and social (satisfaction of affiliate needs). One can also draw a distinction between motives (that provoke an action) and motivations (the force that drives an individual to take action). Importantly, when studying the complexity and multidimensionality of drug use motivations, qualitative inquiries are playing an important role to explore the nuances. When it comes to understanding or evaluating others' motivations, we need also to recognise the many cognitive distortions, and the attribution theory (Heider, 1958; Gordon & Graham, 2006) that explains how the social perceiver gathers and uses information and how it is combined to form a causal judgement.

NPS use motivations from the perspective of users have been studied using a qualitative methodology. Some studies suggest that the main motivations are internal and, similar to OPS, are guided by curiosity, or enhancement motivations (Werse & Morgenstern, 2012; Corazza, Simonato, Corkery, Trincas & Shifano, 2014; Winstock, Lawn, Deluca & Borschmann, 2015), as well as pleasure-seeking (Soussan & Kjellgren, 2016). Other studies have reported external motivations including widespread availability and affordability (Van Hout & Hearne, 2017) and value for money (Van Amsterdam, Nabben, Keiman, Haanschoten & Korf, 2015; Southerland, Bruno, Peckock, et al., 2017). Additionally, studies argue that the user motivations are more contextual and/or external (pragmatic) for NPS use, and these have revealed that temporary legal status, easy availability, low price, and the high perceived or expected quality/purity of these substances might play an important role in predicting NPS use (e.g. Werse & Morgenstern, 2012; Soussan & Kjellgren, 2016; Sutherland, Bruno, Peacock, et al., 2017). Further reasons for NPS use were connected to boredom and peer socialisation (Van Hout & Hearne, 2017). However, it should not be forgotten that NPS is a category name and users have often little knowledge of what they are actually consuming (Benschop, Bujalski, Dąbrowska et al., 2017; Corkery, Guirguis, Papanti, Orsolini & Schifano, 2018).

Studies exploring experts' perspectives are even more limited than those of users, and mainly focus on their attributions (Campbell, O'Neill & Higgins, 2016; Pirona, Bo, Hedrich, Ferri, van Gelder, et al., 2017). Results highlight the uncertainty of experts caused by their fear of having little knowledge about NPS (Abdulrahim, & Bowden-Jones, 2015; Campbell, O'Neill, & Higgins, 2016; Pirona et al., 2017). Experts working with NPS clients (in low threshold services and/or emergency units) felt less confident and expressed their need for more training and information about the substances, the users, and the harms related to NPS (Campbell et al., 2016; Stogner, Khey, Agnich & Miller, 2016). This finding – the systematically and anecdotally reported uncertainty being present in experts – suggests that comparing the different perspectives of users and experts on different aspects of NPS use (Abdulrahim, & Bowden-Jones, 2015; Campbell et al., 2016; Pirona et al., 2017) might have a fundamental importance in better understanding and tackling this phenomenon. At the same time, the media portrayal of NPS is not based on the perspectives of the users, who are better informed about the drugs and the harms by experience (Abdulrahim & Bowden-Jones, 2015; O'Brien, Chatwin, Jenkins & Measham, 2015), but on the inputs of 'un(der)informed "experts"' (Potter & Chatwin, 2018, p. 334). As a result, experts are giving rise to the image of marginalised NPS users and a moral panic that is shaping the NPS discourse. Thus, again, the attributions by experts are important to understand.

The main aim of the current study is to compare the reported motivations for NPS consumption of recent NPS users and the perceptions of experts, to address two questions:
1) How do experts perceive NPS use motivations? Do these perceptions about the motivations differ between NPS and OPS?
2) What differences and similarities in terms of NPS use motivations can be found between users and experts?

2   Methods

2.1 Data set: transnational project NPS-t

We used the data set of qualitative and quantitative research conducted in 2016 in six European countries within the context of the NPS-t: New Psychoactive

Substances: transnational project on different user groups, user characteristics, extent and patterns of use, market dynamics, and best practices in prevention (the participating countries were Hungary, Poland, the Netherlands, Germany, Portugal, and Ireland).

The source of quantitative data was the large-scale survey among recent NPS users. Data collection was carried out between April and November 2016 with the total sample of 3,023 NPS users in the six European countries composing three different user groups (for a detailed methodological description see Benschop et al., 2017; Korf et al., 2019). The three user groups were:

1. *Socially marginalised users* are 'high-risk drug users', often also frequently using opioids, (crack)cocaine and/or (meth)amphetamine – intravenously or through smoking;
2. *Users in nightlife* are recreational-drug users who frequent clubs, raves, and/ or festivals; and
3. *Users in online communities* are very active on the Internet and take part in drug fora.

The questionnaire contained items that measured demographics, routes of consumption, motives, and frequencies of NPS use and problems related to it, ways of obtaining NPS, and possible perceived ways of tackling NPS problems. Seven categories of NPS were initially included in the study based on their epidemiological and clinical relevance: herbal blends (e.g. 'Spice'); synthetic cannabinoids (obtained pure); branded stimulants (e.g. 'bath salts'); stimulants/ empathogens/nootropics (obtained pure, e.g. mephedrone, MDPV, a-PVP); psychedelics (e.g. 'NBOMe-x', '2C-x'); dissociatives (e.g. methoxetamine); and 'other'. However, survey responses indicated that participants were mostly unable to either properly categorise the NPS they had used or differentiate between certain categories (i.e. between herbal blends and synthetic cannabinoids obtained pure, and similarly between branded stimulants and stimulants obtained pure) (Benschop et al., 2017). The motivation-related items of the survey were based on the revised and psychometrically tested and adjusted version of the Marijuana Motivation Scale with additional items specific to NPS use (Simons et al., 1998; Benschop et al., 2015; Korf et al., 2019).

The NPS-t survey investigated – among other topics – the motivational background of NPS use. A seven-factor motivational factor structure was revealed as follows (Benschop et al., 2017):

1) Enhancement
Users aim to increase the positive effects and experiences caused by the drug. Benschop and colleagues (2017) found this factor relevant among the nightlife, the online community, and in the marginalised sample. The motive is connected it to the use of stimulants and stimulant empathogens.

2) Social
   An enhancement of sociability and skills in social situations. It was relevant within the nightlife and online community sample.
3) *Conformity*
   Peer influence/pressure, which was found to be significant in the marginalised sample.
4) *Coping*
   The survey included items such as reducing the negative effect, which was attributed to the marginalised sample and connected to the dissociative substances.
5) *Expansion*
   An experimental awareness, which was found relevant by the nightlife and the online samples.
6) *Routine motives*
   Routine motives include boredom and habit, and reached high scores in the marginalised sample.
7) *Contextual/external/pragmatic motivational factors*
   These included additional items: poor quality of other drugs, price, alleged legality, expecting different or new experiences, non-detectability, and poor availability of OPS. These items were the least-mentioned motives in all three user groups.

The qualitative data collection was administered by semi-structured interviews with 55 selected experts in the participating countries. The expert interviews were conducted by local researchers and based on the project's interview guide. The semi-structured interviews covered the following topics: definitions of NPS within organisations/work fields; characterisation of types of users; description of NPS use by these users; information of NPS market; definition of harm reduction and prevention; the legal status of NPS; and current drug policy issues discussed by the local experts. The participants were recruited by means of a purposeful sampling technique. The interviews were audio-recorded and transcribed verbatim in their original language by local researchers. The interviews were analysed thematically by the local researchers in each country.

2.2 Secondary analysis of interviews with experts

Our study, using the data set from the NPS-t project, first included a secondary analysis of the qualitative data set (i.e. expert interviews). In other words, our study first involved a re-use of pre-existing data derived from the interviews conducted in six European countries. We then compared our findings with the results of the NPS-t survey's quantitative data set.

As far as the analysis of the qualitative data set is concerned, we used the local research reports, resulting in an overall 38,537-word English-language corpus. All respondents had their own specific expertise in the drug field and were active in specific areas within the judiciary, police, health-care, or harm reduction. Overall, 22 female and 33 male expert respondents were included.

Table 1: Fields of expertise of participants by country

Country	n	Field of expertise	Data source
Netherlands	8	drug enforcement and the judiciary, a chemist, a party doctor, a peer coach, a prevention worker, drug researchers	(Wouters & Nabben 2017)
Portugal	8	psychologists, drug researchers, a chemist, a peer educator, a coordinator of a prevention service, intervention technician	(Silva & Henriques, 2017)
Poland	9	police officer, a pharmacist, a lawyer, and governmental officials, therapists, representatives of NGOs	(Dąbrowska, Bujalski, & Wieczorek, 2017)
Hungary	10	social workers, psychiatrists, a mental health expert, a sociologist, a theologian-priest, and a peer-helper	(Kaló & Felvinczi, 2017)
Germany	7	research (social and toxicology), harm prevention, treatment, and prosecution	(Müller, Kamphausen & Werse, 2017)
Ireland	13	research, prevention, and treatment	(Van Hout, 2017)

A qualitative content analysis was also carried out. The function of the content analysis of the data set of NPS-t was to give an overview of the NPS usage motivations as perceived by selected local experts in Europe. The study used an inductive approach (Braun & Clarke, 2006), which means that after reading and re-reading the qualitative data set, the codes strongly linked to the data were identified. A further step of the analysis was to cluster the codes into thematic domains. Thus, this content analysis can be considered an inductive supra analysis (Heaton, 2008), where the aims and focus of the secondary study transcend those of the original research.

Second, we used a deductive approach in our data analysis: we applied the seven (internal/external) motivational factors (enhancement, social, conformity, coping, expansion, routine motives, and contextual/external/pragmatic) from the NPS-t survey (as summarised above) to the findings of the qualitative analysis. In particular, the thematic domains identified in the first phase were interrelated with the motivational factor model based on NPS-t survey results. We systematically checked the results of the survey and compared these with the thematic domains derived from the qualitative content analysis.

3   Findings

3.1   Motivations for NPS use from the perspective of the experts

The qualitative content analysis identified five thematic domains within the expert interviews: motivations related to legal status, the availability of the NPS, the affordability of the NPS, psychological factors as motivations, and myths and misunderstandings as motivations, and the comparison of OPS and NPS motivations perceived by the experts. Here we give a summary of our main findings. Words in italic come from the codes associated with the thematic domains observed in the qualitative data set.

Motivations related to legal status

This group of perceived motivations were related to the legal status of NPS. This thematic domain included the assumption that NPS are seen as an adequate and *legal substitution* for OPS, especially cannabis (Müller, Kamphausen & Werse, 2017, p. 7). This was closely connected to the topic of *fear of prosecution*. Users were believed to use NPS for the reason of its *supposed nondetectability* (Müller et al., 2017, p. 7), compared with traditional drug-screening methods (e.g. urine tests), which could let the user consume without fear of punishment, e.g. losing their driver licence or their job. The experts argued that this would also make the user perceive themselves to be on different moral grounds, *seeing themselves as good citizens* who are actually recreational users using legal substances *('legitimate citizens [...] with the right to get high'*, Müller et al., 2017, p. 7). The code of anonymity of buying NPS via the Internet also supported the legal motivations thematic domain. The experts identified users with legal motives as being non-addicts (i.e. recreational users), and not marginalised users nor clients of substitution treatments.

The availability of NPS

The availability of NPS as a thematic domain was observed as another group of reasons by the participating European experts. Including the code of easy accessibility meant not only that NPS were found in various settings (clubs, streets, deprived neighbourhoods, social meetings, parties), but that they could be procured via friends and peers and, most particularly, via the Internet and could even be produced in 'one's own kitchen' (Kaló & Felvinczi, 2017, p. 8). These circumstances offered the possibility of *anonymity* and the avoidance of meeting *'filthy dudes at the station'* (Müller et al., 2017, p. 8) – close connections with the thematic domain of motivations related to the legal status. The general availability and *wide variety* of NPS were seen as the reasons for their popularity among users. Some experts also noted that in some particular settings (especially among marginalised users), NPS were the only available psychoactive substances. The *wide variety* could make the users feel they could have a choice of moods, preferences, and expectations which is also connected to the thematic domain of psychological motivations.

The affordability of NPS
The affordability of NPS as a thematic domain reflects the financial aspects of perceived reasons for use and it contains a comparison with OPS. The *low price* of NPS was emphasised by the experts. Based on their observations, the drug market had completely changed in some settings (mainly in deprived neighbourhoods) with NPS completely replacing OPS. They explain this by referring to the low prices. However, they see the low prices as a *scam,* as NPS have to be consumed far more times than OPS: a single price could be lower, but the users were paying the same amount overall. In other words, the experts assume that relative prices were lower but absolute prices are the same or even higher. Then again, from the perspective of the user this might have been seen as more affordable. It is a *cheap high* compared to OPS (Van Hout, 2017, p. 9).

Psychological motivations
The thematic domain of psychological factors as motivations compiles those aspects that are attributed to NPS use as inner motivations. *Curiosity* as a motivational factor was identified by the experts as applying especially to adolescent user groups who are experimenting with drugs. Among the psychonauts, *scientific curiosity* was assumed (Müller et al., 2017, p. 8). *Boredom* and *wanting to try something else* were usually seen as a motivational factor for psychonauts. The need to get high was identified with problematic drug users, who were reported to use whatever they got, regardless of the harm. This was also identified as a new drug user group by some of the experts. NPS (and particularly, mephedrone) as a substitute for OPS (cocaine) was perceived by the users as a *sexual arousal enhancer.* The experts also saw *disappointment* as an important factor. They noticed the users being disappointed with the quality of OPS, thus making NPS a better option for them. The motivation for NPS use was also perceived as a *fashion or trend* but only in special scenes (psychonauts) and specific age groups of users (adolescents), and also connected to a particular NPS (herbal blends). The users were also thought to *gain credibility* by using NPS and *becoming experts* by experimentation with them. Use was seen as *normalised,* a *general commodity,* where users were becoming experts.

Myths and misunderstandings of NPS as motivations
The last thematic domain includes the myths and misunderstandings about NPS that are indirectly linked to the perceived motivations for their use. Experts noted that these specifics of NPS can be attributed to the motivations. They assumed that a *postulated high purity* had been present among the users. NPS,

being seen as generally available, seemed *less risky* in terms of not being as addictive as OPS, especially among adolescent users. They were seen as less risky despite the fact that media reports were communicating a 'dreadful' picture of NPS (Dąbrowska, Bujalski & Wieczorek, 2017, p. 7). Some user groups also assumed that NPS are actually *natural and healthy*, as well as helping in the recovery process from OPS.

3.2 Motivations for using NPS compared to OPS

When explaining how they perceived the motivations for NPS use, experts almost always made a comparison between NPS and OPS. Experts believed that users had assumed NPS were *less harmful* than OPS. Motivations similar to OPS were mentioned: being *bored, curiosity, the need to get high*. The marginalised drug users were seen to be *disappointed* by the quality of OPS, and a *higher level of purity* and *easier availability* were perceived. One motivation that differed was that the psychonauts who used NPS were thought to be *interested in self-experimentation* with pharmacological effects: the so-called *scientific curiosity* (Müller et al., 2017, p. 4). NPS were regarded as *less risky* (Dąbrowska et al., 2017, p. 9), *more natural,* and *healthier* (Kaló & Felvinczi, 2017, p. 8), and, most of all, as *cheaper, offer a wider variety,* and have *high purity*. With NPS the concept of drug use has changed: it was not a taboo any more. Compared to OPS, the experts thought that NPS seemed to discard the social taboo aspect and became *'normal commodities'* (Dąbrowska et al., 2017, p. 10).

3.3 Comparing the user and expert perspectives of NPS motivations

The findings on the users' motivations are derived from the NPS-t survey (see above). In comparing the user and expert perspectives, the seven (internal/external) motivational factors (enhancement, social, conformity, coping, expansion, routine motives, and contextual/external/pragmatic) were used. For simplicity, these seven factors were merged into two categories: internal factors and contextual/external/pragmatic factors.

When comparing the categories of motivational factors between the users and the experts, we could interrelate all the factors. In other words, the experts gave examples of all of the motivational factors addressed by the users themselves. Enhancement was mentioned among the psychological motivations with the example of *sexual arousal enhancer* (related to mephedrone) and the social motivational factor was covered by the experts when referring to the codes of *gaining credibility* and *becoming experts*. The aspects of the conformity, the coping, and the routine motives were covered – among other examples from the various psychological motivations – by the codes of the *disappointment* in OPS, and the *need to get high.* In addition, the contextual/ external/pragmatic motivational factors were richly described within three of the thematic domains such as the availability and the affordability of NPS, and the legal motivations, including codes of *anonymity, easy accessibility, general availability, low price,* etc.

In comparing the motivations provided by experts with the motivations of the users, we found that the NPS specific contextual/external/pragmatic motivational items (lack of traditional drugs, detectability, price, quality, alleged legality) were found to be the least-mentioned individual motives among all groups of users (Benschop et al., 2017, for further details see Figure 1 and Table 2). In contrast, these factors that were included as NPS-specific motivational items were richly described by the experts.

Figure 1: Means of internal and external (contextual) motives among recent NPS users (*N* = 2,994; Source: Benschop et al., 2017

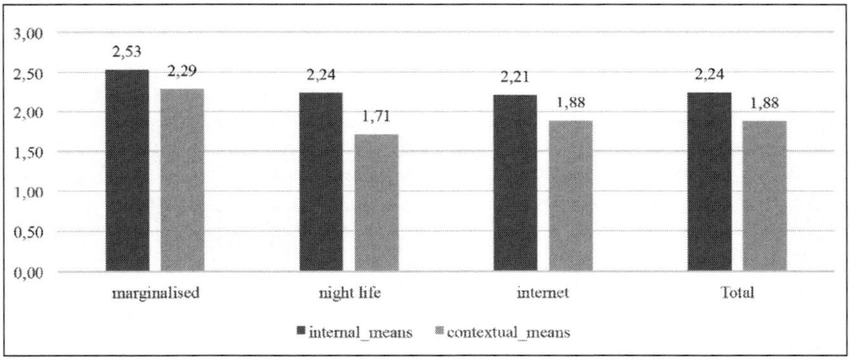

We also recognised that NPS users are a diverse drug user population including – among others – recreational users, psychonauts and party goers (users in the nightlife and online communities), and the NPS-t survey allowed us to check the differences of motivations between these groups. The expert interviews hardly distinguished between the user groups defined by the survey, although, for example, the social motivational factors are connected to the nightlife and online community user groups, as they were in the NPS-t survey results (Benschop et al., 2017). The NPS-t survey found that external/contextual motivational factors do not play a decisive role in motivations for any of the three user groups. The marginalised groups form an exception here. It seems that low availability and poor quality of the controlled substances and the relatively low price of NPS play a role in the motivations towards NPS use most in case of

Table 2: Summary table of the means of internal and external (contextual) motives among recent NPS users (*N* = 2.994; Source: Benschop et al.. 2017)

Respondent group		Internal	Contextual_means
Marginalised	Mean	2.53	2.29
	N	250	251
	Std. Deviation	0.79	0.91
Nightlife	Mean	2.24	1.71
	N	640	639
	Std. Deviation	0.62	0.62
Internet	Mean	2.21	1.88
	N	2,104	2,102
	Std. Deviation	0.58	0.79
Total	Mean	2.24	1.88
	N	2,994	2,992
	Std. Deviation	0.62	0.78

marginalised users compared to other user groups. The experts from countries where the number of marginalised NPS users were high (Hungary and Poland) and those experts from the European countries who were involved in fieldwork highlighted the external motivational factors. But when looking at the whole sample, the expert interviews expanded the external motivational factors to all user groups (recreational users, new user groups, adolescents). They identified external factors as an important motivational background and as an explanation for observing NPS from a regulatory perspective, as well as assuming NPS was becoming a 'normal' commodity.

4   Conclusion

In this chapter, we have argued that, at certain points, the experts' perceptions about the motivations of NPS consumption are different from the reported motives of recent NPS users. This difference can be captured mostly in relation to contextual motivations. The 55 experts from the six European countries stressed the importance of the external/contextual motivations, among them the alleged legality, affordability, and availability of NPS. In contrast, the NPS-t survey results of the user motivations (Benschop et al., 2017; Felvinczi, Benschop, Urbán & et al., unpublished) showed that NPS users consider the NPS-specific items (such as poor quality of other drugs, price, alleged legality, expectation of different or new experiences, non-detectability, and poor availability of other

OPS) less important than internal motivation items (i.e. coping, enhancement, social, etc.). Conversely, legal motives, affordability, and availability are vividly described by the experts as important motivations for taking NPS. This was especially true for those experts who were dealing with marginalised NPS users. Related to this, the importance of these external factors, labelled otherwise as a circumstantial motivational factor (Soussan & Kjellgren, 2016) or opportunistic reasons (Southerland et al., 2017), are also highlighted by previous qualitative studies on NPS users' motivations (Van Hout & Hearne, 2017; Corkery et al., 2018). We conclude that the external/contextual factors of NPS use were more visible to experts, especially those working with marginalised drug users, and, as the phenomenon was new and demanding in many ways for experts at treatment facilities, they attributed the contextual/external motivational factors to marginalised users and generalised it to all NPS users.

Similar to previous qualitative research about users' motivations for taking NPS and OPS (e.g. Van Amsterdam et al., 2015; Van Hout, 2017), experts in our study perceived that the price and value for money ('cheap high'; Van Hout, 2017, p. 9) of NPS is an important (external) motivational factor. However, the NPS-t survey results of users did not support this (Benschop et al., 2017), except for the marginalised users (Felvinczi et al., unpublished). Obviously, the experts saw psychological motivational factors (curiosity, boredom, need to get high, enhancement) as similarly important in using NPS and OPS. When comparing the NPS to OPS, the experts assume that NPS are regarded as 'less risky' by the users and it makes drug use more 'normalised' with the users becoming the 'real experts'.

Overall, we have also argued that if we want to better understand the NPS motivations, we need to study the perspective of experts too. Our research findings have confirmed that, from the perspective of the experts, the information regarding the specificities of NPS is rather lacking (see also Griffiths et al., 2009; Mounteney et al., 2010; Pirona et al., 2017). Their perceptions about the motivations for NPS use remain based on their everyday experiences. Therefore, those experts who frequently meet problematic drug users in their service provisions might have biased concepts regarding the motives towards NPS use, and these biased concepts might shape their perceptions. Importantly, these perceptions might be shaping drug policy responses as well. It may be that experts primarily reason in terms of problems (patients, clients) and addiction, or policy (legality must play a role, whether from a prohibitionist or legaliser's view). Also, they may primarily have specific user groups (such as marginalised users) in mind. This might also explain why marginalised NPS users were more likely to be reported to have external motives. This is probably the group that experts are most likely refer to when thinking about NPS (especially in Hungary and Poland, Felvinczi et al., unpublished). In addition, users may overlook more structural factors and perceive themselves as more autonomous individuals than they in reality are.

Our study supports the notion that expert opinions have a great importance, as they have an impact on formulating treatment, policy options, legislative directions and they also may influence the public discourse related to the issue. The application of mixed method approaches (quantitative and qualitative data collection targeting the same phenomenon) can better reveal the true nature of the issue at stake and can better substantiate the measures to be taken to tackle more effectively the problem.

5 Strengths and limitations of the study

The main strength of the study is its unique access to a data set that has a geographic perspective and a recent timeframe. The study, whilst small-scale, is unique in terms of providing different national and regional snapshots of expert and user perspectives around NPS use in six European countries in 2016. The advantage of this mixed-methods research is the transferability of research methods in studying the particular research object, namely, the exploration and comparison of motivations for NPS use from the perspective of the users and of the experts. However, we must be cautious about the extent to which the findings can be transferred or applied in different settings. The main limitation is that the quantitative study was carried out on a convenience sample, so the information gathered should not be considered as representative for Europe as a whole nor of any of the participating countries.

Using a multilingual qualitative data set condensed into English summaries for secondary analysis left little room for understanding the nuances, but understanding different countries' perspective was not approachable in any other way. The diverse background of the interview experts might also be considered as a possible limitation: dividing the expert groups by the field of expertise could be a direction for further studies of the topic.

Acknowledgements

The study analyses data that were collected within the framework of an EU funded transnational project: New Psychoactive Substances: transnational project on different user groups, user characteristics, extent and patterns of use, market dynamics, and best practices in prevention; European Commission JUST/2014/Action Grant.

We want to thank all members of the research group for their contributions. Members of the NPS-transnational Project (apart from the authors) include: Annemieke Benschop (Bonger Institute of Criminology, University of Amsterdam, The Netherlands), Michal Bujalski(IPIN, Warsaw, Poland), Katarzyna Dąbrowska (IPIN, Warsaw, Poland), Dirk Egger (Center for Drug Research, Goethe-Universität, Frankfurt, Germany), Susana Henriques (CIES-IUL University Institute of Lisbon, Portugal), Gerrit Kamphausen (Center for Drug Research, Goethe-Universität, Frankfurt, Germany), Dirk J. Korf (Bonger Institute of Criminology, University of Amsterdam, The Netherlands), Ton Nabben (Bonger Institute of Criminology, University of Amsterdam, The Netherlands), Joana Paula Silva (CIES-IUL University Institute of Lisbon, Portugal), Marie Claire Van Hout6, Bernd Werse (Center for Drug Research, Goethe-Universität, Frankfurt, Germany), John Wells (Waterford Institute of Technology, Ireland), Lukasz Wieczorek (IPIN, Warsaw, Poland) & Marije Wouters (Bonger Institute of Criminology, University of Amsterdam, The Netherlands).

One of the authors was also supported by OTKA thematic research projects or National Research, Development and Innovation Office, thematic research projects number 128604, title: Addiction problems in the general population; monitoring the trends and renewal of the applied research methods.

References

Abdulrahim, D., & Bowden-Jones, O. on behalf of the NEPTUNE Expert Group (2015). *Guidance on the management of acute and chronic harms of club drugs and novel psychoactive substances.* London: Novel Psychoactive Treatment UK Network (NEPTUNE).

Benschop, A., Bujalski, M., Dąbrowska, K., Demetrovics, Z., Egger, D., Felvinczi, K., Henriques, S., Kalo, Z., Kamphausen, G., Korf, D.J., Nabben, T., Silva, J.P., Van Hout, M.C., Werse, B., Wells, J., Wieczorek, L., & Wouters, M. (2017). *New psychoactive substances: transnational project on different user groups, user characteristics, extent and patterns of use, market dynamics, and best practices in prevention (NPS-transnational project; HOME/2014/JDRU/AG/DRUG/7077). Final report.* Amsterdam: Bonger Institute of Criminology, University of Amsterdam.

Benschop, A., Liebregts, N., van der Pol, P., Schaap, R., Buisman, R., van Laar, M., van den Brink, W., de Graaf, R., & Korf, D.J. (2015). Reliability and validity of the Marijuana Motives Measure among young adult frequent cannabis users and associations with cannabis dependence. *Addictive Behaviors, 40,* 91–95.

Benschop, A., Urbán, R., Kapitány-Fövény, M., Dąbrowska, K., Van Hout, M.C., Felvinczi, K., Hearne, E., Henriques, S., Kaló, Z., Kamphausen, G., Silva, J.P., Wieczorek, L., Werse, B., Bujalski, M., Korf, D., & Demetrovics, Z. (n.y.). *Why do people use new psychoactive substances? Development of a new measurement tool in six European countries.* Unpublished.

Braun, V., & Clarke, V. (2006). Using thematic analysis in psychology. *Qualitative Research in Psychology, 3 (2),* 77–101.

Campbell, A., O'Neill, N., & Higgins, K. (2017). Health and social care workers' perceptions of NPS use in Northern Ireland. *International Journal of Drug Policy, 40,* 93–101.

Cooper, M.L. (1994). Motivations for alcohol use among adolescents: development and validation of a four-factor model. *Psychological Assessment, 6 (2),* 117–128.

Corazza, O., Simonato, P., Corkery, J., Trincas, G., & Schifano, F. (2014). 'Legal highs': safe and legal 'heavens'? A study on the diffusion, knowledge and risk awareness of novel psychoactive drugs among students in the UK. *Rivista di Psichiatria, 49 (2),* 89–94.

Corkery J.M., Guirguis A., Papanti D.G., Orsolini L., & Schifano F. (2018). Synthetic cathinones – Prevalence and motivations for use. In: J. Zawilska (Ed.), *Current topics in neurotoxicity* (Vol. 12, pp. 153–191). New York: Springer.

Dąbrowska, K., Bujalski, M., & Wieczorek, Ł. (2017). *National report on new psychoactive substances expert* interviews in Poland. NPS-transnational project (HOME/2014/JDRU/ AG/DRUG/7077). Amsterdam: Bonger Institute of Criminology, University of Amsterdam.

EMCDDA: European Monitoring Centre for Drugs and Drug Addiction (2016). *Perspectives on drugs: legal approaches to controlling new psychoactive substances.* Lisbon: EMCDDA.

Felvinczi, K., Benschop, A., Urbán, R., Van Hout, M.C., Dąbrowska, K., Hearne, E., Henriques, S., Kaló, Zs., Kamphausen, G., Silva, J.P., Wieczorek, L., Bujalski, M., Demetrovics, Zs., & Korf, D. et al. (n.y.). *Discriminative characteristics of marginalised novel psychoactive users: a transnational study.* Unpublished.

Gordon, L.M., & Graham, S. (2006). 'Attribution theory'. In: *The encyclopedia of human development* (Vol. 1, pp. 142–144). Thousand Oaks: Sage.

Griffiths, P., Vingoe, L., Hunt, N., Mounteney, J., & Hartnoll, R. (2000). Drug information systems, early warning, and new drug trends: can drug monitoring systems become more sensitive to emerging trends in drug consumption? *Substance Use & Misuse, 35,* 6–8, 811–844.

Heaton, J. (2008). Secondary analysis of qualitative data: an overview. *Historical Social Research/Historische Sozialforschung, 33, 3 (125),* 33–45.

Heider, F. (1958). *The psychology of interpersonal relations.* New York: Wiley & Sons.

Kaló, Z., & Felvinczi, K. (2017). *National report on new psychoactive substances – expert interviews in Hungary. NPS-transnational project (HOME/2014/JDRU/AG/DRUG/7077).* Amsterdam: Bonger Institute of Criminology, University of Amsterdam.

Korf, D., Benschop, A., Werse, B., et al. (2019). How and where to find NPS users: a comparison of sampling methods in a cross-national survey among three groups of current users of new psychoactive substances in Europe. *International Journal of Mental Health & Addiction.* https://doi.org/10.1007/s11469-019-0052-8

Mounteney, J., Fry, C., McKeganey, N., & Haugland, S. (2010). Challenges of reliability and validity in the identification and monitoring of emerging drug trends. *Substance Use & Misuse, 45, 1–2,* 266–287.

Müller, D., Kamphausen, G., & Werse, B. (2017). *National report on new psychoactive substances – expert interviews in Germany. NPS-transnational project (HOME/2014/JDRU/ AG/DRUG/7077).* Amsterdam: Bonger Institute of Criminology, University of Amsterdam.

O'Brien, K., Chatwin, C., Jenkins, C., & Measham, F. (2015). New psychoactive substances and British drug policy: a view from the cyber-psychonauts. *Drugs: Education, Prevention and Policy, 22 (3),* 217–223.

Pirona, A., Bo, A., Hedrich, D., Ferri, M., van Gelder, N., Giraudon, I., Montanari, L., Simon, R., & Mounteney, J. (2017). New psychoactive substances: current health-related practices and challenges in responding to use and harms in Europe. *International Journal of Drug Policy, 40 (1),* 84–92.

Potter, G.R., & Chatwin, C. (2018). Not particularly special: critiquing 'NPS' as a category of drugs. *Drugs: Education, Prevention and Policy, 25 (4),* 329–336.

Silva, J., & Henriques, S. (2017). *National report on new psychoactive substances – expert interviews in Portugal. NPS-transnational project (HOME/2014/JDRU/AG/DRUG/7077). Amsterdam:* Bonger Institute of Criminology, University of Amsterdam.

Simons, J.S., Correia, C.J., Carey, K.B., & Borsari, B.E. (1998). Validating a five-factor marijuana motives measure: relations with use, problems, and alcohol motives. *Journal of Counseling Psychology, 45 (3),* 265–273.

Soussan, C., & Kjellgren A. (2016). The users of novel psychoactive substances: online survey about their characteristics, attitudes and motivations. *International Journal of Drug Policy, 32,* 77–84.

Stogner, J.M., Khey, D.N., Agnich, L.E., & Miller, B.L. (2016). They were getting high on what? Evaluating novel psychoactive drug knowledge among practitioners. *American Journal of Criminal Justice, 41 (1),* 97–111.

Sutherland, R., Bruno, R., Peacock, A., Lenton, S., Matthews, A., Salom, C., Dietze, P., Butler, K., Burns, L., & Barratt, M. J. (2017). Motivations for new psychoactive substance use among regular psychostimulant users in Australia. *International Journal of Drug Policy, 43 (1),* 23–32.

Thurn, D., Kuntsche, E., Weber, J. A., & Wolstein, J. (2017). Development and validation of the Amphetamine-type stimulants motive questionnaire in a clinical population. *Frontiers in Psychiatry, 8,* 183.

Van Amsterdam, J.G., Nabben, T., Keiman, D., Haanschoten, G., & Korf, D. (2015). Exploring the attractiveness of new psychoactive substances (NPS) among experienced drug users. *Journal of Psychoactive Drugs, 47 (3),* 177–181.

Van Hout, M.C. (2017). *National report on new psychoactive substances – expert interviews in Ireland. NPS-transnational project (HOME/2014/JDRU/AG/DRUG/7077).* Amsterdam: Bonger Institute of Criminology, University of Amsterdam.

Van Hout, M.C., & Hearne, E. (2016). User experiences of development of dependence on the synthetic cannabinoids, 5f-AKB48 and 5F-PB-22, and subsequent withdrawal syndromes. *International Journal of Addiction and Mental Health.* doi:10.1007/s11469-016-9650-x

Werse, B., & Morgenstern, C. (2012). How to handle legal highs? Findings from a German online survey and considerations on drug policy issues. *Drug and Alcohol Today, 12,* 222–231.

Winstock, A.R., Lawn, W., Deluca, P., & Borschmann, R. (2015). Methoxetamine: an early report on the motivations for use, effect profile and prevalence of use in a UK clubbing sample. *Drug and Alcohol Review.* doi:10.1111/dar.12259

Wouters, M., & Nabben T. (2017). *National report on new psychoactive substances – expert interviews in the Netherlands. NPS-transnational project (HOME/2014/JDRU/AG/DRUG/7077).* Amsterdam: Bonger Institute of Criminology, University of Amsterdam.

4
Emotional mapping: towards a geographical explanation of drug use

Luise Klaus & Mélina Germes

In Europe, most open drug scenes have similar spatial and social characteristics, especially in the growing dynamic of gentrification. This may potentially marginalise more drug users in public spaces. The cities face the same challenges in terms of governance. Within a perspective rooted in critical cartography and social geography, we propose emotional mapping as a method of conceiving urban lived spaces of drug users in European cities, with the aim of considering marginalised drug users as the subjects of their narratives and spatial representations. The method allows a complex analysis of the spatial experiences of urban space. It shows how the emotional appropriation of space by drug users is embedded in the structural socio-spatial exclusion phenomenon in Europe.

Keywords: drug user, urban, space, emotion, mapping

1 Introduction

In Europe, most open drug scenes have similar spatial and social characteristics. European cities are structured around historically dense inner-cities with a high intensity of activities and a wide diversity of social groups. Inner-city areas, e.g. main stations, are the places where inhabitants, tourists, partygoers and homeless drug users cohabit. Inner-city places are flashpoints for conflict, which – especially in the growing dynamic of gentrification – potentially marginalise more drug users in public spaces. These cities face identical challenges in terms of governance.

Today, drug use is widely understood as a socially-embedded phenomenon that is constructed and determined through social environment. The specificity of the urban geographical approach is to consider the relation between places, spaces and drug use and to understand the spatial embeddedness of drug use (Moreno & Wilton, 2014; Parkin, 2013; Duff, 2007). As Potter (2018, p. 13) points out, the taking of drugs 'are physical events that happen in specific locations': these are consumption settings, so place and context do matter. Our aim is to provide geographical answers to the question 'why do marginalised drug users use drugs in the public places of the city?' Thus, we do not aim merely to localise consumption places, but to ask 'where do the lives of marginalised drug users take place?'

Inspired by social geography and critical cartography, we chose a theoretical and methodological framework able to consider marginalised drug users as the subjects of their narratives and spatial representations. We consider their everyday lives as a whole and their complex – and emotional – relationships with the urban spaces. We developed a mapping interview methodology known as emotional mapping in order to consider the users' knowledge, which is beyond the cartographic practices of official (police) statistics, media representations and other institutional instruments of knowledge production.

The development and first results of the emotional mapping interviews presented in this chapter are part of an ongoing Franco-German research consortium that focuses on drug use in public settings and urban security (DRUSEC). The interviews we rely on took place in Nuremberg and Munich (cities without drug consumption rooms/DCRs), as well as in Berlin and Frankfurt (cities with DCRs).

2   From 'maps in minds' to a map on paper

As geographers, we highlight the spatiality of social practices. Space is not only location, background or context, but also a meaningful dimension of social practices. In this sense, drug consumption has its own geographies – on a world scale, regional scale or on the scale of places – which are embedded in economic, political and social practices (Potter, 2018). In this chapter, we focus on the scale of urban places within the city. Emotional mapping is a qualitative methodology, aimed at focussing on urban subjects and, as such, it differentiates itself strongly from other drug mapping practices. Our aim was to find a method able to portray how marginalised drug users – the particular group on which we focus here – have specific routines and emotions regarding the places of their everyday lives. The interpretation of interviews and maps enables us to provide an overview on the drug geographies of cities from the perspective of marginalised users.

2.1 Mapping drugs in the city: positivist approaches and fear maps

There is increasing research interest in spatial approaches to understanding drug issues, including mapping drugs on an urban scale. Spatial approaches understand space mostly as a physical phenomenon, which enables quantitative and spatial modelling based on geocriminological theories (Gruenewald, 2013; Gorman, Gruenewald & Waller, 2013). Such projects raise questions about the data they rely on. Available data for mapping drug practices generally derives from the work of different institutions, such as police, harm reduction and social workers, and pharmacists. The maps based on this data reflect not drug practices but the respective work of these institutions (Germes, 2014). Such positivist approaches reduce the complexity of the social (Belina, 2009), taking neither the everyday lives of marginalised drug users, nor broader urban structures into account. Therefore, geocriminological theories fail to understand drug use practices.

Other drug mapping practices focus on perceived safety, perceived risk or fear as immediate emotion, often conflating them (Hinkle, 2015). In neoliberal times of securitisation, local residents' fear and insecurities are often used to legitimise public policies (Shirlow & Pain, 2003) in order to repress, displace, and erase non-conforming marginalised drug users from particular neighbourhoods. We refrain from such an approach. Instead, we prefer a subject-related approach of positive as well as negative emotions – because drug use is about both pleasure and risk – and we prioritise questioning the emotions of drug users, as shown by our panel of interviewees.

2.2 Qualitative mapping with social geography and critical cartography

Contrary to a positivist understanding of maps representing an objective space mostly with quantitative data, our approach to mapping is based on social geography and critical cartography (Downs & Stea, 1977).

In our understanding, space is not a mere objective physical dimension, but produced (Lefebvre, 2000), through the time and histories of individuals, through scales and interdependencies. Space also materialises power relationships, structures everyday lives and destinies, yet is inhabited and transformed by subjectivities. Spaces are complex social constructions often involved in conflicts between social groups and their different uses of these spaces. That is why the presence of drug users in public spaces, their access to places and resources, as well as the autonomy or control of every person in public are central questions for public debate and research. These questions are fundamental to understand the where and why of drug use, and we will address them through the lenses of individual lives of marginalised drug users. In order not to objectify their lives in the city, we refer to the distinction made by social geography between living and lived spaces, terms derived from the French social geographical concepts espace de vie and espace vécu (Pichon, 2015). The living space is the area of our everyday lives, a mere list of places (such as home, friends' homes, frequently visited public places, routes). The lived space

designates the way we inhabit these places and interact with others, the relationships we establish with them, and the representations we have from them.
With the concept of lived spaces, the research focuses on the ways in which
our participants inhabit spaces, their everyday practices and the emotions they
associate with these spaces.

How can subjective lived spaces be mapped? We follow the critical cartography perspective (Harley, 1989; Crampton & Krygier, 2005; Kindynis, 2014;
Belina & Germes, 2016), which not only criticises the abstractions and objec-
tifications of positivist maps, but also proposes methods to create, produce
and work with maps in a qualitative way, enhancing the complexities of the
production of urban spaces. Qualitative drawn maps have long been developed
as a research method in different disciplines such as urban planning, psychology or geography (Lynch, 1960; Downs & Stea, 1977; Ziervogel, 2011). The
process of mental mapping is often a semi-directed interview during which
interviewees draw the places of their everyday lives and their representation
of these spaces. We enhanced this process in developing our own method of
emotional mapping as one contribution to the lasting interest of researchers in
mapping emotions (Nold, 2009; Olmedo & Roux, 2014; Mekdjian & Olmedo,
2016; Rekacewicz, 2016; Muis, 2016; Dernat, Bronner, Depeau, Dias, Lardon
& Ramadier, 2018).

2.3 Mapping emotions

In order to obtain maps and narratives about lived spaces (and not only living spaces), and in order not to fall back into the traps of neoliberal use of
fear maps, we decided to include emotions as a major part of the mapping
process. Recently, there has been growing interest in the role of emotions, especially the role of pleasure within the context of drug use (Duncan, Duff,
Sebar & Lee, 2017). Emotions are increasingly recognised as an important factor that influences how and why people use drugs. We consider emotions as
constructed and individual lived expressions of social conditions. For the mapping interviews, our first aim was to integrate a diverse but uniform spectrum
of emotions, which enables an understanding of them in relation to both drugs
and space, and of the comparability of drawn maps and transcribed texts. We
developed a colour wheel of chosen emotions with a range of positive feelings
such as relaxation (green), happiness and pleasure (yellow) or bliss and desire
(orange), along with a range of negative emotions such as blue (worry and insecurity), violet (disgust) and red (hostility and aggression). We did not choose the
colours of emotions according to any particular theory, since we do not build
this research on an underlying theory of emotions. The relationship between
colour and signification (emotion) is the one of a legend: a contingent code for
a specific purpose. As in Figure 1, the colours are arranged on a continuous

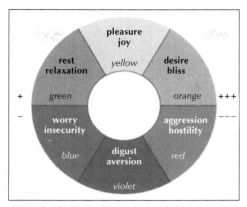

Figure 1: DRUSEC colour wheel of emotions

wheel for hue gradations between positive and negative, as well as more or less intense emotions.

2.4 Procedure of emotional mapping

We conducted qualitative semi-directive interviews, first asking our interviewees about their living spaces – from housing to visiting friends – or working

Figure 2: The process of the emotional mapping interview

places. We explained the process of mapping, and step-by-step they drew each space and place in black on a large blank sheet of paper (there was no need for accurate localisations). Later, the interviewees talked about their everyday life experiences in relation to drugs and places: they chose colours from the colour wheel and circled or coloured particular places according to their different emotions (Figure 2).

The drawn maps are representations of individual geographies and enable us to gain a deeper understanding of specific drug users' geographies (Behnken & Zinnecker, 2013). The entanglement of visual and textual material, the emotional map, and the interview transcript represent the lived space and are therefore a lens into the way drug users experience urban space, producing further knowledge about the pleasures and insecurities of a potentially vulnerable population group, as well as about cities as complex landscapes of drug consumption.

2.5 Experiences and practices from the field of research

After 26 interviews conducted by the authors of this chapter, our experience of emotional mapping had proven enriching. First, we noted that the paper, colour pens, and map were mediating objects between interviewee and interviewer,

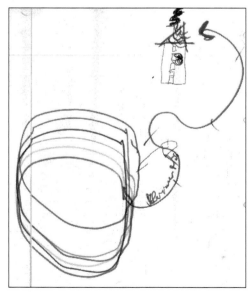

Figure 3: Chris's map: 'If you want me to, I take all [the colours of] pens'

helping to structure the dialogue. The interviewees appreciated the recognition of the importance of their knowledge. Some noted enhancement of feelings at being heard and the possibility of expressing themselves in a creative way. Thus, the mapping enhanced the quality of the interview itself as the map mitigated the typical researcher-subject situation and enabled the interviewees to be experts of their own maps. Nevertheless, there were huge variations in the mapping results. Despite our efforts to standardise the interview process with common guidelines and emotion legends, each of the interviewees approached the method in their own way, which also depended on their ability. Individuals' representation of space sets limits in the drawing of the maps: some maps do not show more than a few signs (see Figure 3). Furthermore, as in other social research methods, the results depend on the willingness of the interviewees, especially if they are asked to draw criminalised acts like drug use

In this chapter, we use two different citation methods: interviewee statements and pictures taken from the maps. In order to anonymise the data, only some details of the maps are quoted, or the map was re-drawn by the authors excluding any personal data that was in the original drawing. Everything was then translated into English. All names of interviewees quoted here are pseudonyms.

3   Urban lived spaces of drug users

Marginalised drug users in urban drug scenes face many challenges in their everyday lives. Mapping interviews with drug users from open drug scenes in Munich, Nuremberg, and Berlin give a unique view of the drug users' perspectives on, and their experiences of these cities. From housing to encounters with institutions, these urban experiences are associated mainly with negative feelings. The visual and text material collected during the interviews confirms how emotions are the results of the encounter between subjectivity and social structures, thereby drawing a social geography of the city.

3.1 The anxieties of precarious housing situations

The people we interviewed are part of a heterogeneous group. Their diversity was shown in their age, gender and housing conditions. Some have a home, sometimes shared with a non-drug-consuming family. The living space of home may lead to very positive or negative emotions, and, as such, is lived in different ways according to whether a person is autonomous or lives with family or a partner (see Figure 4). However, the majority of our interviewees did not have a permanent home. Most of them had lived in insecure and impermanent housing conditions for years. These included homeless shelters, friends' places,

Figure 4: The living space home: hostility or joy

squats in cellars and attics, drug services' sleeping accommodation, and the street.

In the maps, the participants sketched sleeping accommodation which is often decentralised and at the edges of the paper, indicating a peripheral location in the city, but also playing a minor role in the lived spaces (see Figures 5 and 6) They used these places mainly to sleep and were not willing or not allowed to stay there during the day. The housing situation was very stressful for most of the drug users and influenced their drug use habits. The interviewees described an increase in drug consumption with each step towards precarity. Martin, a 36-year-old drug user from Munich, outlined the situation in the homeless shel-

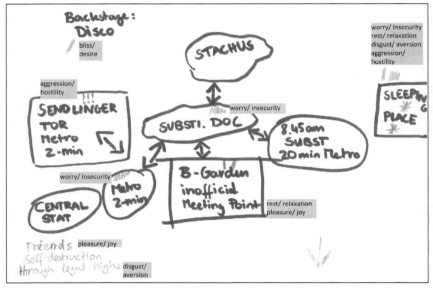

Figure 5: Martin's map: decentralised sleeping accommodation

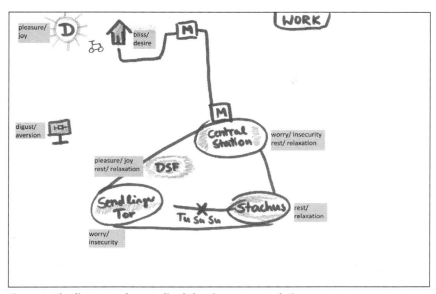

Figure 6: Charlie's map: decentralised sleeping accommodation

ter where he was staying as unbearable and linked this situation to his (increasing) drug use: 'So it's ... you won't make it without being high. I don't know anyone who doesn't drink or blaze or take other stuff' (Martin, 30, Munich). In his experience, one's mere presence in the shelters leads to increased drug use. Nevertheless, the pressure to consume drugs in the sleeping accommodation must be understood as socially constructed. Consuming in safe spaces, such as homes or shelters, generates mixed feelings due to the transgression and the perceived risk of eviction.

3.2 Ambivalent joys and worries of urban routines

Our interviewees spent most of their time outside, going through their principal routine: making money, buying, and using drugs. Here, public space plays a major role as a lived space and particularly as a social meeting space. The term 'open drug scene' is often negatively connoted and used as a catchphrase by politicians, journalist, and other actors. Open drug scenes are a heterogeneous group of drug users, depending on earnings, housing, etc. Beside drug-related issues, these social meeting places have an important function for coping in everyday life (Weber, 2011).

The people who meet at these places can be friends, acquaintances or strangers, while many highlight that their 'street buddies' are in no way 'real friends'. Social meeting places can be in public spaces such as the edge of a square, the bench of a train station or alleys or other interstices between buildings, which permit them to linger. These places are often located next to dealing places, substitution doctors or harm reduction facilities. Alternatively, the facilities of drug services also have an important function as social meeting places. The wide range of emotions visually represents the important role of social meeting places in the maps. In some maps, these places are covered by most of the colours in the emotion wheel, appearing as a rainbow (see Figure 7).

Figure 7: L. Schweino's map: social contact and the rainbow of emotions

The emotions associated with these everyday places may be described as inconsistent or conflicting. On the one hand, these are the places where one can meet one's friends and experience a social life or get what one needs. On the other hand, one's mere presence at these places is often connoted with drug use and the continuation of daily habits. Therefore, many wanted to change the everyday routine of drug consumption and subsequently their marginalisation by changing the spatial environment:

'I just want to leave. I have to change my social contacts somehow. (…) I just need a new and stable environment around me. (…) Again, and again, you go back to the places you know. And again, and again, you meet the people you know. That's very difficult.' (Miriam, 39, Nuremberg)

Miriam saw changing her lived space as the only possibility for changing her drug habits. Nevertheless, she struggled to do so.

3.3 Avoiding the risks of repression and conflict

Within the autonomous routine, encounters with particular institutions – such as police, traffic controllers, emergency services, hospital personnel – made up the lived spaces of marginalised drug users. Places known as hotspots of police surveillance and repression were avoided as much as possible. As Alf (27, Berlin) put it:

> 'From my point of view, they [the police] bother... Then comes the whole confiscation stuff... that's, off again, collecting bottles, working... Evictions ... when they see you again in the next 48 hours, they take you with them... From my point of view, it is harassment.'

In response to the question 'Are there places where you never go?', Alf replied:

> 'Mainly where there is the police! I don't want to have to do anything with them... There are places where they always go through and drive through, such as Kotti, Hermannplatz, Ku'damm, etcetera.'

Our interviewees reported experiencing hostility from institutions, mainly because of repeated experiences of humiliation and violence. Users also experienced hostility (such as threats and assault) from residents while trying to consume drugs in staircases, cellars and attics. The avoidance of such public and private places influenced their mobility in their own neighbourhoods and shaped their representation of a city that is made up of hostile public or private places.

Police checks significantly structure the movements and mobility of drug users in the lived space. For example, with 'junky jogging', drug users described the daily routine of getting evicted from one public place and moving collectively to another, until checks and banishment start over again. It reinforces the experience of not being a proper part of civil society, as several interviewees from Munich pointed out.

4   The emotional geographies of drug use

The lived spaces of marginalised drug users are characterised by a high spatial precariousness and vulnerability. Their emotional geography stresses unrest, hostility and aggression. Therefore, we should focus on the emotional geographies of their consumption places.

For the few interviewees who had a home, it was their preferred place for drug use. In case of cohabitation with sober partners or parents, consuming at home would often be a transgression, so it occurred only in secret. Homes, shelters and assisted housing are mostly peripheral and far away from the city centre, where a routine and harm reduction interventions take place. Therefore, drug consumption in a personal or private space happens only in the evening, for the 'last shot', and once the day is over. Thus, it can be said that drug use is driving consumers into the city.

4.1 Drug consumption rooms (DCR) as anchors of daily life

In Berlin, all interviewees were clients of the same DCR. Some went there almost every day, others occasionally, and most of them did not go to any of the other three DCRs in Berlin.

All emotional maps highlighted the DCR with positive emotions of safety, quiet and happiness: it was the place with the most positive and safe feelings around it. The possibility of drug consumption in a safe context responds to a need for quiet, hygiene, and overall safety: facilities including sterile equipment, meals, showers, and laundry are a significant relief for most of the homeless clients. The availability of information and support from the health and social workers also makes DCRs a helpful resource. Most interviewees were regular DCR users and reported how important this place had become to their every-

Figure 8: Zet's map: quietness and joy at the DCR

day lives, particularly because they felt accepted and welcomed there, did not have to face moral prompting to quit drugs and were spared from the discrimination of police and health workers. In this place, marginalised drug users found acceptance and relief. For many of them, it was the only room or closed space available to them and was an anchor of their precarious routines spent traversing adverse and dangerous public spaces (see Figure 8).

The DCRs are essential for drug users, because drug consumption is possible and support is available. These are the places where one can autonomously conform to addiction. Nevertheless, most of the time, our interviewees consumed drugs outside of the DCR. Neither the schedule of DCRs, nor their restricted number in each city could respond to the needs of the interviewees. Their opening times are limited to the afternoons of certain days, meaning that they are closed over whole weekends, as well as every evening and morning. Even within opening hours, the distance between the places where drugs are retrieved and the DCR for a person experiencing withdrawal symptoms is significant. In such circumstances, only a small proportion of consumption practices might take place in a DCR. Nevertheless, DCRs still play a crucial role for drug users.

4.2 Fragile existences of drug users in public

Marginalised drug users, homeless or not, even in cities with DCRs, are banned from finding places for drug use within public spaces and their interstices. Regularly, withdrawal symptoms lead interviewees to use the drug immediately after buying it. They have to find places for drug injecting and smoking: these must be places within their reach, among the spaces they are allowed to be present while affording some privacy. Indeed, the places of drug use are not adequate drug consumption places and the injecting process at these places is characterised by hurrying and worries for the user. Public consumption places are almost exclusively connoted with negative emotions such as insecurity, worry or disgust (see Figure 9). Charlie, a 28 year-old from Munich, describes this process: 'In underground car parks as well as on the stairs. Just between the cars, kneel down, boil it up, get ready.' The hurry, however, stems from the risk of getting caught, as well as the craving to consume drugs as soon as one gets them:

'If you don't feel well, you have the seal (consumption unit of heroin) in your mouth, you buy yourself a syringe and then you want to absorb the stuff as soon as possible. And then you just go in the next best backyard.' (Charlie, Munich)

Most of the drug users would prefer a DRC instead of 'the next best backyard' and reported aggressive encounters while consuming. A proportion of the re-

Figure 9: Zet's negative emotions associated with consumption in public places

spondents named non-specific places for drug use or refused to draw them. This leads us to interpret that these places are part of an unavoidable situation that these people have to confront in their daily life, rather than a choice for the lived space. Public drug consumption places are neither stable nor secure, but situations of frailty that change due to factors such as (police) checks, public construction work or other measures that influence the urban environment for drug users. In consequence, the emotional geography of drug use itself is polarised between DCRs and public spaces – that is, in those cities where DCRs exist.

5 Geographical explanations: between emotional appropriation and socio-spatial exclusion

Social drug research has shown how the question of why people use drugs has to take into account many factors, such as biographical or medical issues, drug-taking as an act of reward-seeking, as a strategy to avoid distress, or as a cultural practice of late capitalism. All these factors are materialised in urban spaces. The provisional results of emotional mapping show how place plays a huge role in explaining drug consumption. Marginalised drug users use drugs in the public places of the city obviously because there is no other place where they can do so, but also it is precisely because they are excluded from private spaces and institutional support and evicted from public spaces that they use more drugs than they would otherwise. This operates on two scales. On an (inter-)individual scale, the emotional appropriation of spaces explains drug use in the moment. On a broader urban and social scale, socio-spatial exclusion processes explain how marginalised drug users are easily trapped in a day-to-day drug consumption routine.

5.1 Emotional appropriation of spaces

Aside from urban (drug) policies, which affect the lived spaces of drug users – by creating, suppressing or criminalising drug practices – the users themselves have constructed their lived space and influences on cities' geographies, as well as their internalised drug habits. Due to what we call emotional appropriation, drug users experience different places within the city and overlay them with subjective emotions and spatial knowledge. The emotional mapping interviews illustrate that places related to drugs are highly intertwined with specific and inconsistent emotions. Experiences stabilise in the all-day places where they are experienced. During this process, drug users appropriate specific places emotionally. The emotional appropriation of drug places becomes the individual justification of behaviour such as drug use. Indeed, the desire for drugs can be understood as an emotion regarding drug use. As a result, drug users themselves find answers to the question 'why use drugs' in the place itself. Through the emotional appropriation of a specific place, this space becomes the emotional cause for drug use.

From our perspective, these drug places are constructed not only through the lived experiences and appropriation of drug users, but also through urban (drug) policies, which influence the geographies of drug consumption within the urban space. The way drug users experience public places is determined through political (il)legalisations and harm reduction policies as well as through measures of repression and displacement effects. The reasons for using drugs in public places are few and are rather individual preferences, even among a lack of alternative possibilities. Drug users with neither a permanent home nor immediate access to a DCR have to remain in public places in order to consume drugs out of necessity.

5.2 Socio-spatial exclusion and day-to-day drug use routines

From our perspective, the illegalisation, tabooing, and moralising of some substances and their consumption foster social exclusion for some drug user groups. The individualisation of personal vulnerabilities – such as social isolation or psychological issues – fails to point out the production of both isolation and interpersonal violence in neoliberal times and records the failure of the social and medical system to address these issues. In this theoretical perspective,

71

drug use leads to social exclusion (Becker, 1973), exclusion from social relationships, the work market, sufficient healthcare, and stable housing. Exclusion is expressed spatially, as more places become inaccessible to certain individuals due to a lack of financial resources, economic capital, poor health and physical appearance. The near-impossibility of access to private or semi-private spaces, permanent eviction back to public spaces and subsequent eviction from these public spaces are also examples of socio-spatial exclusion. Evelyn (28, Berlin), now living in a shelter, refers to her eviction from supported housing: 'I didn't really inject for three years, and I've been doing it again for six weeks. Probably because of all the things that come together'.

In turn, spatial exclusion deprives marginalised drug users of access to determinant resources. The public spaces appropriated by marginalised drug users are the last ones in which they can stay alive despite all this hostility. The interviews showed clearly how each step toward more socio-spatial exclusion was a step towards greater consumption. Exclusion fosters subjective and objective vulnerability, and thus explains consumption.

6 Conclusion

Within an original perspective rooted in critical cartography and social geography, we proposed emotional mapping as a new method of describing and conceiving urban lived spaces of drug users in European cities. Suitable for researchers, stakeholders and harm reduction institutions, this method is not only helpful for understanding marginalised urban drug users, but is also suitable for understanding the lived spaces of other social groups – whether marginalised or not, occasional or regular users, or non-consumers frequenting public places used for drug consumption and dealing.

With our method of emotional mapping, we highlighted the manner in which places play an important role in explaining drug consumption. On a micro scale, personal emotional appropriation explains individual patterns of drug use. Emotions are intertwined with personal experiences as well as with structural power relationships and their spatialisation reflects both. On a macro scale, the structural phenomenon of socio-spatial exclusion in European metropolises explains how neoliberal, social, economic, and health policies produce massive anomie. Spatial eviction can lead to a feeling of helplessness, abandonment by institutions and social loneliness, thereby fostering drug use.

Emotional mapping is still in the explorative phase within the broader DRU-SEC-Project. Our aim is to extend emotional mapping by individuals from different social groups within the city as a way to better understand urban space and the contentious geographies of the city as a complex production. We applied emotional mapping to cities in Germany and are also applying it to cities France. Furthermore, we suggest that this method may be applied to other

European cities which present similar mixed inner-city neighbourhoods known for being drug places, similar intricate living spaces for many different groups and similar patterns of urban policies.

References

Becker, H.S. (1973). *Outsiders: studies in the sociology of deviance.* New York: Free Press.

Behnken, I., & Zinnecker, J. (2013). Narrative Landkarten. Ein Verfahren zur Rekonstruktion aktueller und biographisch erinnerter Lebensräume. [Narrative maps. A reconstruction process of current and biographical remembered living spaces.] In: B. Friebertshäuser, A. Langer, & A. Prengel (Eds.), *Handbuch Qualitative Forschungsmethoden in der Erziehungswissenschaft* [Manual qualitative research methods of education science] (pp. 547–553). Weinheim: Beltz Juventa.

Belina, B. (2009). Kriminalitätskartierung – Produkt oder Mittel neoliberalen Regierens [Crime maps – products or means of neoliberal government]. *Geographische Zeitschrift* [Geographical Journal], *97 (4)*, 192–212.

Belina, B., & Germes, M. (2016). Kriminalitätskartierung als Methode der Kritischen Kriminologie? [Crime mapping as a method of critical criminology?]. *Kriminologisches Journal* [Criminological Journal], *48 (1)*, 24–46.

Crampton, J. W., & Krygier, J. (2005). An introduction to critical cartography. *ACME: An International E-Journal for Critical Geographies, 4 (1)*, 11–33.

Dernat, S., Bronner, A.C., Depeau, S., Dias, P., Lardon, S., & Ramadier, T. (2018) Représentations socio-cognitives de l'espace géographique [Socio-cognitive representations of geographic space]. *Réseau Cartotête* [Network Cartotête]. Retrieved from https://hal.archives-ouvertes.fr/hal-01934636/document

Downs, R.M., & Stea, D. (1977). *Maps in minds: reflections on cognitive mapping.* New York: Harper & Row.

Duff, C. (2007). Towards a theory of drug use contexts: space, embodiment and practice. *Addiction Research and Theory, 15 (5)*, 503–519.

Duncan, T., Duff, C., Sebar, B., & Lee, J. (2017). 'Enjoying the kick': locating pleasure within the drug consumption room. *International Journal of Drug Policy, 49 (1)*, 92–101.

Germes, M. (2014). Cartographies policières. La dimension vernaculaire du contrôle territorial [Police mappings. The vernacular side of territorial control]. *EchoGéo, 28, Online Journal*, published on 09.10.2014. Retrieved from http://journals.openedition.org/echogeo/13856.

Gorman, D., Gruenewald, P.J., & Waller, L.A. (2013). Linking places to problems: geospatial theories of neighborhoods, alcohol and crime. *GeoJournal, 78 (3)*, 417–428.

Gruenewald, P.J. (2013). Geospatial analyses of alcohol and drug problems: empirical needs and theoretical foundations. *GeoJournal, 78 (3)*, 443–450.

Harley, B. (1989). Deconstructing the map. *Cartographica: The International Journal for Geographic Information and Geovisualization, 26 (2)*, 1–20.

Hinkle, J.C. (2015). Emotional fear of crime vs. perceived safety and risk: implications for measuring 'fear' and testing the broken windows thesis. *American Journal of Criminal Justice, 40 (1)*, 147–168.

Kindynis, T. (2014). Ripping up the map: criminology and cartography reconsidered. *British Journal of Criminology, 54 (2)*, 222–243.

Kübler, D., & Wälti, S. (2001). Drug policy-making in metropolitan areas: urban conflicts and governance. *International Journal of Urban and Regional Research, 25 (1),* 35–54.

Lefebvre, H. (2000). *La production de l'espace* [The production of space]. Paris: Anthropos.

Lynch, K. (1960). *The image of the city.* Cambridge, MA: MIT Press.

Mekdjian, S., & Olmedo, E. (2016). Médier les récits de vie. Expérimentations de cartographies narratives et sensibles [Reaching life's narrative. Experimentations on narratives and sensible cartographies]. *M@ppemonde* [Mappemonde]. Retrieved from http://mappemonde.mgm.fr/118as2/

Moreno, C.M., & Wilton, R. (2014). Using space: critical geographies of drugs and alcohol. New York: Routledge.

Muis, A.S. (2016). Psychogéographie et carte des émotions, un apport à l'analyse du territoire? [Psychogeography and emotion maps, a contribution to the analysis of territories?]. *Carnets de Géographes* [Geography Notebooks], *9 (3),* 1–17.

Nold, C. (2009). (Ed.) Emotional cartography: technologies of the self. *Online: Softhook.* Retrieved from http://emotionalcartography.net/EmotionalCartography.pdf

Olmedo, E., & Roux, J.M. (2014). Conceptualité et sensibilité dans la carte sensible [Conceptuality and sensibility in the sensible cartography]. *Implications philosophiques* [Philosophical implications]. Online Journal, published on 31.04.2014. Retrieved from: http://www.implications-philosophiques.org/actualite/une/conceptualite-et-sensibilite-dans-la-carte-sensible-12/.

Parkin, S. (2013). *Habitus and drug using environments. Health, place and lived-experience.* Aldershot: Routledge.

Pichon, M. (2015). Espace vécu, perceptions, cartes mentales: l'émergence d'un intérêt pour les représentations symboliques dans la géographie française (1966–1985). [Lived space, perceptions, mental maps: the emergence of an interest for symbolic representations in the French geography (1966–1985)]. *Bulletin de l'association de géographes français* [Journal of the association of French geographers], *92 (1),* 95–110.

Potter, G.R. (2018). Introduction: Drugs, place, space and time. In: G.R. Potter, J. Fountain, & D.J. Korf (Ed.), *Place, space, time in European drug use, markets and policy* (pp. 11–25). Lengerich: Pabst Science Publishers.

Rekacewicz, P. (2016). Cartographier les émotions [Mapping emotions]. *Carnets de Géographes* [Geography Notebooks], *9 (3),* 1–22.

Shirlow, P., & Pain, R. (2003). The geographies and politics of fear. *Capital & Class, 27 (2),* 15–26.

Weber, M. (2011). *Szenenalltag. Über die Lebenspraxis abhängiger Drogengebraucher in Frankfurt am Main* [Everyday life of the scene. Life praxis of addicted drug users in Frankfurt on Main]. Frankfurt amMain: Verlag für Polizeiwissenschaften.

Ziervogel, M. (2011). Mental-Map-Methoden in der Quartiersforschung. [Mental-Map-Method in research of neighbourhood management]. In: O. Frey, & F. Koch (Eds.), *Positionen zur Urbanistik I. Stadtkultur und neue Methoden der Stadtforschung* [Position of Urbanism. Urban culture and new methods of urban research]. (pp. 187-206). Wien, Berlin: LIT.

5

'I have no clue' – a qualitative study on crack cocaine use in Frankfurt, Germany

Bernd Werse & Lukas Sarvari

Together with heroin, crack cocaine has been the joint number one drug in the marginalised drug users' scene in Frankfurt for almost two decades. Recent increases in the use of the drug as well as in the public discussion called for a closer look at the users, their motivations for using crack and links to the local discourse on drug policy. Semi-structured interviews were employed to gather data from 30 persons (12 female, 18 male), recruited by approaching them in public, mainly around harm reduction services. The participants of the study used crack cocaine regularly, as well as several other drugs. Half of the users received opioid maintenance therapy. Patterns of use varied between 'binges' of several hours or days and more regular modes of use. Many respondents could not refer to particular motives for crack use. Instead, the drug was often described as dominating one's mind and routine. A majority described staying in the core area of the drug scene as the strongest trigger for use. This perception underlines the significance of social factors for the users' habits. Public and individual beliefs about the addictive potential of the drug have reinforced each other, leading to the observed ubiquitous 'motiveless' use of the drug.

Keywords: crack, cocaine, marginalised users, motives of use, craving

1 Introduction

While crack cocaine nearly disappeared from the focus of social drug research after the 1990s, together with heroin, it has been the joint number one drug in the marginalised drug users' scene in the city of Frankfurt for almost two decades. This setting is relatively unique in Germany and throughout Europe, since many of these drug users stay in the streets of the *Bahnhofsviertel* (the area near the central railway station), where several harm reduction facilities have also been established since a relatively liberal approach in drug policy (the 'Frankfurt way') began in the early 1990s. Thus, marginalised users in Frankfurt (as well as Hamburg) are a rare example for a continuing open 'hard drugs' users' scene. Moreover, Frankfurt is one of the three German cities (along with Hamburg and Hannover) with a significant amount of crack cocaine use (Robert Koch Institut, 2016), with nine out of ten members of the scene having used the drug in the prior month (Werse, Kamphausen, & Klaus, 2019), which is higher than in any other German city. This feature makes the Frankfurt scene also relatively unique in the European context: there is evidence of some level of crack use in urban settings of marginalised drug users only from some Dutch, French, and British cities, (EMCDDA, 2007).

In the last three years, there has been a growing discussion about the Frankfurt scene and particularly the use of crack cocaine in local media and among policy stakeholders. Gradually, the use of the drug in public places got more attention from different actors: passers-by and business people felt disturbed, wealthy residents complained about noise and dirt, journalists fanned the flames of the (political) debate, and finally, law enforcement officials and local politicians were forced to react. The frequency of individual police checks grew, as well as the number of major raids on crack dealers (Kamphausen, Werse, Klaus & Sarvari, 2018). At the same time, the issue was discussed as if crack use was a new phenomenon in the city (Kamphausen, 2018). Indeed, the use of the drug increased to new record levels in recent years (24-hour prevalence: 2002: 79%, 2004: 62%, 2006: 65%, 2008: 59%, 2010: 64%, 2012: 75%, 2014: 83%, 2016: 84%, 2018: 81%, Werse, Kamphausen & Klaus, 2019). However, these numbers also show continuously high levels of crack prevalence since the first quantitative survey in this setting in 2002, when prevalence was nearly as high as recently.

These developments called for a closer look at the users, their motivations for using crack cocaine and links to the local discourse on drug policy. Little is known about the reasons behind the 'success story' of crack cocaine in Frankfurt. The research presented in this chapter aims to get more information about site-specific conditions that may have favoured the rise of the drug, as well as the users' motives for using it.

To a large extent, the existing social scientific literature on crack cocaine centres around the US 'crack epidemic' of the mid-to-late 1980s, starting from sensationalist pamphlets (e.g., Chatlos, 1987), followed by explorations of the users (e.g., Boyd & Mieczkowski, 1990). At the same time, the first critical publications on the media scare that accompanied the phenomenon were released (e.g., Rosenbaum, Murphy, Irwin & Watson, 1990; Gieringer, 1990), culminating in a critical anthology on the issue (Reinarman & Levine, 1997). A highly discussed topic in this context is the question of the 'social pharmacology' (Morgan & Zimmer, 1997) of crack: to what extent can the effects and particularly the intense craving associated with crack (which is, pharmacologically, the same drug as cocaine) be linked to the social context (predominantly marginalised black people as opposed to mainly white middle-class powder cocaine users)?

Further publications on the drug from the USA include several other empirical views of users and settings (e.g., Bourgois, 1995; Sterk, 1999; Baumer, Lauritsen, Rosenfeld & Wright, 1998; Jackson-Jacobs, 2004). In recent years, non-European publications on the use of the drug focused on Brazil, that has 'recently experienced a nationwide increase in crack cocaine use and trafficking' (Toledo, Cano, Bastos, Bertoni & Bastos, 2017, p. 66).

As early as 1993, the first larger European publication on crack was released, including similar critical views on the 'Promotion of an epidemic' (Bean, 1993b, p. 59) in the UK, as had occurred some years previously in the USA. Ever since, there have been only few publications on crack use in Europe, with a focus on the UK (e.g. Green, Day & Ward, 2000; Gossop, Marsden, Stewart & Kidd, 2002). A European multi-centre study (Haasen, Prinzleve, Zurhold, et al., 2004) also found focuses of crack use in the UK and Germany (Frankfurt and Hamburg) only.

The first larger overview on crack cocaine use in Germany was a study by Stöver (2001), assessing crack use in different settings, including the early notion that Frankfurt and Hamburg were the only cities with significant prevalence. Some pilot projects at that time researched the specifics and effects of crack use in these two cities (Vogt, Schmid & Roth, 2000; Thane & Thiel, 2000; Langer, Behr & Hess, 2004). An online survey in Germany (Hößelbarth, 2014) managed to recruit a rather small number of recreational crack users (28 less-than-weekly users), indicating that this seems to be a rare phenomenon compared to users from marginalised settings. The development of crack use in the Frankfurt scene has been documented bi-annually since 2002 in a longitudinal quantitative survey (Werse et al., 2019). Qualitative research focused on women in this setting (Langer, 2004; Bernard, 2013), highlighting that particularly women who work as prostitutes often use crack intensively to cope with problems associated with sex work. Other qualitative research on persons from such settings in Frankfurt, Hamburg and Hannover (Hößelbarth, 2014) indicated a certain variety of patterns of use and of users' capability of controlling crack use, although bingeing seems to be a common feature.

Nevertheless, no evidence about the question why people use crack cocaine in certain German urban hard drugs users' settings exists, let alone the connections of such motives with spatial conditions. This is the focus of the present research. Some of the results can be applied to urban crack-using settings in other European countries, particularly with regard to

a) general reasons for crack use in such settings,
b) patterns and dynamics of crack use, e.g. in connection to other drug use,
c) perceptions of quality, effects and craving,
d) possible alternatives to the drug, and, on a meta-level,

e) collective and individual social constructions surrounding the drug and its connections to motives and dynamics of use.

2 Methods

The subject was researched with a qualitative study, funded by the city of Frankfurt. We used a special guideline-based form of the focused interview (Merton & Kendall 1946) with biographical elements. With these interviews, we gathered data from 30 persons (12 female, 18 male) with an average age of 41 years, mostly identified as members of the local scene of marginalised hard drug users. Interviewers were instructed to recruit a relatively high number of females, in order to be able to draw gender comparisons (general estimates from drug services for the proportion of females in this setting are around 25%). The interviews took place between July and September 2017. Respondents were recruited by approaching them on the streets or around harm reduction facilities (e.g. drug consumption rooms) in Frankfurt-Bahnhofsviertel. The respondents received 20 Euros for a completed interview. The guideline contained questions about general socio-demographic features; drug-using career; definitions, (local) specifics and opinions of crack use, patterns and functions of use, dependence potential, alternatives to crack, social work, and repression.

For qualitative analysis, we used a semi-open coding strategy, largely following the principles of grounded theory (Glaser & Strauss, 1967) and qualitative content analysis (Mayring, 2000), taking into account some existing categories from prior research and the interview guidelines. Following established modes of research on anonymous respondents, the study did not need to be approved by an ethics committee.

3 Results

3.1 General situation and patterns of drug use

The daily grind of the interviewees can be characterised by the procurement of money to buy drugs in order to use them. In the vast majority of cases, respondents had used various legal and illegal drugs (including) heroin before their first crack use. Most interviewees showed a physical opioid dependence and half of the respondents were currently in methadone or buprenorphine maintenance treatment. When looking at drug use in the last 24 hours, crack cocaine was the most frequently used psychoactive substance (90%), followed by alcohol (47%), cannabis (43%), heroin (40%), and benzodiazepines (17%).

3.2 Definitions and quality perceptions

The drug itself is usually called *Stein* (stone or 'rock' in English): 'crack' as a term is rather uncommon in the Frankfurt scene. There were diverging opinions about quality and potential adulterants of crack cocaine. Most of the respondents believed that in addition to 'good stones', there are also 'bad stones' around, which are often called 'chemo-stones', because they presumably include synthetic drugs, mainly of the amphetamine-type. This presumption could not be confirmed in a recent toxicological investigation of drug residues from drug consumption rooms in Frankfurt, where none of the (crack) cocaine samples contained any other stimulants (Peter, Kempf & Auwärter, 2018). Surprisingly, the alleged effects of 'bad stones' are less typical for amphetamine-type stimulants, but rather for high dosages of ordinary crack cocaine, e.g. unrest, insomnia, paranoia, anorexia, sexual dysfunction and strong craving. At the same time, many users qualified the effects of 'good stones' – paradoxically – as psychologically calming and relaxing:

'[The effect is] Short and calming. Quickly take a deep breath. That's it. Simply unwind.' (Roxana, aged 36)

In addition, according to several respondents, common physical side-effects of crack cocaine such as insomnia and lack of appetite do not seem to occur with 'good' or 'real stones':

'There is crack that makes you jittery and greedy, because there is an awful lot of speed [amphetamine] or whatever in it. And then there is crack, you smoke it and you come down really cool. You can eat, drink, sleep.' (Petra, aged 50)

'If it is real [crack] cocaine, then it is totally chilling. You can eat, sleep and have a normal conversation. Although you get a dry mouth and you get really thirsty at some point, you are completely relaxed. Because [crack] cocaine hits you really slowly and also decays really slowly. You are not pushed.' (Tanja, aged 48)

3.3 Patterns of crack use

While crack cocaine was mostly smoked, there was also a considerable amount of intravenous use of the drug: only around one third of the respondents stated that they exclusively smoked it, while the others mostly used both modes of administration. Two basic patterns of use could be identified: the first one, commonly associated with the drug, is bingeing, which may last from several hours up to several-day episodes of use, followed by breaks of varying lengths:

> *'Twenty-four/seven; always chasing the 'stone'. I accept I'm that tired, like six or seven days awake, but I also know that I cannot just stay somewhere on the street – I mean, I am in clear mind at this moment, I do not like others … here on the street … I retreat to a safe place, could be the café above or in the daytime sleeping facility, where I won't just faint.'* (Nilhan, aged 48)

The second pattern of use is a more regular one, with respondents using comparatively small amounts daily (sometimes not starting before afternoon) and having a regular sleeping pattern and place:

> *'Usually I used to smoke all day, until the evening. Until just before going to bed, in the evening rather less, because that's all in vain, actually. That's also the case with heroin. Before bedtime I used to shoot up a cocktail [of heroin and crack cocaine], which is also nonsense. Now it's just like… morning, noon, most consumption. Then in the evening it's getting less.'* (Giovanni, aged 45)

3.4 Crack and other drugs

Although many respondents claimed that powdered cocaine has a better reputation on the scene than crack cocaine, and the effect of cocaine powder was described as more pleasant, many users preferred to use crack even if powdered cocaine was available, since the smokable form of the drug was perceived as 'more convenient'. Some users even mentioned cooking their own crack when they have access to powder cocaine.

Other drugs, particularly sedatives, are often used along with crack cocaine to alleviate unwanted effects, but the drug is also combined directly with heroin (a 'cocktail', see above). In addition, opioid-substituted respondents (half of the sample) mention the desire for the 'kick' achieved by crack cocaine. It should be mentioned that almost all respondents were physically dependent on opioids – those who did not get opioid replacement therapy were daily heroin users. However, apart from the fact that non-substituted respondents had to buy their opioids, we could not observe substantial differences in the drug use patterns of both groups.

3.5 Motivations for use

When asked for reasons why they use crack cocaine, relatively many respondents were not able to figure out any motive. The drug often did not fulfil a certain function in the everyday life of the interviewees. They mainly used crack cocaine because the drug was available and associated with the Frankfurt open drug scene, sometimes referring to the dependence potential of the drug. Jennifer (aged 41) said 'No, it's simply like … I have no clue, I just like the kick… Why or how, that's … really no one knows here.' Marco (aged 25) added:

'I'm trying to get rid of it, but that's just the addiction, and if I've taken it – every time – I get annoyed every time I did it again. But with regard to a certain [function] in everyday life … you cannot say anything, actually.'

In addition, some interviewees reported being able to 'perform' better after consuming crack. The performance-enhancing effects influence different areas of life, e.g. of some of the female users working as prostitutes, but also in terms of common routines. Two respondents compared the use of crack cocaine with a cup of coffee in the morning. Marco commented that 'most people need their coffee to do anything and I need this' and Dennis (aged 32) said:

'Then I just didn't smoke for two days, because I didn't feel like it. But then I got such a performance slump, because every day I need it somehow to get going, somehow I need a pipe, right. I'm so lazy without it.'

Furthermore, the effect of crack use applies to certain activities, especially for raising money:

'I think if I use crack, I'm more efficient. I don't know if I'm right, but I feel more efficient. … So, I have the feeling, if I got crack, then I can afford more as I do without it. So it seems like… Because I also run a lot, I collect deposit bottles [a relatively common activity among poor people in Germany], and if I got crack, then I'll speed up and I think that just makes me more efficient, that I can do more than usual.' (Turbo B, aged 30)

Conversely, many respondents stated that the drug determines everyday life, especially when the first pipe had already been smoked and the craving for more crack had set in:

'That's very determining, you have to say. You run after the stuff more than it is necessary at all. So back then, I did not get it right to do the things in the morning I needed to do. I just ran around from morning to night to make money, buy a stone, make money.' (Marco, aged 25)

3.6 Addiction potential of crack cocaine

While most interviewees considered themselves as 'addicted' to crack cocaine, this addiction is different from the steady, physical opioid dependence: most of the users referred to their crack-smoking habit as 'completely in the head'. More specifically, they described the craving associated with their crack addiction as an irresistible desire. In line with common images of the dynamics of crack use, most respondents report that after the first hit of the day, they need to use more:

'I don't know what they mix in here, but when you smoke it, you always want more. That makes you greedy. There is no end. And with money in your pocket you can't stop.' (Mandy, aged 36)

Another interviewee pointed out that a person needs a certain disposition to get 'hooked' on crack:

'The bad thing with the stuff is, either you like it right away or you don't like it. And if you like it, then you're already lost.' (Petra, aged 50)

Many respondents named the mere presence of drug users in the Bahnhofs-viertel as an essential factor that triggers the desire to use. If the drug users are elsewhere, it is much easier for them to get around without the drug. One user stated that he managed to stop using crack cocaine, which he achieved mainly by not visiting the Bahnhofsviertel anymore. However, to practically every other respondent, such a move would be unthinkable, given the long-term histories of life in this (social and geographical) setting. Some of the respondents imposed self-limiting rules of use to restrain the use of crack cocaine. These interviewees had in common that they identified heroin or other opioids (e.g., methadone) as their main drug.

When respondents stopped using crack, many of them experienced different symptoms such as nervousness, aggressive behaviour, and depressive moods. A smaller proportion of them also reported physical withdrawal symptoms like headaches or heavy sweating. In addition, some respondents felt feeble after waking up when they have not slept for days before. They felt they could regain their strength only through crack. At the same time, they felt the need to fight rising negative emotions with the use of the drug:

*'You're getting more and more nervous. So, you don't feel pain, but it's
such a pricking and drilling in the soul, like "ah, I want it now" and you
get more and more nervous and you're getting pissed off and obnoxious
and so on.'* (Giovanni, aged 45)

3.7 Alternatives to crack

When respondents were asked for possible alternatives or substitute products
for crack cocaine, such a possibility was often denied. However, a noteworthy
proportion named cannabis as the possibly most useful compensation, mainly
because of the similar form of consumption, along with a relatively quick onset
of the effect. It seems like the users mainly sought the act of smoking itself (including the sensory perception) plus any psychoactive effect – even though the
effect of cannabis is a completely different one:

*'When I smoke cannabis, I just do not think about stones. Then I just
want to be a bit for myself, just relax. [...] It helps me completely. Then I
do not have the desire [for stones]. I do not have withdrawal symptoms
or anything else.'* (Paul, aged 41)

A few respondents mentioned other drugs or sports as a possible substitute.
However, much more common was the view that only a significant change in
their living conditions, including a change of location, could lead to a reduction
or cessation of crack cocaine use:

Interviewer: *'Do you have any idea what could personally help you to
smoke less stones?'*
Maria (aged 38): *'Just, away from Frankfurt, that's it.'*
Interviewer: *'Okay, why is it especially Frankfurt, where so many stones
are around?'*
Maria: *'I don't know. Here I started and here ... if I'm somewhere else, I
never use any stones, but as soon as I'm back here, I start again.'*

3.8 Crack, Frankfurt and the Bahnhofsviertel

As highlighted in the quote above, there is a strong association of crack cocaine
with the social space of the Bahnhofsviertel. Most respondents blamed the area
as the key trigger that makes it impossible to change their life. When asked
'What role does Frankfurt play?', Nilhan (aged 48) replied:

'Absolutely, absolutely. I can tell you – during the time when I was clean, these nine years … when I sometimes brought my mum here to the Kaiserstrasse by car, because there are some Persian shops, where you can buy specialties from Iran. My mum told me, I have to go there with her once a month. Then we got into the car, and when I was on the highway, just before the gas station, my blood was running cold, my hands were dripping with sweat, and I got such a rumbling in the stomach, like I'll get diarrhoea. It really only has to do with Frankfurt. When I'm in Frankfurt. But I always got through this and did not use, only because my mother was always there. If she had said, come and take the money, go there and buy these things for me, I would have surely relapsed at that time. Frankfurt plays a very, very important role.'

Many users lacked access to basic everyday features such as work, housing, etc. (or close contact to family members, as was temporarily the case with the respondent quoted above), severely limiting the general possibility of leaving the scene and stopping using the drug. However, most still imagined that they would be able to get out of this setting. Thus, the following quote of a self-confessed 'crack junkie' is a rare exception:

'That smell, that red light district, these bitches, these gays, all of this simply belongs together somehow. I know that, I can… I'm a Bahnhofs-junkie, a hard-core Bahnhofs-junkie, absolutely.' (Giovanni, aged 45)

When asked why the drug plays such a big role in the 'open drug scene' in Frankfurt, the respondents gave various possible reasons. These included the perception that 'Frankfurt has been a cocaine city for a long time' and that cocaine became prevalent among marginalised users during the 1990s when methadone maintenance was established, but the users still had a desire for a 'kick'. The fact that back then, there were many US citizens (e.g. from the army) in town, might have contributed to the move from powder to crack cocaine in the late 1990s. At that time, cocaine dealers in the marginalised scene completely switched to the smokable form, making the sale of the drug more convenient.

4 Conclusion and discussion

Nearly all participants of the study were regular users of crack in addition to several other drugs. The typical Frankfurt-based crack user started their career of compulsive drug use with heroin addiction (half of the users currently received opioid maintenance therapy), but has been a polydrug user for many years. While a significant number reported binges of several hours or days as typical patterns of crack use, others used the drug in a more regular way, e.g. on few occasions per day. Thus, our results confirm the observation that patterns of crack use can be variable (e.g., German & Sterk, 2002; Hößelbarth, 2014). Apart from some who referred to the performance-enhancing effects (see below), a crucial finding of this study is the observation that often no particular motives for crack cocaine use were stated. Instead, the drug was frequently described as dominating one's mind and routine after the first 'hit' of the day. A vast majority described staying in the core area of the drug scene (Bahnhofsviertel) as the strongest trigger for using crack cocaine. It is worth noting that most of the respondents referred to crack as the most relevant drug, although nearly all of them were physically dependent on opioids and a majority used a number of other drugs.

The fact that nearly all users assumed that there were 'bad stones' around, adulterated with amphetamine-type stimulants (which has been refuted by analyses) is an interesting case of a social construction by the users. We can only speculate about the reasons for this very prevalent myth: perhaps bad conditions of set and setting, along with an uncommon texture of crack that was adulterated with non-psychoactive substances, might lead to a negative expectation and thus also a negative perception of drug effects. Moreover, the respondents' descriptions of the effects of bad stones fit the characteristics of highly potent crack cocaine, while at the same time, their descriptions of 'good stones' resemble the effect of crack with a low purity level. Hence, a possible explanation might be that many users, despite their subjectively strong dependence, may actually dislike the specific crack cocaine high and therefore favour stones with lower doses. Accordingly, relatively many of our respondents were not able to describe the drug's supposed positive effects. These observations are particularly noteworthy when taking into account 'humans' extensive homeostatic responses to stimulant drugs' (Morgan & Zimmer, 1997, p. 155), which are responsible for the intense 'low' after a short cocaine 'high', particularly in the accelerated form of smoked crack, and which, in some users, is made responsible for craving and bingeing. It seems like, unknowingly, a considerable proportion of crack users aims to limit the drug's effects and particularly its after-effects.

Although it can be assumed that a strong craving after the use of crack is a characteristic effect of the drug, this does not explain the strong craving of users through the mere presence in the core area of the scene – we suggest a highly social interplay between deviant identity, stigmatisation, ritualisation and drug effects, which seems like a collective form of very effective autosuggestion. The respondents' ubiquitous wish to change their lives stands in stark contrast to their long-practiced life routines. Many had been living in precarious conditions for most of their lives, including the hard drug users' scene as the source of their only social contacts, making it extremely difficult to change. The habits described here are the results of long psychosocial processes, reinforced by stigmatisation, criminalisation and peer influence. In this respect, Frankfurt-based crack users resemble the marginalised users in US inner city neighbourhoods: the intensity of their mental 'addiction' may at best in part be explained by the pharmacology of smokable cocaine, but much more by social contexts and life histories (Morgan & Zimmer, 1997).

The only concrete function of crack use mentioned by a substantial number of respondents is performance enhancement. Considering the desire for change of almost all respondents and the fact that their everyday life is characterised not only by raising money, drug procurement and drug use, but also by (often procrastinated) visits to authorities, doctors and social counsellors, the functionality of crack consumption, which is in turn responsible for the dysfunctionality of users, is possibly easier to understand.

Some of the users shared the narrative that crack might give them the energy that they need for all the tasks they have to complete to realise their desire for change: to get a flat, medical treatment, a place in a treatment programme, insurance, unemployment benefits or even a job. At the same time, crack use is linked to the (often illicit) procurement of money. Stealing, selling stolen goods, sex work or drug dealing are daily features of many scene members (Werse et al., 2019). While they had to do this work in order to fund their drug use, it, in turn, consumes all of their energy. There are periods of extreme tiredness and listlessness after long binges. In summary, at least some of the users are taking a drug (even though they often dislike its effects) for the purpose of their day-to-day work that they do to afford this very drug, which they hope will provide them with the energy to achieve the goals of life associated with getting away from the drug. This vicious and somewhat paradoxical circle is difficult to break and, moreover, gives those who are trapped in it the opportunity to achieve just enough small successes at the level of daily money and drug procurement to prove to themselves their abilities, their efficiency and their stamina – requirements that are imposed on everyone in the modern work society. To some degree, we may understand crack cocaine as the engine of an economic microcosm (Frankfurt-Bahnhofsviertel) in which drug use stands under the paradigm of 'work' and self-assertion.

Regarding potential harm reduction efforts, another particularly notable finding is that several respondents stated that cannabis helped them to use less crack and that some of them even considered cannabis a potential substitute product for crack cocaine. As mentioned above, and despite the different effects of the two drugs, cannabis saturates the indefinite need for some 'high', is inhalable and therefore provides a rapid onset of the 'kick', just like crack does. Apart from these compensatory effects described by some respondents, cannabis can also help to reduce negative side-effects of crack, in line with findings from Gonçalves and Nappo (2015) who examined the benefits of combined cannabis-crack use among Brazilian drug users:

'The interviewees emphasized that the improved quality of life as a result of eliminating or reducing cravings and paranoid symptoms was the most positive effect of using the cannabis-crack combination. [...] the interviewees slowed or even stopped their crack use due to the state of relaxation induced by cannabis' (Gonçalves & Nappo 2015, p. 6).

In addition to the reduction of craving, paranoia and/or mental stress, cannabis also has also sleep-inducing and appetising properties, potentially benefiting the physical health of users. Gonçalves and Nappo (2015) suspect that these anti-psychotic effects and health benefits are mainly due to the active agent cannabidiol (CBD). CBD, which in Germany, unlike tetrahydrocannabinol (THC) is legally obtainable (e.g. in drugstores), could easily be implemented into a health plan for crack users, although the demand for a 'high' described above would not be satisfied with the almost non-psychoactive CBD. However, minimising cravings, improving mental health, and promoting regular sleeping patterns through CBD medication could have a positive impact on the lives of marginalised crack users.

While these results might be transferable to other places where crack use is prevalent, there are various limitations for some of the other findings: e.g. with regard to the 'trigger effect' of the geographical setting, or to the specific patterns of drug use. Thus, further research on these issues, particularly in other European cities with crack users, is required.

Returning to the question why the average member of the Frankfurt-based marginalised drug users' scene uses such considerable amounts of crack, we can conclude that, while many of these persons subjectively cannot give any concrete reason, the drug has an important function in a psychosocial-pharmacological-spatial nexus. This complex may be regarded as one of several paradoxes in the particular lifestyle of such persons: they always come back to the *Bahnhofsviertel* although they blame this place for their habit; they dream of an 'ordinary life' although their long-term acquired habitus would never fit with it; and they use a stimulant drug in order to be able to get money to fund further doses of this stimulant drug.

References

Baumer, E., Lauritsen, J.L., Rosenfeld, R., & Wright, R. (1998). The influence of crack cocaine on robbery, burglary, and homicide rates: a cross-city, longitudinal analysis. *Journal of Research in Crime and Delinquency, 35 (3),* 316–340.

Bean, P. (Ed.) (1993a). *Cocaine and crack. Supply and use.* Houndmills, London, New York: Macmillan/St. Martin's Press.

Bean, P. (1993b). Cocaine and crack: the promotion of an epidemic. In: P. Bean (Ed.). *Cocaine and crack. Supply and use* (pp. 59–75). Houndmills, London, New York: Macmillan/St. Martin's Press.

Bernard, C. (2013). *Frauen in Drogenszenen. Drogenkonsum, Alltagswelt und Kontrollpolitik in Deutschland und den USA am Beispiel Frankfurt und New York City* [Women in drug scenes. Drug use, everyday life, and control policies in Germany and the USA with Frankfurt and New York as examples]. Wiesbaden: Springer VS.

Boyd, C.J., & Mieczkowski, T. (1990). Drug use, health, family and social support in 'crack' cocaine users. *Addictive Behaviors, 15 (5)*, 481–485.

Bourgois, P. (1995). *In search of respect. Selling crack in El Barrio.* Cambridge: Cambridge University Press.

Chatlos, C. (1987). *Crack. What you should know about the cocaine epidemic.* New York: Perigee.

EMCDDA: European Monitoring Centre for Drugs and Drug Addiction (2007). *Selected issue – cocaine and crack cocaine: a growing public health issue.* Luxembourg: Office for Official Publications of the European Communities.

German, D., & Sterk, C.E. (2002). Looking beyond stereotypes: exploring variations among crack smokers. *Journal of Psychoactive Drugs, 34 (4)*, 383–392.

Gieringer, D. (1990). How many crack babies? *The Drug Policy Letter, 4.*

Glaser, B.G., & Strauss, A.L. (1967). *The discovery of grounded theory. Strategies for qualitative research.* New Brunswick, London: Aldine Transaction.

Gonçalves, J. R., & Nappo, S. A. (2015). Factors that lead to the use of crack cocaine in combination with marijuana in Brazil: a qualitative study. *BMC Public Health, 15 (1)*, 706.

Gossop, M., Marsden, J., Stewart, D., & Kidd, T. (2002). Changes in use of crack cocaine after drug misuse treatment: 4–5 year follow-up results from the National Treatment Outcome Research Study (NTORS). *Drug Alcohol Depend, 66 (1)*, 21–28.

Green, A., Day, S., & Ward, H. (2000). Crack cocaine and prostitution in London in the 1990s. *Sociol Health Illn, 22 (2)*, 27–39.

Haasen, C., Prinzleve, M., Zurhold, H., Rehm, J. et al. (2004). Cocaine use in Europe – a multi-centre study. *European Addiction Research, 10 (2)*, 139–146.

Hößelbarth, S. (2014). *Crack, Freebase, Stein. Konsumverhalten und Kontrollstrategien von KonsumentInnen rauchbaren Kokains* [Crack, freebase, stone: consumption behaviour and control strategies of smokable cocaine users]. Wiesbaden: Springer VS.

Jackson-Jacobs, C. (2004). Hard drugs in a soft context: managing trouble and crack use on a college campus. *The Sociological Quarterly, 45 (4)*, 835–856.

Kamphausen, G. (2018). Steine auf dem Frankfurter Weg – Crack in Frankfurt am Main [Stones on the Frankfurt Way – crack in Frankfurt am Main]. In: akzept e.V. & Deutsche Aidshilfe e.V. (Eds.), *5. Alternativer Drogen- und Suchtbericht* (pp. 135–142). Lengerich: Pabst Science Publishers.

Kamphausen, G., Werse, B., Klaus, L., & Sarvari, L. (2018). *MoSyD Jahresbericht 2017. Drogentrends in Frankfurt am Main* [MoSyD Annual Report 2017. Drug trends in Frankfurt am Main]. Frankfurt a. M.: Centre for Drug Research, Goethe-Universität.

Langer, A. (2004). Prostitution von Stein zu Stein [Prostitution from stone to stone]. In: H. Stöver, H. & M. Prinzleve (Eds.), *Kokain und Crack. Pharmakodynamiken, Verbreitung und Hilfeangebote* (pp. 159–178). Freiburg i. Br.: Lambertus.

Langer, A., Behr, R., & Hess, H. (2004). Was dir der Stein gibt, kann dir keine Nase geben [What the rock can give you, no nose would be able to]. *Forschung Frankfurt, 22 (1),* 28–32.

Mayring, P. (2000). Qualitative content analysis [28 paragraphs]. *Forum Qualitative Sozialforschung/Forum Qualitative Social Research, 1 (2),* Art. 20. Retrieved from http://nbnresolving.de/urn:nbn:de:0114-fqs0002204

Merton, R.K., & Kendall, P.L. (1946). The focussed interview. *American Journal of Sociology, 51 (4),* 541–557.

Morgan, J.P., & Zimmer, L. (1997). The social pharmacology of smokeable cocaine: not all it's cracked up to be. In: C. Reinarman, & H.G. Levine (Eds.), *Crack in America: demon drugs and social justice* (pp. 131–170). Berkeley, CA: University of California Press.

Peter, R., Kempf, J., & Auwärter, V. (2018). *Substanzmonitoring in Konsumräumen – Analysenergebnisse der Untersuchungen des Jahres 2017* [Substance monitoring in drug consumption rooms – results of analyses from the year 2017]. Poster, Freiburg i. Br.: Universitätsklinikum, Institut für Rechtsmedizin. Presented at a press conference of the city of Frankfurt a. M., 18.03.2018.

Reinarman, C., & Levine, H.G. (Eds.) (1997). *Crack in America: demon drugs and social justice.* Berkeley: University of California Press.

Robert-Koch-Institut (2016). *Abschlussbericht der Studie „Drogen und chronische Infektionskrankheiten in Deutschland' (DRUCK-Studie)* [Final report of the study 'Drugs and chronic infectious diseases in Germany' (DRUCK study)]. Berlin: RKI.

Rosenbaum, M., Murphy, S., Irwin, J., & Watson, L. (1990). Women and crack: what's the real story? In Trebach, A.S. & Zeese, K.B. (Eds.). *Drug prohibition and the conscience of nations* (pp. 69–71). Washington, D.C.: Drug Policy Foundation.

Sterk, C.E. (1999). *Fast lives: women who use crack cocaine.* Philadelphia: Temple University Press.

Stöver, H. (2001). *Bestandsaufnahme „Crack-Konsum" in Deutschland: Verbreitung, Konsummuster, Risiken und Hilfeangebote. Endbericht* [Inventory of 'crack use' in Germany: prevalence, patterns of use, risks and available services. Final report]. Bremen: BISDRO/ Universität Bremen.

Thane, K., & Thiel, G. (2000). Eine explorative Studie zum Crack-Konsum in der Hamburger 'offenen Drogenszene' [An explorative study on crack use in Hamburg's 'open drug scene']. *Wiener Zeitschrift für Suchtforschung, 23 (2),* 15–19.

Toledo, L., Cano, I., Bastos, L., Bertoni, N., & Bastos, F.I. (2017). Criminal justice involvement of crack cocaine users in the city of Rio de Janeiro and Greater Metropolitan Area: implications for public health and the public security agenda. *International Journal of Drug Policy, 49 (1),* 65–72.

Vogt, I., Schmid, M., & Roth, M. (2000). Crack-Konsum in der Drogenszene in Frankfurt am Main: Ergebnisse empirischer Studien [Crack use in the Frankfurt drug scene: results of empirical studies]. *Wiener Zeitschrift für Suchtforschung, 23 (2),* 5–13.

Werse, B., Kamphausen, G., & Klaus, L. (2019). *MoSyD Szenestudie 2018 – Die offene Drogenszene in Frankfurt am Main* [MoSyD Scene Survey 2018 – the open drug scene in Frankfurt am Main]. Frankfurt: Goethe-Universität, Centre for Drug Research.

6
On aging cannabis users:
a welfare economics analysis

Marco Rossi

This chapter reports on a study of the implications of an increasing share of adults in the population of cannabis users, using a welfare economics approach. This demographic process is already significant in Italy, which is leading European 'greying': a decrease in birth-rate and youth, and an increasing proportion of older people in the general population. We hypothesise that adult users go through a process of social integration and normalisation, through which they change their patterns of use and socio-economic status. In order to verify the empirical relevance of the share of adults and the above hypotheses, we interviewed a targeted, non-representative, sample of cannabis users: visitors at the biggest Italian cannabis fair. Our data suggest that the role and weight of adults in the cannabis market is quantitatively significant and qualitatively different from that of younger people. We analysed the links between the aging issue and the views supporting cannabis market restrictions (defined as paternalism, economics externalities, and moral externalities). Finally, we developed a model where we demonstrated how the utility of cannabis market restrictions decreases as the share of adults in the cannabis user population increases.

Keywords: cannabis, aging, normalisation, social integration, paternalism, externalities, welfare, regulation.

1   Introduction

The literature on the cannabis market has been mostly focused on consumption by young people, such as students (e.g. European School Survey Project on Alcohol and Other Drugs/ESPAD studies). The reason for this may be twofold. Firstly, it is supposed that cannabis consumption may severely harm adolescent development (Zammit, Allebeck, Andreasson, Lundbers & Lewis, 2002; Hall, 2009). Secondly, because for many years the dominant view has been – and often still is in the public and political discourse – that cannabis consumption is mostly limited to young people. However, several indicators suggest that the share of adults in the cannabis consumer population is increasing, and it is no longer negligible (e.g. European Monitoring Centre for Drugs and Drug Addiction/EMCDDA statistics). This demographic transition, which we define as aging, is already visible in Italy, a country that is leading European 'greying': a decrease in birth-rate and youth, and an increasing proportion of older people in the general population. In Italy, the share of adults (aged 30 years and above) reported for illegal drug possession has steadily increased: from 11 percent in 1990 to 27 percent in 2015 (DPA, 2016). In 2017, the share of adults reported for illegal cannabis possession was 21 percent (DPA, 2018). If the typical evolution of cannabis consumers' careers goes through a process of normalisation (Parker, Williams & Aldrige, 2002; Duff et al., 2012) and social integration (Duff & Erikson, 2014), where consumers' habits (i.e. patterns of use and supply) and socio-economic status change during the transition from adolescence, through young adulthood to adult, this change in cannabis consumers' age distribution may have policy implications. This chapter investigates these by using a welfare economics model.

In this welfare economics approach to the cannabis market, the aim is to identify the optimal tolerable quantity of cannabis consumption. The quantity that, when comparing the benefits of cannabis consumption restrictions and the cost of their implementation, maximises social welfare. Therefore, we define an objective function, which includes the benefits coming from market restrictions. In particular, we hypothesise that these benefits decrease as the share of adults in the population of cannabis consumers increases. Then, we cross this objective function with a cost function, which includes the cost of the implementation of market restrictions. The result of this social welfare maximisation process is that the optimal tolerable quantity of cannabis consumption is increasing as the share of adults in the population of cannabis consumers increases.

In order to verify the empirical relevance of the normalisation and social integration process, we collected a dataset on the consumption habits and socioeconomic status of cannabis consumers through semi-structured interviews of visitors at the biggest Italian cannabis fair event, Canapa Mundi IV edition in 2018. The particular setting of the interviews biased the sample toward an over- representation of frequent consumers (those that are more significant from an economic standpoint). Our data confirms the normalisation and social integration hypotheses as: cannabis consumption by adults (in this chapter defined as 30 years and older) is more solitary, more frequent and less exhibited than that of young people. Adults, contrary to young adults, consume cannabis for relaxation rather than for intoxication. Adults' supply comes more from domestic cultivation than from the (more visible) street dealers. Finally, adult cannabis consumers' education, employment and job level are akin to the rest of the contemporary population.

2   Three approaches supporting cannabis market restrictions

The objective function of our model includes the benefits coming from cannabis market restrictions. The views supporting these restrictions may be classified into three categories: paternalism, economic externalities and moral externalities. These are three kinds of market failures. According to paternalism, the market fails because of consumers' irrationality. In the presence of negative externalities, the market may fail to capture the negative impact that cannabis consumption causes on society. Because of these failures, the quantity of cannabis consumed in the market is excessive. Therefore, restrictions are useful to contain consumption within its optimal tolerable quantity. If these restrictions are effective, social welfare benefits from the containment of excessive cannabis consumption.

2.1 Paternalism

Paternalism may be defined as a solution to a market failure, where agents (the economic term for 'people') may make irrational choices, and therefore regulations are useful to prevent this risk. Rationality is defined as the ability of an economic agent to process their available information in order to prevent the risk of systematic errors (Fama,1970). By irrational choices we mean that agents may be unable to use their endowments, including available information, in order to maximise their expected lifetime utility. Irrational choices may be caused by agents having limited information and/or their inability to correctly process their information (while it is assumed that the regulator is better informed and/or it has better processing abilities). As time is needed both to collect information, and to develop the abilities to process this information, the paternalistic view fears that before a certain age, it is unlikely that agents' information and/or abilities are sufficient enough to allow them to make rational choices. Therefore, this view may support the many restrictions applied to young people, who, before a certain age, have limited civil rights.

In the case of cannabis, the application of paternalistic restrictions for young people may be motivated by the fear that they may not yet be conscious of the health risks caused by smoking cannabis and, therefore, they may be involved in an irrational consumption, which reduces their expected lifetime utility. The paternalistic view seems less suited for adult consumers, who have had more time to collect and process information about the health risks implied by smoking cannabis. In fact, assuming agents' rationality, Becker & Murphy (1988) showed that it is theoretically possible to have a rational drug consumption: that is a consumption of a drug which is compatible with the maximisation of expected lifetime utility (where 'drug' is defined as a substance that is dangerous for health and which may cause addiction and/or tolerance).

93

In Europe, the distinction between young and adult consumers is traditionally applied in the market regulation of tobacco and alcohol, where paternalistic restrictions are applied to young people, who cannot purchase these drugs. In the case of cannabis, paternalistic restrictions were motivated by the wider consumption of this substance among young people, especially teenagers, while the number of adult consumers was negligible. Therefore, from this standpoint, the paternalistic approach loses generality as the share of adults in the population of users increases.

2.2 Economic externalities

In the economic literature, externalities are the effects on society caused by the action of another agent j, which are not compensated in the market. In particular, negative economic externalities are defined those cases where j's actions reduce i's utility without a monetary compensation. When there are economic externalities, the market equilibrium is sub-optimal. In particular, if agent j's consumption causes negative externalities, the resulting market equilibrium is one of over-consumption, i.e. the quantity consumed is above that which would maximise social welfare. This result supports market regulations aimed at reducing excessive consumption.

In the case of cannabis, the negative economic externalities are the costs, caused by individual consumption, which are paid for by society. These costs accumulate mainly in health care costs, production losses, and damages to others caused by consumers' misconduct (such as driving accidents). The healthcare costs are caused by the risk of incurring in diseases caused by cannabis consumption, in particular by smoking cannabis. The cost of treating these diseases are, at least partially, paid for by society through their national health system. Moreover, as well as the risk of incurring these diseases, the productivity of cannabis consumers may be reduced. This productivity loss reduces the supply of goods and services available to society and, therefore, reduces social welfare. In actuarial terms, the expected value of these two kinds of externalities is proportional to consumer life expectancy. In particular, expected production losses are inversely proportional to the residual consumers' working life, so that they are negligible for retired people.

A different kind of economic externality consists of the revenues accruing to those criminals, who are (illegally) supplying cannabis. In fact, this is not an externality caused by consumption itself, but an unintended consequence of prohibition, which constrains cannabis trade to the illegal market. In addition, the criminals may use the revenues coming from cannabis sales to finance other illegal activities, whose successes reduces social welfare. We suppose that, compared to young users, adults' cannabis supply comes more from domestic cultivation than from street dealers. Accordingly, the revenue from (illegal) cannabis sales is decreasing as the share of adult users increases. Moreover, we suppose that their heavier reliance on domestic cultivation makes the adult supply less detectable, so that it is costlier to implement restrictions.

2.3 Moral externalities

We define moral externality as the non-monetary damage that agent i's action imposes upon another agent j, without compensation. While economic externalities may be quantified in monetary terms (such as health care costs or value of production losses), moral externalities do not reduce income or production, but they harm society through the exhibition of behaviour that is ethically disapproved of. Note that moral externalities come from the exhibition of immoral behaviour. According to this, if a behaviour is not public exhibited, it does not cause moral externalities. Moreover, in order to cause a moral externality, agent j's behaviour should be judged as immoral by some other agent i. In sociological terms, we define moral externalities as caused by the exhibition of immoral behaviour by deviant people. When moral externalities are present, agent j may try to restrict agent i's behaviour to prevent them from causing the externalities and, if the people affected by the moral externalities are powerful enough, restrictions on agent i's behaviour may be imposed.

Cannabis consumption may be associated with immoral behaviour (Hathaway, Comeau & Erickson, 2011), but we suppose that the moral externalities caused by adult consumption are less than those caused by young consumers. We believe this is because of the qualitative shift in consumption and supply patterns and status, which seems to occur along cannabis consumers' careers between adolescence and adulthood. According to Grosso (2018), the typical drug consumer's career starts at adolescence, it is often motivated by emulation within small groups of peers, and it is mainly occasional and collective. Then, around the age of 30 years, the typical cannabis consumer's habits change. Most leave the market before reaching the age of 34–35 years, but a minority of them continues to consume cannabis, although in a quite different way. Adult cannabis consumers who continue to use cannabis go through a process where their consumption becomes an individual daily habit, and they become 'socially integrated' (Sznitman, 2007; Duff et al., 2012; Duff & Erikson, 2014). Given our above definition of moral externality, we think that the change in the users' habits and status from young adult to adult causes less moral stigma because we suppose that:
a) there is less exhibition (because of the shift from collective to individual consumption, and from street dealers to domestic cultivation) and
b) adult users are socially integrated people.
We suppose that there is also a significant difference between young users and adults on the side of cannabis supply. We suppose that adult users supply

comes relatively more from regular dealers and, specifically, from domestic cultivation, while young users rely more upon street dealers, whose trade is often conducted in public. Therefore, this difference in supply habits makes cannabis purchases by adults less visible or inexistent. As there is a reduction in the exhibition of the drug immoral trade by adults, there is also a decrease in the moral externalities caused by drug supply to adults compared to young people.

3 Empirical analysis

The empirical analysis studies a dataset collected through semi-structured interviews to a non-random sample of visitors at the biggest Italian cannabis fair event Canapa Mundi in 2018. Given its suburban location and a non-trivial entrance fee, it may be presumed that we got a distorted sample, where very involved people are over- represented. The (printed) questionnaire was administered to 626 visitors, and asked about consumption and supply habits, considerations for consumption, and socio-demographic characteristics. The data collected was both quantitative and qualitative. The qualitative variables were measured through self-reported and/or structured grading. The respondents were grouped according to their class of age (Table 1). Thereafter, we split the sample into two subsets, where we grouped the first two age classes into young consumers, while people 30 years and above were grouped as adult consumers. This cut-off age (30 years) is similar to the one standardly used by EMCDDA statistics, which uses the term 'young adults' for the group aged between 15 and 34 years. We picked a lower cut-off age because, firstly, our main sources of official data (DPA, 2016, 2018, and DCSA, 2016), use this kind of partition, and secondly, it is at the age of 30 that the process of normalisation usually starts, as it is revealed by the structural shift in our sample data (particularly for female users).

Table 1: Age and gender distribution

Age (n)	< 20 (55)	20–29 (346)	30–39 (159)	40–49 (43)	50+ (19)	Total (622)
Gender						
Male	7%	54%	29%	8%	3%	72%
Female	14%	60%	17%	5%	3%	28%

3.1 Consumption patterns and habits

An overwhelming majority of participants declared themselves as regular and/ or frequent consumers (Table 2). In fact, most of them (three quarters) reported consuming cannabis every day, a minority once a week or once per month, and very few once a year. Accordingly, most of the participants (about two thirds) declared consuming more than ten grams of cannabis per month, while a minority (one quarter) of them declared consuming between three and nine grams, or less. Because the estimates for the total population of Italian cannabis consumers are lower than the findings by Van Laar, Frijns, Traumann and Lombi (2013a), who estimated use as 41 percent chippers (i.e. infrequent users); 37 percent occasional; 12 percent regular; and 10 percent intensive, our results confirm that our sample is distorted. But this sample distortion allows us to focus on those consumers, regular and frequent, that are more important from an economic standpoint, because they demand most of the cannabis (Van Laar et al., 2013a, estimated that in Italy almost three quarters of the cannabis is consumed by intensive consumers, and one quarter by regular consumers).

Table 2: Cannabis consumption patterns by age group and gender

	Occasional	Daily	> 10 grams	Socially		Alone	
				mostly	only	mostly	only
Age							
Adults	21%	79%	70%	49%	6%	39%	6%
Youth	26%	74%	60%	65%	10%	23%	2%
Gender							
Males	8%	79%	67%	58%	8%	31%	4%
Females	15%	68%	54%	63%	12%	22%	2%

Almost all of the participants (96%) claimed to consume cannabis through direct inhalation of burnt fumes, a way of consumption (a joint) that is very dangerous for consumers' health. About two thirds of participants declared consuming cannabis together with other people, while the remaining third did so alone.

Our data shows that there are differences in the frequency and quantity consumed throughout a cannabis consumer's career. Occasional consumption is higher for young users than for adults, and, conversely, daily consumption is higher for adults than for young users. Our findings confirm the positive correlation between consumers' age and frequency of consumption already found in Van Laar, Frijns, Trautmann and Lombi (2013b). Accordingly, the quantity of cannabis consumed by people older than 30 is higher than that consumed by younger ones. These figures suggest that, although the cannabis market is mainly populated by young consumers, the weight of adult demand is higher than its share in the total population of consumers.

Our data also shows that there is another variation in consumption habits between young and adult cannabis consumers: young people consume cannabis socially more than adults do. In particular, three quarters of the under-30-year-old participants declared they consumed company, while adults' share is one half. Conversely the share of those participants who declared consuming alone is higher for adults (almost one half) than for young users (one quarter).

3.2 Motives for cannabis use

The questionnaire investigated two motives for cannabis use: recreation and relaxation. We asked the participants to assign a value ranging from 0 to 5 to each of these categories. Recreational consumption (getting high) scored an average value of 3.25; the average value of cannabis consumption for relaxation was 4.25 (Table 3). Our findings are in line with Van Laar et al. estimates (2013b), where, among the population of Italian cannabis consumers, other considerations dominate over potency.

In particular, the recreational properties of cannabis are on average more appreciated by young consumers than by adults. The average value attributed to recreation by young respondents was higher than that attributed by adults. Only a few of young participants attributed none (0) or very low value (1) to the recreational motivation, while one adult in five attributed none (0) or very low value (1) to this motive. Whilst relaxation is more appreciated by adults than by young consumers: the attributed average value was higher for adults and most of them awarded relaxation the maximum value (5).

Table 3: Motives for use and self-perceived cannabis dependence

	Recreation (avg.)	Recreation (0–1)	Relax (avg.)	Relax (5)	Cannabis dependent (5)
Adults	3.0	21%	4.3	62%	31%
Youth	3.4	10%	4.2	53%	19%

3.3 Cannabis dependence

In the questionnaire, participants were asked to rank their cannabis dependence on a scale ranging from 0 (no dependence) to 5 (heavy dependence). The distribution of answers was very skewed toward cannabis dependency (average value: 3.24; asymmetry index = −.496). About two thirds of participants perceived themselves as dependent (attributing a value of at least 3 to their cannabis dependence). In particular, almost one third of adult participants attributed to their cannabis dependence the maximum value (5), while the corresponding percentage among young participants was much lower (Table 3). The Cannabis Abuse Screening Test (CAST) screening on the Italian population of cannabis consumers confirms that, from 2007 on, the modal class of age of problematic consumers is above 35 years old (38.6%; DPA, 2018).

3.4 Supply

In the questionnaire, participants were also asked about their cannabis supply sources (Table 4). The modal source of supply was through friends, followed by home dealers and domestic cultivation, while a few of participants said they relied on street dealers. According to these figures, it may be that the supply to frequent consumers comes from a kind of customer market, where transactions occur mostly within permanent customer relations, instead of arm's-length transactions with other dealers. This finding contrasts the IFC-CNR estimate that, in Italy, street dealers supply cannabis to most users (DPA, 2018). It looks as if the cannabis market is dichotomous: while most consumers are occasional and rely on street dealers, the minority of frequent consumers rely more on customer relations. Moreover, our data shows that cannabis supply to adults is different from the one to young people. Adult consumers rely more upon domestic cultivation than young ones, while young consumers' supply comes more from friends and dealers.

Table 4: Cannabis supply source, in percent per age group

Age	< 20	20–29	30–39	40–49	50+	Total
Domestic cultivation	6	18	28	35	16	21
Friends	53	48	40	30	53	45
Home dealers	36	29	25	26	21	28
Street dealers	6	5	6	9	5	5
National Health System	0	1	1	0	5	1
Total	*100*	*100*	*100*	*100*	*100*	*100*

3.5 Consumers' socio-economic status

Age

In our sample, most of participants were aged between 20 and 40 years, and a few were over 40 years or teenagers (Table 1). Moreover, the share of adult consumers (over 30 years) was about one third of the total sample, a share slightly higher than the share of adults reported by Italian police for illegal cannabis possession (DPA, 2016). Therefore, our results show that adult cannabis consumption is very significant. Moreover, this result is interesting because it comes from the analysis of a selective biased sample, where very involved people are over-represented. Therefore, we can suppose that the weight of adult consumers in the cannabis market is more than proportional to their share in the users' population.

Gender

In our sample, most of participants were male (Table 1). Moreover, men consume more cannabis than women (Table 2). The percentage of daily consumers is higher for males than for females, while the percentage of occasional consumers is higher for females. Along with a higher frequency of consumption, the share of male participants who declared consuming more than ten grams of cannabis per month is larger than that of females, while the share of participants who declared consuming less than two grams of cannabis per month is larger for females. Altogether, these results confirm the traditional belief that cannabis is mostly consumed by males (Van Laar et al., 2013b).

However, we found a significant difference in consumers' cannabis-using careers between genders (Table 1). The representation of consumers in the younger age classes (< 30 years) is higher for females than for males. But the proportion of females suddenly drops in the age group 30–39 years, and it continues to decrease at older ages. Conversely, the male rate remains relatively more stable as consumers get older. In particular, its drop in the age group of 30–39 years is less dramatic. Therefore, we can suppose that female cannabis consumption is more concentrated in younger age groups, while, given the sudden drop in female rate after the critical age of 30, adult cannabis use is dominated by males.

Finally, females consume cannabis together with others relatively more than males. The percentage of those who consume cannabis mostly, or only, together is higher for females than for males, while the percentage of those who consume cannabis mostly, or only, alone is higher for males than for females (Table 2).

Perceived health

Our questionnaire asked participants to declare their self-perceived health on a scale ranging from 0 to 5. An overwhelming majority of participants declared themselves to be very healthy people: two thirds ranked themselves in the highest class of health, and one fifth in the second one. Only one participant in ten ranked themselves in the lowest categories (from 0 to 2). The very high perception of good health is common among participants was irrespective of their consumption habits (as frequency of use or quantity consumed). In our sample, the perceived good health initially increases from young consumers until the age group 30–39, where it peaks, then it decreases along with participants' age, but not dramatically, as most of participants aged 50 or over still ranked themselves in the highest class of health. Altogether, we guess that these results indicate that cannabis consumption is not very harmful for health, or, that it systematically alters consumers' perceptions, making them feel healthy.

Education

As to their level of education (Table 5), most participants declared themselves as educated people: many reported having a high school degree, and over one quarter a university degree (a level of education well above the Italian standard). In particular, the highest rate with a high school degree was in the age group 20–29 years, while the highest rate with a university degree was in the age group 30–39 years. The highest rate with high school degree was among those who declared monthly use of cannabis, while the highest rate with a university degree was among those who declared a yearly rate of consumption. But intensive consumers also declared having a high level of education: most of the daily consumers declared having a high school diploma and one quarter of them a university degree. We should not forget that our sample is distorted. Firstly, it mostly consists of school-age people and secondly we suppose that it is the result of self-selection process, caused by entrance fees and transportation costs. Therefore, it is likely that our sample overestimates the education level of cannabis consumers in the general population. The finding that the education attainment of intensive users is similar or better than the

Table 5: Education and occupation per age, in percent per age group

Age	< 20	20–29	30–39	40–49	50+	Total
Education						
None	0	0	1	0	0	0
Elementary school	0	0	0	2	0	0
Primary school	67	11	14	12	32	17
Secondary school	33	63	45	51	53	55
University degree	0	26	41	35	16	28
Total	*100*	*100*	*100*	*100*	*100*	*100*
Occupation						
Blue collar	2	6	4	2	0	5
Skilled blue collar	8	26	45	29	38	30
White collar	4	19	42	56	56	27
Student	85	33	1	2	0	27
Unemployed	2	15	6	10	6	11
Total	*100*	*100*	*100*	*100*	*100*	*100*

general population was also found in Dutch and Australian samples of heavy or long term users (Reilly, Didicott, Swift & Hall, 1998; Copeland, Swift & Rees, 2001; Van der Pol, Liebregts, de Graaf, et al., 2013).

Occupation

Participants reported a very high occupation rate, as only one in ten declared they were unemployed or out of the workforce. This employment rate is much higher than that of the whole Italian population (National Statistical Institute, 2019). Our results are in line with those of Van Laar and colleagues (2013b); Copeland and colleagues (2001), and Reilly and colleagues (1998). Van der Pol and colleagues (2013) found that frequent users are more often unemployed or unable to work. The above remarks on sample distortion are also applicable here: it may be that non-negligible entrance fees and transportation costs inhibited low income (unemployed) people from attending the fair. Therefore, it is likely that our data overestimate the employment rate of the total cannabis consumer population.

We classified the participants' occupations into three categories: high, medium and low. The highest one consists of managers, entrepreneurs, and high-skill white-collar positions; the second category includes clerks and skilled blue collar jobs; and the lowest category includes all low or no-skill blue collar occupations. The average level of participants' occupation was quite high (Table 5). In fact, most reported to have high or medium level occupations. Over one quarter of participants were students. Although the above statement about sample bias still applies, the occupation rate and level in our sample are better than that of the general Italian population, so we can suppose that our data empirically deny the hypothesis that cannabis consumption is incompatible with the achievement of users' social integration.

4   Conclusions

This study was motivated by the observation of the increasing share of adult cannabis consumers. According to police data, this demographic phenomenon, defined as aging, is already significant in Italy, a country which is leading European greying. Although the literature is still focused on the young populations' consumption, some studies have suggested that cannabis consumption by adults is different from that of young people (Maturo, 2008; Buso & Grosso, 2009; Duff, Asbridge, Brochu, et al., 2012). In fact, most of the consumers reduce, or quit, consumption as they become adult. But a minority of them who continue to consume into adulthood go through a process through which they change their habits and status. Therefore, we suppose that these changes may have policy implications, the relevance of which is going to grow because of the current European demographic trend.

We studied this aging issue in a welfare economic approach, as in Becker, Grossman & Murphy (2006). In our model, the issue was to find the optimal tolerable quantity of consumption: that is, the quantity that maximises social welfare. We identify this optimal quantity by crossing the benefits of cannabis market restriction with the cost of implementing this restriction. In particular, we group the views supporting market restrictions into three categories: paternalism, economic and moral externalities. Then, we showed the actuarial motives whereby the utility of restrictions, dictated by paternalism or by economic externalities, is inversely related to the residual consumers' expected life. Moreover, we argued that the above changes in adult consumers' habits and status reduce the moral externalities caused by their consumption.

In order to empirically verify the normalisation hypothesis, we interviewed visitors at the biggest Italian cannabis fair Canapa Mundi in 2018. Because of this location, we collected a distorted sample, where frequent consumers were over-represented. From an economics point of view, this sample distortion allowed us to focus on these important consumers, who, although being less numerous than the occasional consumers, demand most of the cannabis and are more likely to suffer from the harmful health consequences of cannabis dependence. From this point of view, the most important result coming that came from our sample data is that, on average, adult people consume more cannabis than young ones, and more frequently, so that the economic relevance of adults' demand on the market is more than proportional to their share in the population of consumers. This finding increases the economic relevance of cannabis consumption by adults.

Moreover, compared to young people, adults consume cannabis relatively more individually than socially, and for relaxation purposes rather than as a recreational activity. Adults' cannabis supply comes relatively more from domestic cultivation than from street dealers. Finally, the education and occupation of the adult respondents are better than the average of the whole Italian population. Altogether, we believe that our results support the hypotheses of normalisation and social integration of adult cannabis users.

Ultimately, our model shows that the benefits of restrictions are inversely related to the share of adult consumers in the population. That is, as aging progresses, the social benefit of market restrictions is lower, and the optimal tolerable quantity of cannabis consumption increases. We acknowledge that it is not very simple this quantification of the optimal degree of tolerance to translate into operational terms. Nevertheless, our results may suggest the use of different policies for adults or young people. That is, keeping the current restrictions on young users, but lowering the restriction on adult cannabis consumption. An age-based regulation already applied in several cases (tobacco, alcohol, gambling, pornography, etc.).

5 Addendum: the model

This is a welfare economics model, where the issue of regulating the cannabis collapses in finding the cannabis market size which maximises social welfare, that is the optimal tolerable quantity (Q*) of cannabis consumption. The value of Q* is found by comparing benefits and costs of market restriction. Therefore, we define an objective function [4], which includes the benefits coming from market restrictions, and a cost function [7] that includes the cost of restriction implementation. Crossing this objective function with the cost function, we get the optimal tolerable quantity of cannabis market size (Q*), that is the quantity which maximizes social welfare [9]. Because we guess that the benefits of market restriction are inversely related to the share of adult consumers in the cannabis consumers' population (t), we show that the optimal tolerable quantity of cannabis market size (Q*) is increasing as this share (t) grows [10].

Defined (t) as an index of the share of adult consumers in the population of cannabis consumers, and (Q) as the quantity of cannabis consumption, we define a PATERNALIST utility function as:

$P = p(t,Q)$;   [1]
where: $p'(t) < 0$ and $p'(Q) > 0$.

Then we define a moralist utility function as:
$M = m(t,Q)$;   [2]
where: $m'(t) < 0$ and $m'(Q) > 0$.

Finally, we define externalities as:
$E = e(t,Q)$;   [3]
where: $e'(t) < 0$ and $e'(Q) > 0$.

The objective function, defined as the Social Cost of cannabis consumption, is:
$SC = s(P(t,Q), M(t,Q), E(t,Q))$ [4]
where: $s'(P) > 0$; $s'(M) > 0$; $s'(E) > 0$.

We assume that the amount of cannabis consumption (Q) depends on prohibition implementation effort (e):
$Q = q(e)$,   [5]
where $q'(e) < 0$;

but, if this effort is costly:
$C = c(e)$,   [6]
where: $c'(e) > 0$,

then, the cost function is:
C = c(e(Q)),   [7]
where: $c'(Q) < 0$.

We define a Social Welfare Function as:
SWF = f(SC(t,Q), C(Q))   [8]
where: $f'(SC) < 0$ and $f'(Q) < 0$.

According to the above assumptions, maximizing this SWF respect to Q results a quantity of optimal consumption (Q*) which is positively related to the share of adults among the population of cannabis consumers:
Q* = q(t),   [9]
where:
$q'(t) > 0$.   [10]

References

Becker, G. S., & Murphy K.M. (1988). A theory of rational addiction. *Journal of Political Economy, 96 (4),* 675–700.

Becker, G.S., Grossman M., & Murphy K.M. (2006). The market for illegal goods: the case of drugs. *Journal of Political Economy, 114 (1),* 38–60.

Buso, G., & Grosso L. (2009). Evoluzione e caratterizzazione del consumo di cannabis in Italia. [The evolution of cannabis consumption in Italy]. In: R. Pavarin (Ed.), *Cannabis e problemi sanitari* [Cannabis and health problems] (pp. 81–90). Milano: Franco Angeli.

Copeland, J., Swift, W., & Rees, V. (2001). Clinical profile of participants in a brief intervention program for cannabis use disorder. *Journal of Substance Abuse Treatment, 20 (1),* 45–52.

Dipartimento per le Politiche Antidroga (DPA) (2016). *Relazione annuale al Parlamento, anno 2016* [Anti-Drug Department. Annual report, 2016]. Roma: Presidenza del Consiglio dei MInistri. www.politicheantidroga.gov.it/it/attivita-e-progetti/relazioni-annuali-al-parla mento/relazione-annuale-al-parlamento-2016/presentazione/.

Dipartimento per le Politiche Antidroga (DPA) (2018). *Relazione annuale al Parlamento anno 2018* [Anti-Drug Department. Annual report, 2018]. Roma: Presidenza del Consiglio dei Ministri. http://www.politicheantidroga.gov.it/media/2445/339911.pdf.

Direzione centrale per i servizi antidroga (DCSA) (2016). *Relazione Annuale, 2016* [Antidrug Directorate. Annual report, 2016]. Roma: Ministero degli Interni. http://www.interno.gov. it/it/direzione-centrale-i-servizi-antidroga.

Duff, C., Asbridge A., Brochu S., Cousineau M.M., Hathaway A., Marsh D., & Erikson P.W. (2012). A Canadian perspective on cannabis normalization among adults. *Addiction Research and Theory, 20 (4),* 271–283.

Duff, C., & Erikson P. (2014). Cannabis, risk and normalization: evidence from a Canadian study of socially integrated, adult cannabis users. *Health, Risk & Society, 16 (3),* 210–226.

EMCDDA: European Monitoring Centre for Drugs and Drug Addiction (2015). *Perspective on drugs – characteristics of frequent and high-risk cannabis users.* Lisbon: EMCDDA.

Fama, E. (1970). Efficient capital markets. *Journal of Finance, 25 (2),* 383–417.

Grosso, L. (2018). Un'opportunità per una migliore tutela della salute [A chance for a better health care prevention]. In: L. Grosso (Ed.), *Questione cannabis* [The cannabis issue] (pp. 31–68). Torino: Edizioni Gruppo Abele.

Hall, W.D. (2009). The adverse health effects of cannabis use: what are they, and what are their implications for policy? *International Journal of Drug Policy, 20 (6)*, 458–66.

Hathaway, A.D., Comeau N.C., & Erickson P.G. (2011). Cannabis normalization and stigma: contemporary practices of moral regulation. *Criminology & Criminal Justice, 11 (5)*, 451–469.

Maturo, A. (2008) L'habituation come categoria della dipendenza da cannabis [Habituation as a category of cannabis addiction]. In: C. Cipolla, (Ed.), *La normalità di una droga* [Drug normalisation] (pp. 182–201). Milano: Franco Angeli.

National Statistical Institute (2019). *Employment rate table – Italy*. Retrieved from http://dati.istat.it/Index.aspx?DataSetCode=DCCV_TAXOCCU1 on 5/7/2019.

Parker, H., Williams L., & Aldrige J. (2002). The normalization of 'sensible' recreational drug use: further evidence from the North West England longitudinal study. *Sociology, 36 (4)*, 941–964.

Sznitman, S.R. (2007). *Social integrated drug users: between deviance and normality*. Stockholm: CRAD, Stockholm University.

Reilly, D., Didicott P., Swift W., & Hall W. (1998). Long-term cannabis use: characteristics of users in an Australian rural area. *Drug and Alcohol Dependence, 93 (6)*, 837–846.

Van der Pol, P., Liebregts N., de Graaf R., tenn Have M., Korf D.J., van den Brink W., & van Laar M. (2013). Mental health differences between frequent cannabis users with and without cannabis dependence and the general population. *Addiction, 108 (8)*, 1459–1469.

Van Laar, M., Frijns, T., Trautmann, R., & Lombi, L. (2013a). Surveys on user types, availability and consumption estimates. In: F. Trautmann, B. Kilmer, & P. Turnbull (Eds.), *Further insights into aspects of the EU illicit drugs market: summaries and key findings* (pp. 15–22). Luxembourg: Publications Office of the European Union.

Van Laar, M., Frijns, T., Trautmann, R., & Lombi, L. (2013b). Part I, Report 1, Cannabis market: users' types, availability and consumption estimates. In: F. Trautmann, B. Kilmer, & P. Turnbull (Eds.), *Further insights into aspects of the EU illicit drugs market: summaries and key findings* (pp. 73–182). Luxembourg: Publications Office of the European Union.

Zammit, S., Allebeck P., Andreasson S., Lundbers I., & Lewis G. (2002). Self-reported cannabis use as a risk factor for schizophrenia in Swedish conscripts of 1969: historical cohort study. *BMJ, 325 (7374)*, 1199–1201.

7

Exploring and (re)negotiating the question of (not) being: narrative identity constructions of people who use illegal drugs

Michelle Van Impe

Qualitative social research on identity constructions of people who use illegal drugs (PWUDs) shows that drug users (still) experience stigma. A way for users to narrate a positive identity is by engaging in boundary work, whereby they separate themselves from other drug users (mostly stereotypical 'addicts') whom they perceive as worse. Stories about why people use drugs and why they do so in particular ways are central to boundary work. While we know that intra-group stigma exists, the question of how we can better understand and deconstruct these discourses among PWUDs remains pressing. By means of qualitative meta-synthesis (QMS) – an interpretative integration of qualitative research – this chapter seeks to partly answer this question by investigating empirical qualitative work on stigma, identity, boundary work and illegal drug use. The analysis focusses on identifying gaps in the literature and empirical findings that conflict with the prevailing view of boundary work, such as narrating empathy towards other PWUDs. Based on this QMS, it was found that elements of PWUDs' narratives incorporate more than negative 'downward comparisons' to other 'lesser' PWUDs. Given this, it is concluded that future critical drug research could undertake more participatory and interactive research with PWUDs in order to (try to) challenge, and renegotiate stereotypical representations of drug use(rs), apparent both outside and within the drug-using community.

Keywords: Narrative identity constructions, illegal drug use, symbolic boundaries, intra-group stigma, qualitative meta-synthesis (QMS)

1   Introduction

Stories have a central function in how we make sense of our world, others and ourselves because they tend to 'explain what we did and therefore what kind of being we are.' (Presser, 2016, p.138). Nevertheless, identities and narratives are extremely complex because they are always in process, fluid and situated in particular contexts and social interactions (Bamberg, 2010). Moreover, the stigmatised and illegal status of drug use has inspired several studies on how drug use is connected to people's sense of self (Pereira & Carrington, 2016). Within social psychology, the principle of downward social comparison describes situations whereby subjective well-being can be increased – for instance when feeling excluded – by juxtaposing onself against other people who are less fortunate (Wills, 1981). A related, and often cited, concept in the study of narrative identity constructions among people who use drugs (PWUDs) is symbolic boundary work (Lamont & Molnár, 2002). Defining who you are, is inherently also a practice of representing who you are not or do not want to be (Van De Mieroop & Clifton, 2016).

PWUDs engage in boundary work in order to separate themselves from other drug users, whom they perceive to be worse (Rødner, 2005; Copes, 2016). These boundary constructions revolve around the difference between being a functional or a dysfunctional drug user, where the latter reflects charachteristics of the 'stereotypical addict' (Copes, 2016). Furthermore, this assesment of what establishes (dys)functional use is closely related to the explanations people provide for using drugs: having an acceptable or understandable answer to the 'why?' question is important (Copes, 2016; Willis, 2016). Stories about (drug) experiences and what they mean(t) to users, can tell us much about how people consider themselves in relation to illegal drugs (Sandberg & Tutenges, 2015). While most drug users reject stigmatising discourses when it comes to their own drug-using behaviour, they give them credit by applying them to other users. Although boundary work might be positive for the narrator's identity, the repetition of stereotypes about PWUDs is worrying. Hence, the question of how we can understand and potentially deconstruct prevailing stigmatising discourses through research remains pressing (Lancaster, Santana, Madden & Ritter, 2015). In the search for (some) answers to this question, this book chapter presents a qualitative meta-synthesis (QMS) of existing empirical literature regarding narrative identity and boundary work by PWUDs.

2   The nexus between narratives and identity constructions

People rely on available stories when telling their own (Van De Mieroop & Clifton, 2016). Master narratives can be regarded as largely accepted cultural frames, ideologies and practices through which we can understand our experiences (Loseke, 2007). A relevant example of the relationship between master and personal narratives is how mothers who consume illegal drugs have to negotiate the ideal image of 'clean' motherhood and the seemingly contradictory practice of using drugs (Stone, 2016). However, a critique on the relation between master and personal narratives is the simplified division between agency and structure for analytical reasons and clarity. From this dualistic perspective, agency can then be located in personal stories, while structural influences can be found in dominant discourses (for instance, spread by media and policy) (Bamberg, 2010). In response, Jennifer Fleetwood (2016) developed the concept of narrative habitus based on the theoretical concept of habitus, as developed in the theory of social practice by Pierre Bourdieu (1990), who suggested that human agency and social structures exist in a dialectical relationship.

The concept of narrative habitus (Fleetwood, 2016) posits that the stories known to us are sources for our personal identity constructions, which implies that individuals are herein limited by the stories they are actually familiar with. In the case of illegal drugs, the discourse of risk, harm and loss of control remains dominant and anchored in prohibitionist drug policies (Taylor et al., 2016). However, the ongoing process of constructing the social world – and entering (new) contexts – also means that the narrative habitus can incorporate new stories and perspectives. This contextuality of stories is closely connected to the fluidity of identities. As such, Hall (1996) describes how:

'... identities are never unified ... increasingly fragmented and fractured; never singular but multiply constructed across different, often intersecting and antagonistic, discourses, practices and positions. They are subject to a radical historicization, and are constantly in the process of change and transformation' (Hall, 1996, p. 4).

Although we cannot define ourselves completely freely through narrative identity work, the framework of narrative habitus acknowledges that speakers can become aware of and resist – even transform – the various storied conventions that bind them (Fleetwood, 2016). In other words, we can position ourselves within the storied world and (re)interpret prevailing dominant discourses for our own life situations. To this end, the constitutive nature of stories is important because it informs thought, reflection and action which can lead to social change. Applied to the topic of this chapter, stigmatising dominant narratives of who drug users are – as well as the incorporation and reproduction of such stories by PWUDs – can be (re)negotiated, (re)interpreted, and deconstructed by PWUDs themselves.

3   Stigma and symbolic boundary work

Illegal drug use is still largely considered to be 'unacceptable' (Taylor, Buchanan & Ayres, 2016). Goffman (1963) argues that stigma is constituted when a personal attribute – in this case drug use – is perceived as negative and when the affected person is aware of this status (for instance being a 'junkie'). Such stigmas can become part of a persons' self-understanding, which is also known as internalised stigma (Goffman, 1963). In the case of drug use, stigma is not merely enacted from the outside. PWUDs can likewise experience harms, oppression and stigma imposed by other (legal and illegal) drug users (Lancaster et al., 2015). The occurrence of boundary work in the construction of illegal drug users' identities has been exhaustively described by Copes (2016). This boundary work is pivotal in both (re)producing and managing stigma because it allows for the representation of the self and the other. Copes' (2016) QMS on this topic highlighted how boundary work is present across several illegal drug user groups, i.e. those who use different illegal drugs, polydrug users, those who had experienced treatment and those who had not, people who self-identified as 'addicted', and those who identified as 'recreational' users.

Copes' (2016) analysis also resulted in the identification of six recurring dimensions of boundary constructions amongst PWUDs. A first dimension concerns physical appearance and health, which implies that (dys)functional use can be inferred from physical markers (skin, teeth, sores, hygiene, etc.). A second dimension addresses mental health, such as having a good memory and the absence of paranoid behaviour. A third dimension concerns maintaining obligations, which refers to drug use that can be combined with the responsibilities such as work and family. The fourth dimension Copes (2016) identified concerns the way of consuming. A common example is that injecting drug use is seen as a sign of desperation (Soller & Lee, 2010; Edland-Gryt, Sandberg & Pedersen, 2017; Askew & Salinas, 2018). The fifth boundary dimension involves motivations for use. For instance, using to perform better at work is more acceptable than using drugs as a form of escapism. The last dimension refers to the procurement of substances: (not) engaging in illegal activities in order to secure money to obtain substances was paramount in the discursive division between functional and dysfunctional users.

4   Research methodology

The qualitative meta-synthesis (QMS) by Copes (2016) inspired the QMS that is described in this chapter. Because intra-group stigma seemed so present in PWUDs' identity narratives, the aim of this QMS – drawing on the framework of narrative habitus (Fleetwood, 2016) – was to analyse empirical qualitative studies on narrative identity and boundary work by PWUDs and search for data that does not comply with this well-documented principle of intra-group stigma. While Copes' (2016) review focussed on the occurrence of boundary work between types of illegal drug use(rs), this QMS concentrates on elements that (can) blur or somehow challenge these boundaries (for instance, what PWUDs have in common within their stories; whether boundaries are narratively challenged and if so, how). The attention is aimed at such counter-indications in order to reflect on how to proceed with research on intra-group stigma between PWUDs and on strategies for deconstructing stigmatising representations of drug use(rs) more generally.

QMS is a method for interpretively synthesising qualitative research in order to broaden knowledge on a specific phenomenon or discover new pathways for research (Walsh & Downe, 2005). QMS goes beyond providing an overview of findings from individual qualitative studies. The approach aims to construct a more complex understanding of a particular topic by comparing, interpreting and integrating findings from qualitative research (Sandelowski & Barroso, 2006).

This QMS was initially performed from March 2018 until October 2018, while an update (using the same search terms and protocol) was conducted between March and April 2019 in order to include more recent publications. Databases used included Web of Science, Google Scholar, Sociological Abstracts and the library database of Ghent University. The search combination used included: 'identity, identity construction, identity work, social identity, self and narrative, story/ies' and 'symbolic boundary/ies, intra-group stigma, boundary work, stigma, othering' and 'illegal drug(s), illegal drug use, substance use, people who use drugs, drug consumption' and 'qualitative'. The initial search across all databases delivered 5,227 results.

The next selection phase consisted of screening the titles and reading through the abstracts. To qualify for inclusion, studies had to apply qualitative methods on the subject of illegal drug use in relation to narrative identity and boundary work. Studies on legal substance use – such as alcohol or licit medication use – or research which did not study drug use experiences (for instance studies about drug dealing), were not included. When multiple publications were based on the same empirical data (after reading the complete works), the most in-depth and relevant article was selected. Research in journals, single or edited books that was not covered by a peer review procedure or was unpublished, was also excluded. However, one exception was made regarding the doctoral dissertation of Dr Laura Willis (2016) because her work specifically addressed narrative identity and boundary work. This screening eventually resulted in 19 selected publications. Lastly, the bibliographies of these 19 publications were screened for other relevant studies, which resulted in the inclusion of an additional 12 works. Hence, the total number of analysed publications is 31. An overview and summary of the selected studies can be found in Table 1.

Table 1: Summary of studies included in the QMS

Study	Sample	Drug(s) used	Setting	Method(s)	Highlighted narratives
Askew & Salinas, 2018	28 recreational users	Cannabis, cocaine, ketamine and ecstasy	U.K.	Semi-structured interviews, ethnography	Stigma narratives
Boeri, 2004	38 active users	Heroin	Atlanta, U.S.A.	In-depth interviews, questionnaires, ethnography	Social role(s) and control narratives
Copes et al., 2018	52 active users	Methamphetamine ('ice' and 'shake')	Alabama, U.S.A.	Interviews, observations, photography	Boundary narratives
Copes et al., 2014	30 female former users	Methamphetamine	Transitional facility, U.S.A.	Semi-structured interviews	Life stories, boundary violations
Copes et al., 2008	28 imprisoned male offenders	Crack cocaine	Two medium security prisons, U.S.A.	Semi-structured interviews	Boundary and identity narratives
Dahl & Heggen, 2014	25 users who had reduced their use (7 women, 18 men)	Cannabis	Norway	Semi-structured interviews	Identity and control narratives
Edland-Gryt, et al., 2017	31 recreational users (61.3% men, 38.7% women)	MDMA and ecstasy	Oslo, Norway	In-depth interviews	Boundary narratives
Fast et al., 2014	75 youngsters aged 14-26	methamphetamine	Canada	In-depth interviews, ethnography	Motivation and identity narratives
Frank et al., 2013	39 cannabis users/growers older than 25	Cannabis	Denmark	Semi-structured interviews	Control narratives
Gibson, et al., 2004	40 participants (26 men, 14 women) recruited from detoxification/recovery units	General	U.K.	Four focus groups and in-depth interviews	Identity and recovery narratives
Green, 2016	Approximately 60 non-service-engaged adolescents	Amphetamines	Perth, Australia	Ethnography, in-depth interviews	Identity and transition narratives
Hathaway, 2004	104 experienced users (64 men, 40 women)	Cannabis	Toronto, Canada	Semi-structured interviews	Risk and stigma narratives
Järvinen & Demant, 2011	Number not specified, youngsters aged 14-19	Cannabis and alcohol	Longitudinal study 2004-2008, Denmark	Focus groups	Identity and neutralisation narratives
Kronbæk & Frank, 2013	32 daily adult users (10 women, 22 men)	Cannabis	Denmark	Semi-structured interviews	Identity and boundary narratives
Lancaster et al., 2015	20 people with experience with injecting use (7 men, 13 women)	Opioids and polydrug use	Canberra and Sydney, Australia	Focus groups	Boundary and stigma narratives
Lavin, 2016	18 Women strippers/dancers	General (legal/illegal substances)	Specific strip club, U.S.A.	Ethnography, interviews	Personal choice narratives
McIntosh & McKeganey, 2000	Former users (36 women, 34 men)	Heroin	Scotland	Semi-structured interviews	Recovery narratives

Study	Sample	Drug(s) used	Setting	Method(s)	Highlighted narratives
McKay et al., 2012	30 young homosexual and bisexual men	Alcohol, cannabis and crystal methamphetamine	Los Angeles and New York	Semi-structured interviews	Boundary narratives
McKenna, 2013	8 active female users	Methamphetamine	Colorado, U.S.A.	In-depth interviews	Stigma narratives
O'Gorman, 2016	Approximately 30 young adults aged 17-24	Polydrug use (cannabis, ecstasy, alcohol, cocaine, NPS)	Dublin, Ireland	Ethnography	Choice narratives
Pennay & Moore, 2010	25 young party-drug users (between 18 -30)	Polydrug use (ecstasy, speed, meth-amphetamine, cannabis, etc.)	Melbourne, Australia	Ethnography	Boundary, motivation and identity narratives
Pereira & Carrington, 2016	29 users (10 women, 19 men)	General	Brisbane, Australia	Semi-structured interviews	Boundary narratives
Plumridge & Chetwynd, 1999	20 young injecting users (13 men, 7 women)	Not specified, general injectables	Needle exchange service, New Zealand	Semi-structured interviews	Life and risk narratives
Radcliffe, 2009	17 Substance misusing women w(pregnant or gave birth in the past 2 years)	Methadone, opiates	Treatment setting, U.K.	Semi-structured interviews	Motherhood and stigma narratives
Rodner, 2005	44 integrated users (16 women and 28 men)	General	Stockholm, Sweden	Informal interviews	Identity and boundary narratives
Sandberg & Tutenges, 2015	100 users (88 men and 12 women)	Cannabis	Norway	Semi-structured interviews	Experience narratives
Soller & Lee, 2010	199 Asian American adolescents (43% women; 57% men)	Cannabis	East San Francisco Bay area, U.S.A.	semi-structured interviews	Boundary narratives
Stone, 2016	30 pregnant women	General	U.S.A.	Semi-structured interviews	Redemption and identity narratives
Thommesen, 2010	17 young people with double diagnosis (10 men, 7 women)	General	Norway	Multiple in-depth interviews with each participant	Self and othering narratives
Webb et al., 2017	17 active female users and 12 women in treatment	Meth-amphetamine	Alabama, U.S.A.	Semi-structured interviews	Boundary and recovery narratives
Willis, 2016	21 users	General	Australia	In-depth interviews	Identity and stigma narratives

After a first reading, and in keeping with the QMS method, the analysis focussed on listing the data in a schematic manner (i.e. theoretical frameworks, methods and main findings) and how these related to each other (e.g. where they differed or aligned). A second reading resulted in a more in-depth juxta-position of the data while the coding-scheme was adapted to new emerging patterns. The analysis was deductive (e.g. relying on the existing knowledge on boundary work) and inductive (e.g. focussing on deviating data and gaps). The coding scheme reflected the following eight themes: boundary work; (in-ternalised) stigma; explanations for use; critical selves; resistance; personal vs. group narratives and methods; sample-composition; and theoretical/empirical focus. This ongoing comparative analysis resulted in an overview of how nar-rative identity and boundary work among PWUDs has generally been studied and more importantly, how it has not been studied or has been studied only to a limited degree.

A significant limitation of this study is that the analysis is not based on the raw qualitative data of the selected studies, but instead is based on their rep-resentations by the authors of the chosen works. It is possible that the selected studies contain more data that challenges boundary work than is present in the broader literature. Furthermore, this QMS was performed by one person (the author), and so the analysis was little discussed with other researchers. Although this is not problematic as such, the results might have differed if this project had been conducted by a team (Walsh & Downe, 2005). Additionally, the limited number of databases consulted – which list mainly sociologically-oriented work – has undoubtly narrowed the dataset. Lastly, the choice to in-clude only peer-reviewed publications can be regarded as a limitation because non-peer-reviewed studies might also contain relevant information (Sandelowski & Barroso, 2006).

5   Results

The QMS resulted in three main reflections, i.e.
1) there are shared elements in the narrative explanations for drug use;
2) there is little variation in the research designs used across the selected stud-ies; and
3) PWUDs can blur boundaries through the stories they tell.

5.1 Explaining drug use in identity narratives

Symbolic boundary work by PWUDs mainly occurs between people who use different drugs or use the same drug but in a 'less acceptable' way (Copes, 2016). While varying types of illegal drugs generate different drug effects and the context of (the) use(rs) shapes their diverse experiences, explanations for drug use display several similarities across user groups. From the QMS, a first prominent set of explanations for consuming drugs revolved around feeling good, having fun, experiencing pleasure and a sense of freedom (Plumridge & Chetwynd, 1999; Rødner, 2005; Pennay & Moore, 2010; Dahl & Heggen, 2014; Sandberg & Tutenges, 2015). Drugs are used to create a buzz in life and to feel more closely connected to friends (Järvinen & Demant, 2011; Frank, Christensen & Dahl, 2013; O'Gorman, 2016; Green, 2016).

A second identified group of explanations for drug use is enhancing performance, managing comedowns, and managing withdrawal symptoms from other drugs (Pennay & Moore, 2010; Fast, Kerr, Wood & Small, 2014; O'Gorman, 2016; Green, 2016). This instrumental use of drugs applied to several drugs and contexts. People used cannabis and amphetamines to increase creativity, productivity and social skills in order to perform better at work (Hathaway, 2004) or in order to cope with jobs they did not always like (Lavin, 2016). Furthermore, the QMS showed that a prominent explanation for drug use was to achieve a state of normalcy and functionality in order to manage daily expectations. This included working, cleaning, cooking, looking for a job, etc. (McIntosh & McKeganey, 2000; Fast et al., 2014). The last identified explanation for using drugs was related to feelings of discouragement, sorrow, internalised stigma and 'rock-bottom' stories (such stories are often told in recovery settings and describe a crisis that eventually became a turning point) (Gibson, Acquah & Robinson, 2004; Radcliffe, 2009; Webb, Deitzer & Copes, 2017). These studies covered narratives about loneliness, illness and exclusion from wider society, family and friends. The use of drugs provided for some participants a chance to enjoy, to forget, to cope and to regain some courage (Boeri, 2004; Thommesen, 2010; McKay, McDavitt, Goeorge & Mutchler, 2012; McKenna, 2013; Kronbæk & Frank, 2013).

The three overarching explanations that resulted from the QMS occurred (also jointly) across people who used different drugs and identified themselves as functional or dysfunctional users. While the personal context of individual users is highly important in shaping sense-making and underlying explanations of drug use (Hammersley et al., 2001), looking for a new or different experience – either to evoke pleasure, resistance, functionality or relief – is something that PWUDs share from a meta-perspective.

5.2 Theoretical and methodological reflections

This QMS also looked at how the selected publications theoretically and methodologically approached identity and boundary work. A commonly identified theoretical stance located identity work in the personal narratives of PWUDs. Although the personal level is essential, identities are also created in relation to other elements (such as institutional or cultural discourses) and are a highly contextual, interactional and momentary (Loseke, 2007; Bamberg, 2010). Although several studies incorporated a complex and contextual theoretical understanding of identity (Gibson et al., 2004; Copes, Hochstetler & Williams, 2008; Pereira & Carrington, 2016), the individual level was (perhaps over-)emphasised. A methodological consequence is that most studies drew on data gathered at this individual level, mostly via interviews. Moreover, there are no detailed reflections on how the interviewer interacted with the identity narratives of the participants (Bamberg, 2010). This means that there is an emphasis on isolated accounts of PWUDs while the social component has received less attention. Only three of the 31 studies explicitly applied focus groups in order to counter opinions and experiences of PWUDs (Gibson et al., 2004; Järvinen & Demant, 2011; Lancaster et al., 2015). Especially when studying boundary work and intra-group stigma, including these interactional layers can lead to a deeper understanding of how stigmatising representations of drug use can be deconstructed.

A connected finding that is present in almost all analysed studies is the focus on rather homogenous groups in terms of the drugs that are used, their patterns of use, or their context of use. Although population-specified research is valuable, engaging in boundary work might be easier among peers. Therefore, this subject of intra-group stigma might benefit from bringing together PWUDs, regardless of the categories we and other participants perceive them to belong to. Related to this reflection, in searching to deconstruct stigmatising discourses it might be beneficial to examine the possible role of empathy (because looking towards what is shared – commonalities), instead of focusing on what establishes difference, is key to bringing people (and their stories) closer together and to challenging stigma (Agar, 2002; Cahill, 2007).

5.3 Theoretical Identity ambivalence and narrative symbolic boundaries

Although the scope of this QMS is to identify elements which (can) blur boundaries between PWUDs, the importance of Copes' (2016) analysis could not be denied. However, the QMS also showed that symbolic boundaries can be (re)negotiated or rejected, and that PWUDs can experience difficulties with identifying themselves within these boundaries. PWUDs narrated conflicting statements about being a functional and a dysfunctional user within the same conversation, behaviour which violated former established boundaries, internalised stigma, and they struggled to identify oneself with particular 'categories' of users (Gibson et al., 2004; Copes et al., 2014; 2018; Willis, 2016). In line with the broader theoretical and empirical literature on narrative identity constructions, it is not surprising to find that people can be contradictory in their actions and stories (Loseke, 2007; Van De Mieroop & Clifton, 2016).

Importantly, in some of the selected studies participants displayed interesting notions of critical self-reflection towards common sense understandings of drug use(rs). The study by Willis (2016) showed that participants were aware of dichotomising ways of being as the blueprint for constructing their own conduct and subjectivities. They felt they had to pin down 'the truth' about what they do and who they are by establishing which of the opposing positions (e.g. functional or dysfunctional users) they occupy. Several participants struggled to do so. In the study by Lancaster et al. (2015) – where focus groups were conducted with opioid users – the boundary work between heroin (regarded as 'soft') and methamphetamine users was apparent. However, a participant countered this reasoning:

> *'Ursula: I find it kind of interesting. We've have a room full of opiate users here, and you're, "Oh no, 'ice' is bad [...]" Well why?'* (Lancaster et al., 2015, p. 228).

Ursula explicitly questioned the arbitrary divisions between users based on their drug of choice. Some other studies in the analysis also contained similar signs of ambivalence, struggle, contradiction, empathy and critical thought within their narrative identity constructions (Gibson et al., 2004; McKenna, 2013; Sandberg & Tutenges, 2015; Green, 2016). This part of the QMS indicates that boundaries and stereotypes of drug use(rs) can be questioned by seeing the personal lived experiences behind categories (Cahill, 2007). These ambivalent notions hint at the inconsistent nature of identities and (life) stories as such (Loseke, 2007). This raises important questions about simplified and essentialising categories through which we (try) to understand and narrate our social wold (Fraser & Moore, 2008). Given that symbolic boundary work is often inspired by dichotomous reasoning (Willis, 2016), personal, shared and messy lived experiences or exchanges between PWUDs might be an inspiring and transformative (research) practice. Indications of ambivalence, struggles, and sometimes outright challenges, hold out the hope that symbolic boundaries and stigmatising accounts of drug use can be actively renegotiated. Social drug researchers, who are interested in the topic of (intra-group) stigma and who want to contribute to the deconstruction of stereotypical representation, can play an engaging role in this renegotiation.

6   Conclusion: 'there's a crack in everything, that's how the light gets in'

In 2015, Lancaster et al. stated that

> *'How negative identities can be successfully converted, and intra-group stigma minimised, so as to empower PWIDs to participate in transforming their own social construction, requires further study'* (p. 230).

In order to reflect on possibilities for such studies, this QMS invoked a vast body of knowledge on narrative identity work and intra-group stigma among PWUDs. Drug users (still) experience stigma and, for storying a 'good self', they rely on boundary work (Copes, 2016). Although the title of this section might create an overly romanticised impression, the quoted phrase from Leonard Cohen's 1992 song 'Anthem' is fitting because symbolic boundaries seem fractured too.

Although hints of narrative struggles are present in some studies, their potential is rather understudied, as this QMS has helped demonstrate. Taking into account that narrative identities are never static and are largely contextual, struggles in drug narratives are not surprising as such (Loseke, 2007). However, this subject has been less situated within the opportunities of the narrative habitus, which is open to new stories and more detailed and personal versions of master narratives (Fleetwood, 2016; Van De Mieroop & Clifton, 2016). Empathy and being aware of commonalities, instead of mainly fixating on differences, are important tools for the blurring of symbolic boundaries, which tend to be based on simplified and partial knowledge (Agar, 2002; Cahill, 2007).

In order to study this potential of both narrative struggles and empathy in (re)negotiating intra-group stigma, the element of interaction is profoundly important. However, most studies in the QMS relied on individual qualitative interviews while a minority applied group research. Moreover, participants were often similar in terms of illegal drugs used and patterns of use. While this renders highly informative data about narrative identity work within these groups, the ability to renegotiate stigmatising discourses may be addressed to a lesser degree. Consequently, further research might benefit from applying interactive group-techniques with more heterogeneous samples of PWUDs. When studying if, and how intra-group stigma can be (re)constructed when PWUDs are brought together, we might apply longitudinal designs to explore the(se) process(es). Most studies in the QMS publications presented here engage only once with participants: this offers a highly situated (and potentially narrow) narrative version of identities (Bamberg, 2010). Additionally, it can be insightful to research these processes simultaneously within the group and on the level of the individual participants. Given that personal and social narrative identities are fluid and interactional, we could gain further insight into how both these levels jointly (re)construct narrative struggles, identities and boundaries.

A final thought is that drug researchers might consider developing more participatory study designs. Following Paolo Freire (1970) and Orlando Fals Borda (2001), people can be critical about their existing situations, selves and others. Renegotiating stigma within a community – and working towards social change – should be done in cooperation with this same community. Scientific knowledge-building can rely more extensively on a diversity of experiences based on people's lives (Cahill, 2007). As academics, this could help our search for opportunities to transcend the (re)production of (intra-group) stigmatising representations of drug use(rs). Appealing to the capacity for understanding others', and our own contradictory subjective positions would be an interesting place to start (Agar, 2002). In doing so, researchers and PWUDs could contribute to challenge the stigma attached to drug use, which profoundly impacts PWUDs' lives to this day.

References

Agar, M. (2002). How the drug field turned my beard grey. *International Journal of Drug Policy, 13 (4)*, 249–258.

Askew, R., & Salinas, M. (2018). Status, stigma and stereotype: how drug takers and drug suppliers avoid negative labelling by virtue of their 'conventional' and 'law-abiding' lives. *Criminology & Criminal Justice, 19 (3)*, 311–327.

Bamberg, M. (2010). Who am I? Narration and its contribution to self and identity. *Theory & Psychology, 21 (1)*, 3–24.

Boeri, M.W. (2004). 'Hell, I'm an addict, but I ain't no junkie': an ethnographic analysis of aging heroin users. *Human Organization, 63 (2)*, 236–245.

Borda, O.F. (2006). Participatory (action) research in social theory: origins and challenges. In: P. Reason, & H. Bradbury (Eds.), *Handbook of action research* (pp. 27–37). London: Sage.

Bourdieu, P. (1990). *The logic of practice.* Stanford, CA: Stanford University Press.

Cahill, C. (2007). The personal is political: developing new subjectivities through participatory action research. *Gender, Place and Culture, 14 (3)*, 267–292.

Copes, H. (2016). A narrative approach to studying symbolic boundaries among drug users: a qualitative meta-synthesis. *Crime, Media, Culture, 12 (2)*, 193–213.

Copes, H., Hochstetler, A., & Williams, J. P. (2008). 'We weren't like no regular dope fiends': negotiating hustler and crackhead identities. *Social Problems, 55 (2)*, 254–270.

Copes, H., Kerley, K.R., Angulski, K., & Zaleski, S. (2014). 'Meth's not my cup of tea'. Perceptions of methamphetamine among black women. *Journal of Drug Issues, 44 (4)*, 430–441.

Copes, H., Tchoula, W., Kim, J., & Ragland, J. (2018). Symbolic perceptions of methamphetamine: differentiating between ice and shake. *International Journal of Drug Policy, 51 (1)*, 87–94.

Dahl, S.L., & Heggen, K. (2014). Negotiating identities: patterns of self-presentations among socially integrated cannabis users. *Young, 22 (4)*, 381–398.

Edland-Gryt, M., Sandberg, S., & Pedersen, W. (2017). From ecstasy to MDMA: recreational drug use, symbolic boundaries, and drug trends. *International Journal of Drug Policy, 50 (12)*, 1–8.

Fast, D., Kerr, T., Wood, E., & Small, W. (2014). The multiple truths about crystal meth among young people entrenched in an urban drug scene: a longitudinal ethnographic investigation. *Social Science & Medicine, 110 (10)*, 41–48.

Fleetwood, J. (2016). Narrative habitus: thinking through structure/agency in the narratives of offenders. *Crime, Media, Culture, 12 (2)*, 173–192.

Frank, V.A., Christensen, A.S., & Dahl, H.V. (2013). Cannabis use during a life course – integrating cannabis use into everyday life. *Drugs and Alcohol Today, 13 (1)*, 44–50.

Fraser, S., & Moore, D. (2008). Dazzled by unity? Order and chaos in public discourse on illicit drug use. *Social Science and Medicine, 66 (5)*, 740-752.

Freire, P. (1970). *Pedagogy of the oppressed*. New York: Continuum.

Gibson, B., Acquah, S., & Robinson, P. G. (2004). Entangled identities and psychotropic substance use. *Sociology of Health & Illness, 26 (5)*, 597–616.

Goffman, E. (1963). *Stigma: notes on the management of spoiled identity*. Harmondsworth: Penguin.

Green, R. (2016). 'I wonder what age you grow out of it?' Negotiation of recreational drug use and the transition to adulthood among an Australian ethnographic sample. *Drugs: Education, Prevention and Policy, 23 (3)*, 202-211.

Hall, S. (1996). Introduction: Who needs 'identity'? In: S. Hall, & P. Du Gay (Eds.), *Questions of cultural identity* (pp.1–17). London: Sage.

Hammersley, R., Jenkins, R., & Reid, M. (2001). Cannabis use and social identity. *Addiction Research & Theory, 9 (2)*, 133–150.

Hathaway, A.D. (2004). Cannabis users' informal rules for managing stigma and risk. *Deviant Behavior, 25 (6)*, 559–577.

Järvinen, M., & Demant, J. (2011). The normalisation of cannabis use among young people: symbolic boundary work in focus groups. *Health, Risk & Society, 13 (2)*, 165–182.

Kronbæk, M., & Frank, V.A. (2013). Perspectives on daily cannabis use: consumerism or a problem for treatment? *Nordic Studies on Alcohol and Drugs, 30 (5)*, 387–402.

Lamont, M., & Molnár, V. (2002). The study of boundaries in the social sciences. *Annual Review of Sociology, 28 (1)*, 167–195.

Lancaster, K., Santana, L., Madden, A., & Ritter, A. (2015). Stigma and subjectivities: examining the textured relationship between lived experience and opinions about drug policy among people who inject drugs. *Drugs: Education, Prevention and Policy, 22 (3)*, 224–231.

Lavin, M.F. (2017). She got herself there: narrative resistance in the drug discourse of strippers. *Deviant Behavior, 38 (3)*, 294–305.

Loseke, D.R. (2007). The study of identity as cultural, institutional, organizational and personal narratives: theoretical and empirical integrations. *The Sociological Quarterly, 48 (4)*, 661–688.

McIntosh, J., & McKeganey, N. (2000). Addicts' narratives of recovery from drug use: constructing a non-addict identity. *Social Science & Medicine, 50 (10)*, 1501–1510.

McKay, T.A., McDavitt, B., George, S., & Mutchler, M.G. (2012). 'Their type of drugs': perceptions of substance use, sex and social boundaries among young African American and Latino gay and bisexual men. *Culture, Health & Sexuality, 14 (10)*, 1183–1196.

McKenna, S. (2013). 'The meth factor': group membership, information management, and the navigation of stigma. *Contemporary Drug Problems, 40 (3)*, 351–385.

O'Gorman, A. (2016). Chillin, buzzin, getting mangled, and coming down: doing differentiated normalisation in risk environments. *Drugs: Education, Prevention and Policy, 23 (3)*, 247–254.

Pennay, A., & Moore, D. (2010). Exploring the micro-politics of normalisation: narratives of pleasure, self-control and desire in a sample of young Australian 'party drug' users. *Addiction Research & Theory, 18 (5)*, 557–571.

Pereira, M., & Carrington, K. (2016). Irrational addicts and responsible pleasure seekers: constructions of the drug user. *Critical Criminology, 24 (3)*, 379–389.

Plumridge, E., & Chetwynd, J. (1999). Identity and the social construction of risk: injecting drug use. *Sociology of Health & Illness, 21 (3)*, 329–343.

Presser, L. (2016). Criminology and the narrative turn. *Crime, Media, Culture, 12 (2)*, 137–151.

Radcliffe, P. (2009). Drug use and motherhood: strategies for managing identity. *Drugs and Alcohol Today, 9 (3)*, 17–21.

Rødner, S. (2005). 'I am not a drug abuser, I am a drug user': a discourse analysis of 44 drug users' construction of identity. *Addiction Research and Theory, 13 (4)*, 333–346.

Sandberg, S., & Tutenges, S. (2015). Meeting the djinn: stories of drug use, and trips, and addiction. In: L. Presser, & S. Sandberg (Eds.), *Narrative criminology: understanding stories of crime* (pp. 150–151). New York: New York University Press.

Sandelowski, M., & Barroso, J. (2006). *Handbook for synthesizing qualitative research*. New York: Springer.

Soller, B., & Lee, J. P. (2010). Drug-intake methods and social identity: the use of marijuana in blunts among Southeast Asian adolescents and emerging adults. *Journal of Adolescent Research, 25 (6)*, 783–806.

Stone, R. (2016). Desistance and identity repair: redemption narratives as resistance to stigma. *British Journal of Criminology, 56 (5)*, 956–975.

Taylor, S., Buchanan, J., & Ayres, T. (2016). Prohibition, privilege and the drug apartheid: the failure of drug policy reform to address the underlying fallacies of drug prohibition. *Criminology & Criminal Justice, 16 (4)*, 452–469.

Thommesen, H. (2010). Master narratives and narratives as told by people with mental health and drug problems. *Journal of Comparative Social Work, 5 (1)*, 1–16.

Van De Mieroop, D., & Clifton, J. (2016). Life stories. In: J. Östman, & J. Verschueren (Eds.), *Handbook of pragmatics* (pp. 1–20). Amsterdam: John Benjamins.

Walsh, D., & Downe, S. (2005). Meta-synthesis method for qualitative research: a literature review. *Journal of Advanced Nursing, 50 (2)*, 204–211.

Webb, M., Deitzer, J., & Copes, H. (2017). Methamphetamine, symbolic boundaries, and using status. *Deviant Behavior, 38 (12)*, 1393–1405.

Willis, L.L. (2016). *Deconstructing divergent constructions of illicit drug use and drug-using subjects: understanding enduring stigma and marginalisation* (Doctoral dissertation, Curtain University, Perth, Australia). Retrieved from https://espace.curtin.edu.au/handle/20.500.11937/1537

Wills, T.A. (1981). Downward comparison principles in social psychology. *Psychological Bulletin, 90 (2)*, 745–271.

8
Buyer motives for sourcing illegal drugs from 'drop-off' delivery dealers

Thomas Friis Søgaard

Research indicates that drug dealing organised as 'drop-off' delivery services is increasing in popularity. Based on the assumption that drug market developments are fuelled by supply-side as well as demand-side processes, this chapter draws on 28 interviews with drug users in Denmark to explore user motivations for purchasing drugs from delivery dealers, as well as the related barriers and experiences of risks. The key findings are that the buyers primarily source mainstream drugs such as cannabis and cocaine from delivery dealers, and that their preference for this method is based on easy access to these dealers, the speed with which drugs can be obtained, and experiences of transactional ease and convenience. Having drugs delivered to their doorstep, however, also entails new anxieties and risks for buyers. These include concerns about potentially violent or criminal dealers knowing where they live, and threats of stigmatisation stemming from decreased abilities to keep their drug purchasing hidden from neighbours.

Keywords: drug markets, delivery services, drug dealing, buyer perspectives, risks

1   Introduction

Contrary to popular imagination depicting the drug market as a monolithic entity, recent studies argue that drug markets and distribution systems vary vertically between levels and horizontally within the same market level (Potter, 2009). Research also suggests that distribution models can change in shape and prominence (May & Hough, 2004). While not a new phenomenon, retail distribution organised as drop-off delivery seems to be accelerating. As an indication of this, the EMCDDA recently described how the European market for cocaine is undergoing a process of '[u]bernisation', where sellers promote additional services beyond the product itself, such as 'fast delivery anywhere at any time' (EMCDDA, 2018, p. 18; see also Winstock, Barratt, Maier & Ferris, 2018).

While there is agreement among scholars that the drop-off delivery model is on the rise in many European countries (EMCDDA, 2018), including Belgium (De Middeleer et al., 2018), France (Cadet-Taïrou et al., 2017) and Denmark (Søgaard et al., 2019), research on the phenomenon remains limited. Most notably, no in-depth research exists on buyers' experiences of sourcing drugs from delivery dealers. This chapter therefore draws on 28 interviews with drug users in Denmark to explore motivations for purchasing drugs in this way, the related barriers and experiences of risks.

2   The drop-off delivery model: a research perspective

Drop-off delivery dealing is essentially a service where buyers contact sellers, for instance by phone, and make appointments for the delivery of low-volume units of drugs at the buyer's home or other buyer-specified locations (Curtis, Wendel & Spunt, 2002; Salinas, 2018; Søgaard et al., 2019). Research suggests that delivery dealing first became a growth area in the 1980s and expanded rapidly in the 1990s, and that this was in large part a result of dealers' adaptation to communication technologies such as pagers and mobile phones. This enabled buyers and dealers to arrange meetings regardless of their physical location (Curtis et al., 2002). The proliferation of delivery dealing has also been described as a drug market response to changes in policy and law enforcement (May & Hough, 2004; Barendregt, van der Poel & van de Mheen, 2006). In comparison to street dealing, delivery dealing is not as easy for the police to detect. Not only does the use of mobile phones, and more recently, encrypted apps on smartphones enable more covert contact between customers and dealers (Curtis et al., 2002; Moyle, Childs, Coomber & Barratt, 2019), delivery dealers are also constantly on the move, which makes traditional hotspot police surveillance ineffective (Barendregt et al., 2006). The growth in delivery dealing is therefore indicative of a more general transformation from open street dealing to less visible and more closed distribution networks (May & Hough, 2004).

More recently, scholars have argued that the current acceleration in the use of drop-off delivery models might also be a result of current market developments and increased competition between dealers. Recent studies have noted that online cryptomarkets are often more customer-service oriented than their traditional offline counterparts. For instance, many cryptomarkets offer systems where buyers can rate vendors and products, escrow systems to reduce transactional scams, and systems for conflict resolution (Barratt & Aldridge, 2016). Winstock and colleagues have speculated that the developments within online markets might be a catalyst for other customer service upgrades, such as more dealers offering convenient and speedy delivery of drugs (Winstock et al., 2018). In line with this, the EMCDDA (2018) recently noted that the emergence of crypto- and social media markets seems to have led to increased competition between a growing number of smaller groups and individual entrepreneurs, who compete for customers by promoting additional services beyond the product itself, such as fast delivery of drugs.

While cryptomarket vendors have traditionally relied on postal services for the delivery of drugs (Barratt & Aldridge, 2016), the provision of rapid delivery services makes good business sense, as it enables retailers to reduce the time between purchase and customers' receipt of drugs. However, the growing popularity of rapid drug delivery services can also be seen as a reflection of more general tendencies in contemporary consumer society. Research shows that a growing number of food chains, restaurants and grocery stores offer rapid delivery services to customers as a way of gaining market advantages. In today's fast-paced life, many consumers cannot or will not go through the hassle of going out for food. Thus, they make the food come to them (Yeo, Goh & Rezaei, 2017). Drug dealing, organised as drop-off delivery, copies the increasingly dominant logistical logic of the legitimate food market and applies it to the illicit market for drugs. More generally, and similar to the county line supply model as described by Coomber & Moyle (2018), the urban drop-off delivery model reflects key characteristics of the neoliberal capitalist market characterised by 24/7 trade, decreased geographical constraints, transaction intensiveness, and much competition between a growing number of suppliers.

Research shows that the socio-technical organisation of drop-off delivery schemes vary. At one end of the scale are local delivery schemes run by individual freelancers or smaller groups, who use traditional mobile phones or smartphone encryption apps to communicate with buyers (Curtis et al., 2002; Salinas, 2018; Søgaard et al., 2019). At the other end are highly organised delivery schemes with either domestic (Curtis et al., 2002; Cadet-Taïrou, Gandilhon, Martinez, et al., 2017) or out-of-country call centres (De Middeleer, Van Nimwegen, Ceulen et al., 2018) that take orders from buyers and coordinate the activities of local deliverers ('runners').

While existing research has primarily been concerned with outlining the historical growth and socio-technical organisation of the supply-side of local delivery schemes, little research exists on buyers' experiences of purchasing drugs from delivery dealers. This is a problem, because exploring what motivates buyers to choose delivery dealers as supplements or alternatives to other channels from which drugs can be sourced can strengthen our understanding of contemporary transformations in drug distribution. Furthermore, a focus on buyers' experiences can also produce insights about how the current changes in supply methods might involve new anxieties and risks for users.

3   Context and data

In Denmark, the first publicly known example of a drug delivery service emerged in Copenhagen in the early 2000s. Since then, the phenomenon has spread to many towns and cities across the country. Though some delivery dealers in Denmark have started using Internet-enabled encryption apps such as Wickr or Signal when communicating with buyers, many still use regular mobile phones with pre-paid SIM cards, which can be bought and used anonymously (Søgaard, Kolind, Haller & Hunt, 2019).

The data for this paper was obtained through face-to-face interviews with 28 drug users with first-hand experiences of purchasing illegal drugs from drop-off delivery dealers. Participants were recruited through chain referrals and snowballing methods. To establish the initial contacts, the principal researcher made use of his network of personal acquaintances and his relations with participants in a previous research project on Danish nightlife. Later on, a research assistant made use of a similar recruitment strategy. After being interviewed, participants were asked if they would help us establish contact with other potential participants in their network. In total, participants were recruited from seven different chain referral networks. The participants included 16 men and 12 women, between the ages of 17 and 37 (average age 26 years). In terms of their occupational status, five were unemployed, ten were students at applied or higher education institutions, two were researchers, two worked in public administration, six were social workers or employed in the service sector, and three worked in the music and entertainment sector. Participants primarily lived in two different cities. While differences exist between delivery schemes in these cities, this chapter focuses on the commonalities in buyer experiences.

Before the interviews, participants were thoroughly informed about the purpose of the study and the voluntary and anonymous nature of their participation. All interviews were conducted using a semi-structured interview guide, and lasted between one and three hours. The interviews were designed to examine issues such as variations in drug sourcing practices; motives for using delivery dealers; buyers' use of communication technologies; and experiences with delivery dealers. The researchers also collected 63 group-based text messages known as 'dealer spam' (Moyle et al., 2019). These were sent by dealers to buyers as a means of advertising their products, and buyers forwarded them electronically to the researchers either during or after the interviews. On average, the group-based text messages are approximately 80 words. All data was coded using NVivo12. The study was approved by the Danish Data Protection Agency. Pseudonyms are used throughout the chapter and specific locations are anonymised.

4 Findings

4.1 An overview of participants' drug use and sourcing practices

Interviews revealed variations in participants' drug use patterns. While some reported being daily users of cannabis, most described themselves as recreational users of cannabis and cocaine but occasionally also MDMA, ecstasy and amphetamine. A few occasionally used mushrooms, LSD and ketamine. All reported sourcing drugs from a combination of social supply channels (Potter, 2009) and commercial dealers, with some mainly using the former and others the latter. Importantly, when purchasing drugs from commercial dealers, participants preferred drop-off delivery dealers, along with offline modes of acquiring drugs. For instance, interviews showed that only two of the 28 participants had ever purchased drugs from a cryptomarket vendor. Three others had tried, but had experienced technical difficulties and abandoned the attempt. More surprisingly, given the recent expansion of social media dealing internationally (Moyle et al., 2019), only five participants had ever purchased drugs from a dealer on Instagram, Snapchat or Facebook. Contrary to this, 19 participants reported having purchased drugs from a street dealer, 17 from an apartment dealer, and eight from a dealer inside a nightclub/bar. All participants had sourced drugs from a delivery dealer, and all but two reported that delivery dealers constituted the primary commercial channel through which they obtained either cocaine and/or cannabis. In addition, 15 participants reported that they had occasionally purchased MDMA, ecstasy or amphetamine from delivery dealers. Data also showed variation in the technology used by participants to communicate with dealers. While most participants (14) reported exclusively using regular phone calls or text messages, six reported using regular phones but rarely encryption apps; seven used encryption apps and phone calls/text messages interchangeably; and only one exclusively used an encryption app (Wickr).

We did not collect systematic data on the quantities of drugs sourced from delivery dealers. Interviews however suggested that the buyers in this study primarily purchase smaller amounts either for personal consumption or to be shared among friends. The dealer spam messages we collected also showed that many dealers operate with very low minimum amounts – typically 0.5–1 gram of cocaine, 2–3 gram cannabis, and 1 pill of ecstasy/MDMA. A few buyers reported group purchases on party nights, but none reported 'stash buying'. While some of the daily users of cannabis reported buying from delivery dealers once or twice a week, many recreational users of cocaine and cannabis reported doing so once a month and some less.

4.2 Good enough quality, a fair price, and little risk of police detection

Quality and price are often important factors informing drug users' sourcing practices. In terms of drug quality, the participants in this study described the delivery market as located in between street markets and darknet cryptomarkets. With the exception of the open-air cannabis market in Christiania, Copenhagen, participants agreed that the quality of drugs sold by street dealers was generally lower than that provided by delivery dealers. Participants also agreed that the best quality and widest range of drugs were available on the darknet. However, many felt that buying drugs on the darknet was not worth the effort. The reason for this was that most participants were primarily interested in mainstream drugs such as cannabis and cocaine, and few considered themselves to be drug connoisseurs, and did not have expert knowledge or a very sophisticated taste. They therefore believed that delivery dealers generally provided products of 'good enough' quality to satisfy their needs.

While most agreed that delivery dealers' prices were generally fair, some complained that the price was sometimes slightly higher than elsewhere because delivery was included. Participants explained that most of the delivery dealers operated with relatively fixed prices. While this had its benefits in reducing the risk of price-related conflicts, some buyers found this annoying as it reduced their ability to strike better deals:

> *'The price is a downside of buying from the delivery guys. You pay a bit extra, because they deliver. Also, you don't have much chance of influencing the price. They set the price and that's it. When I buy from this guy [an apartment dealer] I know, you can negotiate… Try to get a better price.'* (Dennis, aged 37)

While price and quality of drugs were rarely mentioned as key reasons for choosing delivery dealers, concerns about police detection figured more centrally. Participants described buying from delivery dealers as safer than buying from street dealers, on Facebook or from vendors on cryptomarkets. Street transactions often take place in specific areas and are relatively visible, which increases the risk of police detection. By sourcing drugs from mobile delivery dealers, participants felt they could avoid heavily-policed dealing hotspots. Participants' reluctance to buy drugs from dealers on Facebook was rooted in concerns about this being an insecure and potentially police-surveilled platform, while their reluctance to buy from cryptomarket vendors centered on fears of police/customs when drugs are sent by postal service to their address (see also Barratt & Aldridge, 2016):

'For me it doesn't make sense to buy on the darknet. You need to buy a lot for it to make sense. Also, if you order something you have to write your real name and address, and that just scares me. What if it's seized in customs, then the police come knocking on my door?' (Louise, aged 24)

Participants' construction of delivery dealers as a relatively safe channel for sourcing drugs was based on a number of factors. One is that communication with dealers is either conducted through the use of encrypted apps, or, when regular phone or text messages are used, with little or no mention of names, drugs, or codes for drugs. Rather, since many buyers know in advance which type of drug can be bought from a particular phone number (see Søgaard et al., 2019), phone-based exchanges often merely include buyers asking the dealer 'can you help me?' and the dealer replying 'yes', followed by a brief exchange about where to meet. Buyers were convinced that this would make it difficult for police to build a case against them. Most importantly however, many buyers were convinced that police prioritised the targeting of online users and sellers, which meant that buying from delivery dealers was likely to go under the police radar. Possible naively, some also believed that if police did manage to tap a delivery dealer's phone, they would probably go for the 'bigger fish', and not some little fish like themselves:

'In some way I feel ... that I'm protected by the crowd. If there's like 100 customers to one phone number and the police crack it, what's the likelihood that you are the most interesting? Probably not that big, right?' (Tommy, aged 26)

4.3 Easy access to dealers

While drug quality and price seemed to play a secondary role in buyers' decision to use delivery dealers, easy access to dealers was often mentioned as a central factor. Unlike cryptomarkets, where users need a relatively high level of digital competence to participate (Barratt & Aldridge, 2016), dealers providing drop-off delivery services are very easily accessible in terms of the technical knowledge required. This is the case with app-based delivery services (Moyle et al., 2019), and even more so with dealers using traditional mobile phones. However, access barriers might still operate. For example, May and Hough (2004) argue that phone-based delivery services at times operate as closed networks, where sellers and buyers will only do business if they know each other, or if a third party vouches for them. Although this might be true for some delivery schemes, many delivery dealers in Denmark seem to operate with a very low access threshold. As an indication of this, the phone numbers and Wickr user names of delivery dealers were often routinely circulated between users, and dealers did not seem to exercise much, if any, control over who their contact details were passed on to. In fact, some dealers actively encouraged users to share their number with potential new customers:

> *'Some dealers have this thing where if you give their number to three others, and instruct them to tell the dealer that you were the one who gave them the number, the next time you buy you get extra drugs for free.'* (Henrik, aged 28)

Other participants reported that they were occasionally offered dealers' phone numbers by strangers in the street or when going out at nightclubs.

> *'There are so many numbers circulating. I've had people approach me in nightclubs saying "Hey do you need a number"? The marketing has become much more aggressive than it used to be. I've even seen [dealers'] business cards hanging at bus stops.'* (John, aged 33)

The above is illustrative of the aggressive marketing strategies characterising the neoliberal drug market (Coomber and Moyle, 2018), involving not only dealers' distribution of contact details by use of business cards (Spicer, 2018) or dealer spam (Moyle et al., 2019; Søgaard et al., 2019), but also the instrumental use of 'freebies' to incentivise regular customers to recommend them to other buyers (Coomber, 2003). Another reason why many Danish delivery dealers operate with low access thresholds might be that, in comparison to many other European countries, Denmark until very recently had much stricter legislation when it comes to police use of 'agents provocateurs' (Vendius, 2015). This meant that even if police got hold of a dealer's phone number or Wickr username, they were rarely allowed to pose as customers as a means of arresting a dealer. As a consequence, dealer contact details are circulated relatively freely, and many participants reported being in possession of between three and ten different delivery dealer phone numbers or Wickr accounts:

> *'If you are a regular user, then you'll quickly get 5–10 [dealer] numbers on your phone, passed on from friends or people you know. I've even been approached by these smaller boys in the street: "Do you need hash? Do you need a number"?'* (Tom, aged 25)

For buyers, one advantage of being in possession of multiple delivery dealer phone numbers or Wickr accounts is that it reduces the search time for drugs. If a preferred dealer is unavailable, buyers do not need to head to the street or look for dealers online. All they have to do is contact the next delivery dealer on their list.

4.4 Speed and convenience

Interviews showed that speed of delivery and convenience were the two most important reasons for buyers to choose drop-off delivery dealers. Unlike cryptomarkets, where buyers sometimes have to wait days or weeks for packages to arrive, participants reported that most delivery dealers provide relatively swift delivery of products. Obviously, dealers' response time can vary depending on the location of buyers and whether or not it is a busy (time of) day:

> *'I think the longest I have waited is 20 minutes. I don't know how they do it. But it depends on when you call. On weekends, I never call them after eleven o'clock because that's when they are busy.'* (Sofie, aged 26)

Participants also emphasised that part of the appeal of delivery dealers was that many showed considerable flexibility. Not only did many dealers provide home delivery, many also left it to the buyers to decide alternative meeting points:

> *'Normally when you want to buy drugs, it can be quite a hassle. Either you have to know the right people, or you have go out and look for someone [a dealer] (…) But the system here, the first time I heard about it I was very, very impressed. It's extremely flexible… that it's the dealer who comes to you, even if you're at some party, and you say: "I'm at this place". They just say: "Okay, I'll meet you there". You call, they bring. Incredible!'* (Sara, aged 28)

As the above indicates, localised delivery services are tailored to accommodate the needs of an individual consumer by offering rapid and flexible drug delivery. For buyers, this has several advantages. Not only does it give the consumer a sense of control, it also means that they do not need to plan in advance whether or not they want to use drugs on a particular occasion. Rather, the relative ease with which buyers can have drugs delivered to a place of their choosing better enables them to react to spontaneous desires. For the participants, convenience amounted to the time and effort they perceived to be saving when trying to source drugs. According to them, some dealers had adopted two key procedures to minimise customers' experience of wasting time waiting, as this could result in a loss of customers. Similar to when a customer books a taxi, all delivery dealers would, at the time an order was placed, try to give a rough estimate of when the delivery car would arrive. Furthermore, possibly also inspired by taxi companies, some dealers would text customers five minutes before their arrival. The latter procedure greatly increased customers' sense of convenience because it meant that they could get on with other things while waiting. Furthermore, getting notified five minutes in advance also reduced the time buyers had to stand outside their home or on a street corner, in the often cold and rainy Danish weather, waiting for the delivery car.

'I got this routine; I text my guy: "Can we meet"? Then we agree when and where to meet. He texts me five minutes before his arrival, which gives me time to go to an ATM across from where I live. Then he arrives and I get into his car. He gets money and I get the drugs. Then we talk a bit about football or whatever. Then I say: "thank you, and see you". That's it. I go back upstairs to my apartment.' (John, aged 33)

Convenience and time-saving are also important when buyers make assessments of different delivery dealers. Experiences of inconvenience and wasting time waiting were often mentioned as reasons for discontinuing a relationship with a particular dealer:

'One time, me and a friend wanted to buy [drugs], and this guy didn't show up at the time we agreed. We were supposed to meet at the church. He had texted us: "I'll be there in 30 minutes", but it took about an hour and a half. We were just standing there waiting, and we couldn't even sit down because there were no benches. It was really annoying that he didn't show up at the time we agreed. They always say "sorry I'm late", but then they are late again the next time. Then it's just don't use that guy anymore, just try a new number [on the list].' (Lizzy, aged 26)

The above illustrates that while purchasing drugs from delivery dealers entails many benefits for users, it can also have its downsides. For instance, decreased search time for dealers is sometimes superseded by time spent waiting for one to arrive.

4.5 Delivery risks and anxieties

Interviews revealed that, for buyers, sourcing drugs from delivery dealers is coupled with a number of risks and concerns, and that some of these are related to the actual delivery. Similar to the finding of Curtis and Wendel (2007), participants in this study described the delivery market as a low-violence market. With very few exceptions, none had experienced dealer-related violence or threats. In fact, several participants reported that many delivery dealers acted in a strikingly service-minded manner, and that this was part of the appeal of buying from them. Nevertheless, some participants also described how they had initially felt uneasy about getting into a car with dealers because this left them in a vulnerable position. Not only did many dealers drive around with a partner, which meant that a buyer would be outnumbered in a potential violent encounter, being in a car also involved an element of loss of control in that drivers could easily drive them to a remote location and take advantage of them (see also Tzanetakis, Kamphausen, Werse & von Laufenberg, 2016). While concerns about potential violence were most pronounced in interviews with male participants, concerns about potential sexual assault were most evident in interviews with female participants, as illustrated below:

'The first time I was nervous about getting into the car, so I called a [male] friend of mine. Thinking back... It's really sweet, I was almost like a child, like scared. What if they were dangerous, right? So I didn't give them my address. Instead, we met at some parking lot. I told my friend that he should be the one to get in the car, because I was a woman and what if they did something to me. But these guys [dealers], they were so easy-going, and everything was nice and easy. After that I felt confident to do it on my own.' (Sara, aged 28)

As well as voicing concerns about having to enter a dealer's car, some participants expressed concerns about having a dealer deliver drugs to the doorstep of their private home. Some felt uneasy about dealers knowing where they lived, because if a disagreement were to arise it would be relatively easy for dealers to come and find them and possibly harm them. Others expressed concerns about letting 'criminals' know where they lived, as this might render them vulnerable to burglaries:

'There is absolutely no reason to let them know where I live. I don't know what kind of people they are; I don't know them, or even their names. What if they are delivering, and then they look through the window [of the house] and go: "Well, hey! That's an expensive lamp hanging there ... hmm maybe we should come back and steal it". You see, no reason why they should know where I live.' (Peter, aged 28)

For other participants, having drugs delivered to their doorstep by a dealer was associated with social risks and potential stigmatisation. More so than online dealing, which relies on postal services, or street dealing, where buyers sometimes travel a distance to pick up drugs, dealing involving a home delivery service can constitute a threat to users keen to keep their drug habits hidden from neighbours and the wider community where they live:

'They [dealers] are not getting close to my home address, not at all. There are lots of reasons... well for one thing there are the neighbours. You know they can see it... that some guys in a trashy car regularly come to my door. They'll get suspicious, right. I got kids and I live in a small town where gossip spreads faster than wildfire.' (Dennis, aged 37)

To minimise the risks associated with having drugs delivered to their doorstep, some of the more concerned participants arranged to meet with dealers in a neighbouring street, nearby parking lot or a street corner, and a few deliberately chose to meet at locations far away from their home.

5   Conclusion

In this chapter I have argued that if we are to develop nuanced understandings of the seemingly growing popularity of the drop-off delivery model, we need to include the perspective of drug users into our analysis. Though we must be cautious about over-generalising the insights from the small-scale study presented here, it nevertheless provides findings that might also be relevant when trying to understand the proliferation of the drop-off delivery model elsewhere.

Some key findings in this study are that localised delivery services are primarily used to source mainstream drugs such as cannabis and cocaine. This indicates that part of the business success of Danish delivery dealers is that they tend to cater for a large mainstream segment of users who do not consider themselves to be drug connoisseurs. Another finding is that while the price and quality of drugs continue to matter to users, they are sometimes secondary to other factors such as dealers' provision of additional customer-oriented services. Much of the customer appeal of delivery dealers stems from the speed and convenience with which drugs can be obtained. Similar to the growth in the legitimate home delivery sector for food (Yeo et al., 2017), localised drug delivery services are often tailored to accommodate the needs of an individual consumer, who might be relatively well-off in terms of income but time poor. Being able to source drugs pretty much anywhere and at any time not only gives buyers a sense of control, it also gives them a sense of freedom, in that drug access can now be adjusted to their everyday lives and activities rather than the other way around. Related to this, part of the appeal of delivery dealers is that they are relatively easily accessible both in terms of the technological skills required and in terms of their social availability. Obviously, customers' ability to access local delivery schemes will vary depending on the context. While some delivery schemes will function as closed networks with high social access barriers (May & Hough, 2004), others, as demonstrated in this study, are characterised by very low social access thresholds.

The sourcing of drugs from delivery dealers, however, is also coupled with new inconveniences, risks and concerns. For instance, while a growing number of dealers today compete for customers through speed of delivery, the reality is that many are not always as swift as sensationalised media accounts will have us believe. For buyers, this means that decreased search time for dealers is sometimes superseded by time spent waiting for a dealer to arrive. For buyers, the convenience of having drugs delivered to their doorstep by a dealer is at times also coupled with concerns and anxieties. Not only do some buyers fear that home delivery increases their risks of becoming victims of violence and crime, some also feared that home delivery would make their drug habits more visible to neighbours, which in turn increases their risk of being socially stigmatised in their community. Sourcing drugs from drop-off delivery dealers, in this way, then, entails both benefits and new risks to buyers.

Overall, this study supports the notion that an 'ubernisation' of some sections of the cocaine market has occurred, and the findings also show that this supply model has spread to include other drugs (see also Salinas, 2018). Due to its customer appeal, and because it has proven difficult to police, this supply model is likely to proliferate in the coming years. However, the proliferation and the specific socio-technical organisation of local delivery schemes are likely to vary between contexts depending on differences in national drug policies and legislations. In Denmark for instance, the proliferation of delivery schemes based on the use of traditional mobile phones has in part been enabled by the fact that the Danish Administration of Justice Act until recently stipulated that police were only allowed to use agents provocateurs in relation to 'serious crimes' that carry a maximum penalty of at least six years. Since the delivery business-model is based on dealers' provision of a large number of low-volume unit sales, it has often been difficult for the police to prove beforehand that such practices constitute 'serious crime'. In early 2019, however, the Danish parliament changed the Administration of Justice Act to enable police to use agents provocateurs also in cases involving the selling and purchasing of low-volume drugs. Since the amendment of the law was primarily driven by public concerns about drug dealing and other crimes on the Internet, a precondition for police to make extended use of agents provocateurs is that interactions between small-scale drug sellers and buyers must involve an aspect of Internet exchange (Danish Ministry of Justice, 2019). Since many Danish delivery dealers today communicate with buyers by means of traditional non-Internet-based phone calls and text messages (Søgaard et al., 2019), the amendment of the Administration of Justice Act is not likely to have much effect on the drop-off delivery market. The most likely change is that delivery dealers who currently use Wickr or Signal might shift back to using traditional burner phones when communicating with buyers, as this mitigates police abilities to use agents provocateurs. Investigating how differences in national drug policies and legislation influence both the proliferation, organisation and buyer experiences of the drop-off supply model is a task for future research.

References

Barendregt, C., van der Poel, A., & van de Mheen, D. (2006). The rise of the mobile phone in the hard drug scene of Rotterdam. *Journal of Psychoactive Drugs, 38 (1)*, 77–87.

Barratt, M.J., & Aldridge, J. (2016). Everything you always wanted to know about drug crypto-markets* (*but were afraid to ask). *International Journal of Drug Policy, 35 (1),* 1–6.

Cadet-Taïrou, A., Gandilhon, M., Martinez, M., et al. (2017). *Psychoactive substances, users and markets: recent trends (2016–2017). Tendances No 115.* Paris: Observatoire français des drogues et toxicomanies.

Coomber, R., & Moyle, L. (2018). The changing shape of street-level heroin and crack supply in England: commuting, holidaying and cuckooing drug dealers across 'County lines'. *The British Journal of Criminology, 58 (6),* 1323–1342.

Curtis, R., Wendel, T., & Spunt, B. (2002). *We deliver: The gentrification of drug markets on Manhattan's lower east side, final report.* Rockville, MD: U.S. Department of Justice.

Curtis, R., & Wendel, T. (2007). 'You're always training the dog': strategic Interventions to reconfigure drug markets. *Journal of Drug Issues, 37 (4),* 867–891.

Danish Ministry of Justice (2019). *Lov om ændring af retsplejeloven (Styrkelse af politiets muligheder for efterforskning af kriminalitet på internettet)* [Law on amendment of the Administration of Justice Act (Increased police abilities to investigate crime on the Internet)]. 21.01.2019. Copenhagen.

De Middeleer, F., Van Nimwegen, S., Ceulen, R., et al. (2018). *Illegal drug markets in Belgium and the Netherlands: communicating vessels?* Brussels: Belgian Scientific Policy Office.

EMCDDA: European Monitoring Centre for Drugs and Drug Addiction (2018). *Recent changes in Europe's cocaine market. Results from an EMCDDA trendspotter study.* Lisbon.

Winstock, A.R, Barratt, M.J., Maier, L.J., & Ferris, J.A. (2018). Global Drug Survey (GDS) 2018. *Key Findings.* Link: https://www.globaldrugsurvey.com/gds-2018

May, T., & Hough, M. (2004). Drug markets and distribution systems. *Addiction Research & Theory, 12 (6),* 549–563.

Moyle, L., Childs, A., Coomber, R., & Barratt, M. (2019). #Drugsforsale: An exploration of the use of social media and encrypted messaging apps to supply and access drugs. *International Journal of Drug Policy, 63 (3),* 101–110.

Potter, G. (2009). Exploring retail level drug distribution: social supply, 'real' dealers and the user/dealer interface. In: T. Demetrovics, J. Fountain, & L. Kraus (Eds), *Old and new policies, theories, research methods and drug users across Europe* (pp. 51–74). Lengerich: Pabst Science Publishers.

Salinas, M. (2018). The unusual suspects: an educated, legitimately employed drug dealing network. *International Criminal Justice Review, 28 (3),* 226–242.

Søgaard, T.F., Kolind, T., Haller, M.B., & Hunt, G. (2019). Ring and bring drug services: delivery dealing and the social life of a drug phone. *International Journal of Drug Policy, 69,* 8–15.

Spicer, J. (2018). 'That's their brand, their business': how police officers are interpreting county lines. *Policing and Society.* doi:10.1080/10439463.2018.1445742

Tzanetakis, M., Kamphausen, G., Werse, B., & von Laufenberg, R. (2016). The transparency paradox. Building trust, resolving disputes and optimising logistics on conventional and online drugs markets. *International Journal of Drug Policy, 35 (2),* 58–68.

Vendius, T.T. (2015). Proactive undercover policing and sexual crimes against children on the Internet. *European Review of Organised Crime, 2 (2),* 6–24.

Yeo, V.C.S., Goh, S.-K., & Rezaei, S. (2017). Consumer experiences, attitude and behavioral intention toward online food delivery (OFD) services. *Journal of Retailing and Consumer Services, 35 (3),* 150–162.

9

From ancient organic to the newest synth: building trust in drug user communities

Ximene Rêgo, Jakub Greń & Olga S. Cruz

The transformation of drug use patterns and user profiles have been occurring in parallel to broader social and cultural changes. Recent innovations in the digital era, especially information technologies, together with a wider availability of illegal drugs, are catalysts for the diversification of drug phenomena. Drug trade markets have also undergone a shift from face-to-face purchases to virtual locations on the Internet. These interconnected aspects contribute to the increasing complexity of the present-day drug use landscape, and, as with every novelty, have created both challenges and opportunities. Taking into account the social, economic and cultural transformation in which globalisation processes have a distinctive accountability, this chapter focuses on the role of trust in shaping online and offline Portuguese drug user communities. Social connotations ascribed to different categories of substances – natural drugs versus synthetic drugs – and how these appear to be associated with preferences for online versus offline communities are highlighted. Finally, aspects of the role of trust have emerged as key elements to understand how these communities take shape, offering insights that could assist the design of harm reduction interventions.

Keywords: online drug user communities, social transformation, trust, harm reduction, drug markets, cryptomarkets

1   Introduction

The contemporary landscape of drug use is marked by a heterogeneity of drug use patterns, challenging the traditional dichotomy of small numbers of dependent injecting users on the one hand and large numbers of recreational users on the other. This gives rise to studies that focus on drug experiences that do not fit the problematic patterns that have been widely identified. These variations in use seem to be closely intermingled with an individual's worldview – including social meanings ascribed to drugs, motivations for drug use, and social contexts such as drug users' online and offline communities.

Alongside the innovations of the digital era, the emergence of new or novel psychoactive substances (NPS) and a rapidly evolving network of online drug-related forums and communities (Van Buskirk, Griffiths, Farrell & Degenhardt, 2017) underscore the increasing complexity of present-day drug phenomena. As with every novelty, this creates both challenges and opportunities.

Several aspects contribute to the understanding of demand for an ever-increasing variety of drugs as a facet of contemporary cultural and social change. As such, it has been argued that recreational drug use has become an unremarkable feature of life for some young people in their pursuit of leisure and pleasure, discussing those dynamics in the postmodern lifestyles of young individuals who experience life differently than their parents (Pennay & Measham, 2016). Individualism endows each person's trajectory with unlimited flexibility, encouraging a constant search for diversity and making eligibility a pillar of identity (Giddens, 1996). Postmodern consumerism points to a reality in which the individual is increasingly defined by what they choose to consume (Girona, 2003), including drugs.

Taking into account the social, economic and cultural transformations of postmodernity, this chapter focuses on the role of trust in shaping online and offline drug user communities. Trust can be briefly defined as the conviction that most people place in the constancy and predictability of their social environment (Giddens, 1996). While trust is associated with traditional societies, it retains relevance today, especially in contexts of interaction that are anonymous or ephemeral. When context is marked by uncertainty, there exists a need to trust more in others (Gambetta, 2000; Giddens, 2005). Risk and trust are connected, as trust serves to reduce the hazards associated with certain types of activity (Giddens, 2005). In this sense, buying and using illegal drugs is a terrain where trusting others is of particular importance.

Data presented here is from focus groups held with drug users in Portugal as part of the BAONPS (Be Aware on Night Pleasure and Safety) European project. This project seeks to provide governments in the participating countries (Portugal, Italy and Slovenia) with information about NPS use and to establish evidence-based harm reduction interventions (see Rolando, Beccaria, Dovzan, et al., 2017, for further details). The main goal of the focus groups was to highlight unresolved issues from other strands of the BAONPS research, in particular a lack of meaningful results related to understanding the use of web/digital tools by Portuguese drug users seeking to research illegal drugs.

Findings from the focus groups highlighted social connotations ascribed to different categories of illegal drugs (natural versus synthetic) and how these appear to be associated with preferences for different types of interaction (online versus offline). Aspects of the role of trust have emerged as crucial to understanding how online and offline drug user communities take shape, offering insights to assist the design of harm reduction interventions targeting online drug user communities.

2 Old and new trends in drug use

The progressive transformation of drug use patterns in Europe over the past two decades is well documented (e.g., EMCDDA, 2014). The dependent use of heroin that gave rise to social alarm has been replaced by a diversification of drug use patterns (EMCDDA, 2014), moving away from marginalised groups to younger, cosmopolitan users that propone the pleasure/leisure dyad. Heroin plays a less relevant role, whereas cannabis, cocaine and synthetic drugs acquire social meaning as use of them grows. Accordingly, since 2000, Portugal has seen a rising trend in the use of cannabis, synthetic substances and hallucinogens, illustrating diversified consumption patterns (Trigueiros & Carvalho, 2010).

Recent epidemiological data underpins this shift and indicates that trends in Europe appear to be 'particularly dynamic'. Drug availability is high or increasing and polydrug use is common. The use of NPS, although apparently limited, continues to pose challenges in terms of health risks (EMCDDA, 2018). In Portugal, NPS use is mainly focused on synthetic cannabinoids. Knowledge about these types of substances is lacking, while users' assessment of them tends to be negative, especially when compared with other illegal drugs generally considered to be less harmful (Calado et al., 2017).

Globalisation processes and developments in information technology play progressively central roles in users' access to old and new drugs (EMCDDA, 2014, 2018). While online drug distribution accounts for a relatively small part of the overall market, online drug trade is significant and growing. Online markets are particularly prevalent in Europe, which is an important destination for global drug suppliers (EMCDDA, 2018).

Portugal is not exceptional in Europe, although dependent heroin use, which gained visibility during the 1990s when it almost overshadowed other drug use. To an extent, drug use patterns in the country have been evolving in parallel to broader social transformations.

2.1 Drug use in Portugal

Contemporary drug use patterns have formed in the context of new practices of sociability among youth. They are almost always related to the disruptive power, more or less symbolic, ascribed to drugs. In Portugal, this type of expression of drug use was hardly seen until the mid-1990s (Fernandes, 2015). It started taking hold as the institutions of modernity – production, family, church – progressively weakened (Young, 1999), replaced by increasingly diversified mass consumption (Cruz, Seruya, Reis & Schmidt, 1984) and ludic lifestyles (Baptista, 2005). From 1974, the country re-opened itself to the international community, following the revolution that ousted 50 years of fascist dictatorship. Drug use at the time was mostly associated with cannabis.

Changes began taking place as early as the 1960s, gathering momentum from the mid-1970s. In the space of just 20 years, significant social transformations, including metropolisation, gender and generational relations, cultural plurality and increases in gross domestic product, national per capita income and wages (Barreto, 2000), occurred, defining a new relationship with mass consumption made possible by a steady rise in collective and individual well-being.

Concomitant to these changes, younger generations became more complex, reflecting the growing uncertainty of future pathways (Pais, 1990), although they benefited from greater access to culture, education and leisure than before. Consequently, lifestyles homogenised around certain patterns of consumption (Lopes, 1998), reformulating social life. Until then a practice of hidden groups, heroin use grew exponentially in the early 1990s, capturing the attention of the public agenda. This virtually hid other manifestations of the drug phenomenon, including the emergence of new drugs.

Contrary to what has been observed elsewhere – where the discussion on decriminalisation has been linked to the increasing prevalence of cannabis use – the political debate in Portugal has centred on concern about the psychosocial vulnerability of problematic drug users. Heroin use was the second highest in Europe in 2000 (EMCDDA, 2011).

The Portuguese paradigm shift occurred in 2000, when decriminalisation of drug use was adopted: acquisition, possession and use of any illegal substances for personal consumption were no longer charged as criminal offences, but as administrative ones (Quintas, 2011). The profile of those sanctioned for drug use misconduct significantly (and progressively) changed. Nowadays, the vast majority of those charged with an offence are 'non-addicted' users (70%) of cannabis (86%), while most users are young (92%) and employed (47%) or in education (83%) (SICAD, 2016).

While dependent heroin use and related risks were contained (SICAD, 2017), the following years saw a consolidation of harm reduction responses (Fernandes, 2009). Drug use patterns in Portugal, as in other European countries, have diversified, while compulsive behaviours have tended to be replaced by others that denote an informed choice (Carvalho, 2007; Cruz, 2015). The heterogeneity of drug use observed is consonant with Pennay and Measham's (2016) argument that recreational drug use has become commonplace among youngsters who are on a quest for leisure and pleasure.

2.2 Diversification of drug user profiles

Along with the social changes described and fuelled by technological advances and globalisation, a transformation of drug user profiles has been identified. Besides the focus on the normalisation of the use of certain illegal drugs (Parker, Williams & Aldridge, 2002) and on recreational use (e.g. Calado, 2006; Calafat, Gómez, Juan & Becoña, 2007; San Julián & Valenzuela, 2009; Aldridge, Measham & Williams, 2011; Caiata-Zufferey, 2012), research has addressed patterns of drug use that are defined as functional (Smith & Smith, 2005), non-dependent (Keene, 2001), healthy (Whiteacre & Pepinsky, 2002), socially-integrated (Pavarin, 2016) and non-problematic (e.g. Pallarés, 1996; Nicholson, Duncan, White & Watkins, 2012; Cruz, 2015). Portuguese legislation acknowledges this diversity by differentiating between 'addicted' and 'non-addicted' users when determining the appropriate offence with which to make charges.

Moreover, contemporary drug user profiles are affected by innovations in communication technologies and online drug markets (cryptomarkets). Such individuals include those who not only acquire substances online and use online networks to learn about new drugs, but also to experiment and then disseminate their knowledge and experiences to others (Boyer, Lapen, Macalino & Hibberd, 2007). This pattern appears to be particularly prevalent among users of NPS, which constitute a broad range of unexamined and complex substances (Corazza, Schifano, Simonato et al., 2012; Musselman & Hampton, 2014; Potter & Chatwin, 2018).

This profile contrasts with earlier types of drug use that were driven by ideas of mind-expansion and inner-exploration and associated with classic psychedelics (e.g. Willis, 2002), as well as with the more recent types that can be framed as pleasure-seeking, associated mainly with euphoric stimulants like MDMA (Szmigin, Griffin, Mistral, et al., 2008; Nissen, 2012). According to Duxbury (2018), as opposed to those drug use perspectives that are focused on individualistic benefit from hedonistic or 'mind extension', the new perspective employed within online drug communities gives drug use (or rather 'drug experimentation') an ethical valorisation due to its emphasis on social duty and the moral implications of knowledge production and exchange.

2.3 Online user communities and harm reduction

In the last decade, an increasing number of drug transactions have shifted from face-to-face purchases to dedicated virtual platforms known as cryptomarkets (Sui et al., 2015; Aldridge & Decary-Hétu, 2016). These employ advanced encryption to protect the anonymity of users, which makes it possible to acquire illegal substances without direct customer-dealer contact, revolutionising drug markets (Bartlett, 2014; Martin, 2014). Research suggests that online drug distribution, while competitive regarding prices and quality, presents substantially fewer threats and less violence than traditional face-to-face transactions (Martin, 2014; Barratt, Ferris & Winstock, 2016). While ease of access to a wider range of drugs and the increasing diffusion of NPS associated with online markets and forums might be seen as failures of current drug prohibition (Ormsby, 2012; Aldridge & Decary-Hétu, 2016), they represent an opportunity for harm reduction initiatives.

In fact, drug-related online forums have already been recognised as potential vehicles for health interventions (Boyer, Shannon & Hibberd, 2005; Caudevilla, 2016; Champion, Newton & Teeson, 2016; Vale Pires, Caudevilla & Valente, 2016). Discussions on such forums are characterised by a social process in which users support each other, while also exchanging knowledge about specific drugs and management of the related risks (e.g. Chiauzzi, DesMahapatra, Lobo & Barratt, 2013; Soussan & Kjellgren, 2014; Van Hout & Hearne, 2015; Hearne & Van Hout, 2016).

3   Methodology

The Portuguese focus groups taking part in the BAONPS project used the volunteers' network CHECK!N (harm reduction outreach team for party-settings) for initial recruitment of focus group participants. Four focus groups were held, involving 34 participants, whose profile is described in section 4.1. Focus group membership was expanded through snowball sampling (chain referral sampling), which means recruitment occurred 'through referrals […] among people who share or know others who possess some characteristics that are of research interest' (Biernacki & Waldorf, 1981, p. 141). Procedures included asking initial recruits to suggest other individuals that met the inclusion criteria of drug use, Internet use and not using only cannabis. This allowed access to populations that are typically hard for researchers to reach. Focus group discussions were recorded and transcribed in order to undertake qualitative analysis, which led to the establishment of the themes presented below.

4   Results

4.1 Participants

The 34 focus group (hereafter FG) participants (FG1: 9; FG2: 8; FG3: 10; FG4: 7) consisted of 28 men and six women, and were aged between 22 and 46 years old (average age: 31.5). Formal education levels were generally high and heterogeneous: 21 of the participants held a university degree and 13 had had between nine and 12 years of formal education. Twenty-nine participants were employed, two unemployed and three were full-time students. None of the participants mentioned ever being subject to any therapy or counselling service, nor being involved in any legal proceedings related to drugs.

The vast majority of participants showed high levels of drug and NPS literacy and a wide range of drug use patterns were observed. The drugs used were diverse, including cannabis, synthetic cannabinoids, MXC, psilocybin, DMT, LSD, MDMA/ecstasy, speed, GHB, DOB, 2CB, NBOMe, 2C-T-7, MDPV, cocaine, crack cocaine, heroin, salvia, methylone, ketamine, mephedrone, amphetamines, oxytocin, and kratom.

Different drug user profiles were observed, based on drug categories rather than single substances or NPS. As described in the following section, they were inseparable from the different values attributed to natural and synthetic drugs, and related to preferences for online versus offline communities.

4.2 Practices within online drug users' communities

The use of online communities to access information, find out about harm reduction strategies, and to share drug users' experiences was considerable. Two thirds of the participants indicated that they prefer web-mediated exchanges while one third prioritised face-to-face exchanges. Other, less common, ways of gathering information were scientific papers, books, documentaries, Check!n flyers and Facebook posts.

The majority of participants frequented online communities to learn about the differing quality, danger and risks associated with different substances, in addition to the dosage, effects and health impacts, interactions between substances, personal experiences and, less frequently, prices. Participation did not necessarily mirror drug preference, but easy access to information in online communities, and the opportunity to relate to others with similar experiences and interests were valued.

Nevertheless, most respondents used both online and offline communities to access information and experiences despite some of them emphasising that online forums are used only for the reading of information and not for participation. Websites and forums were accessed depending on the goal of the participant: 'Bluelight is more liberal and the people there are more sophisticated (…) Reddit has all types of people (…) Erowid has everything' (Participant 4, FG 2).

Those who produced drugs at home principally searched for cannabis and mushroom production issues, while those more interested in NPS describe the web as the only means to access NPS information. In short, online communities seem to gain more value for users when the level of technical sophistication of the necessary procedures for home production, or of the drugs themselves (for instance, when a drug's pharmacological properties are new and pose spontaneous harm reduction challenges), is greater.

4.3 Natural versus synthetic drugs

Counterintuitively, age and level of formal education did not point to any definitive preference pattern regarding online versus offline means of accessing information and sharing drug experiences. These tendencies seem to be more closely related to the social meanings and beliefs ascribed to drugs, which frequently varied also across different categories of substances. A key difference identified by participants was the type of drug and its association with spirituality, while similar points were made about drugs and online communities. As one participant stated, noting a hierarchy between categories that related to how participants classified substances:

'There are many sites and forums. Long time ago, the difference was between legal and illegal. Nowadays, the difference is between natural drugs and chemical drugs.' (Participant 6, FG 1)

Those who used cannabis and its derivatives as their substances of choice, while occasionally using others (such as mushrooms), tended to favour offline communication. Furthermore, it was often noted that drugs were used not only for recreational purposes, but also medicinal and spiritual reasons. These participants were also often those who produced cannabis and mushrooms themselves. For that reason, being identified by the police and, as a result, being subject to house searches, represented a bigger threat. Offline communications were considered safer. Online drug supply took place only, as one participant stated, 'when the house is 'clean' [drug-free] (...) and the method is always the dark web with bitcoins.' (Participant 7, FG 2).

The participants who chose natural substances as their drugs of choice tended to prefer offline interaction and show more signs of distrust of online research tools. The belief the authorities monitor social media and the resulting fear of being identified were reasons for this choice. Distrust in the Internet was typically accompanied by distrust of the state and societal mechanisms such as capitalism, financial sectors, corporations, and means of production, as well as democratic institutions and police forces. Skeptical attitudes regarding the Internet as a means to communicate were bound together with views and social meanings ascribed to lifestyles and world transformation. Memories were evoked of a world where the Internet and phones were absent and commitment to others used to prevail. This was not exclusively an issue for older participants: some younger participants shared identical views. Thus, the widespread mistrust in the system appears to be associated with a certain nostalgia for traditional societies, where trust among individuals and between individuals and institutions predominates.

The dichotomy between natural drugs and synthetic drugs paved the way to further differentiation among the participants. A recurrent element was that chemical or synthetic drugs are more harmful than natural ones. The belief that natural substances (e.g., cannabis, mushrooms, salvia, ayahuasca) are 'better' was supported by various explanations, including objective aspects and personal beliefs. Among the latter was that plants and herbs are sacred substances, able to give knowledge and precious gifts to those who respect them.

Participants identified that illegal drugs were used not only for recreational purposes but for therapeutic and spiritual purposes too. These participants also tended to advocate the need to be closer to nature, to use 'natural' products – including organic food and organic clothing – and to place drug use in a historical perspective and as a meaningful ritual. This ideological vision of drug use was frequently challenged by 'pragmatic' views, typically displayed by those users that favoured web-mediated interactions. These users – most of whom mentioned synthetic drugs as their preferred choice – did not seem to recognise the boundaries between drugs set by those who justified the virtues of what is natural. Instead, they valued the pharmacological properties of substances (natural or synthetic), as well as their effects. Moreover, online communities were valued for their global aspects and the opportunities they presented for people with shared values to connect with each other. Proximity and experience exchange were emphasised and valued in identical terms to the ones used regarding offline communities, since they presented an opportunity to talk with people who are at least apparently similar to one another.

It is important to note here that participants involved in research discussions tended to show high levels of literacy about both natural and synthetic drugs. The meanings ascribed to drugs and drug use gave rise, in all focus groups, to controversy, as can be seen in the following excerpt of an exchange between focus group 2's participants (P):

'P2: I might prefer GHB. It is among the best I have experienced.
P6: So, more chemical...
P2: Chemical? Yes...
P3: Well, it is synthetic; but all are chemical; the natural ones are still chemical!
P6: But there are the ones that grow in nature, and the ones that are made in a toilet, in a lab!
P2: To be honest, for me, that is irrelevant... natural or chemical.
P6: People who are earthbound understand better.
P7: Well ... but each person has their own path; we have to respect that.'

This hierarchy of synthetic drugs and natural drugs compelled participants to draw boundaries between their practices for using substances. While participants shared motivations for drug use, be it driven by recreational, self-development or spiritual ends – with the exception of uses driven by medical purposes, which was an exclusive feature of those who favour natural drugs – the motivation for drug use for purely recreational purposes was less apparent than others. As such, natural drugs (especially ayahuasca and mushrooms) were perceived as near-sacred and associated with spiritual growth. A similar hierarchy was outlined when psychedelics were compared to, for instance, stimulants. Since NPS users were a minority in all of the focus groups – and no group was exclusively NPS users – it appears that these drugs were often used as a substitute for traditional drugs and not highly regarded by participants, as reported by previous studies in Portugal (Calado, Lavado & Dias, 2017).

4.4 Drug supply preferences

Various channels were used by participants to assure drugs supply. Well-known dealers and cryptomarkets were preferred, although not to the same extent. The concerns and distrust expressed about searching for information via the Internet, especially in forums, deepened when it came to engaging in online drug markets and only some dared to buy drugs online. Uncertainty regarding the predictability of quality, quantity, delivery or the overall process prevailed, prevented others progressing from going online to find information to the online purchase of substances Despite anonymity and the employment of ranking systems and customer reviews, there was considerable distrust among by participants, especially among those who preferred the virtues of natural drugs and who favoured offline interactions. Some participants assumed a pragmatic stance again, finding parallels with other online markets. Although individuals who used cannabis and mushrooms as their drugs of choice did not buy them online, they did purchase production-related paraphernalia via the Internet. While this stance was bound by the social meanings and beliefs identified earlier, it was apparent that participants' distrust of exchanging information about drugs can grow and deepen if online supply is in play. As one of the participants stated, it depends on the drug: 'Nobody buys hashish or weed online!' (Participant 6, FG 1).

Concerns were raised by many participants – both users of natural and synthetic drugs – around issues of security and quality, as well as technical difficulties and the use of bitcoins:

> *'I fear to buy online because, first, it is expensive and, second, I do not know about its level of quality. They say quality is above average, but I don't know. The fact that is expensive is not a problem if I could be sure about the good quality. I have been on Silk Road, but I have feared to order.'* (Participant 5, FG 1)

The different values and practices regarding trust in online drug supply appear again to relate to drugs of choice – natural versus synthetic – and, ultimately, to drug users' preferred settings for interaction – online versus offline drug communities. Those who bought their drugs online did not especially value natural substances thus demonstrating greater pragmatism towards online supply. Participants knew that a diversity of means to ensure security, not much different from other sites or forums – 'procedures are very simple. There are marketplaces in the same way you have eBay' – and to guarantee quality by the use of user reviews. Furthermore, the use of Energy Control (a Spanish harm reduction project) drug-testing services is mentioned as a means of checking quality. Meanwhile, the option for online supply was also related to drug of choice, although not exclusively based on substance category:

> *'Synthetic drugs or research chemicals, the ones that have now appeared, I believe that the web is more reliable. I trust it more. It is difficult to find a friend that really knows how to do it.'* (Participant 4, FG 2)

On the other hand, offline communities were valued and preferred by some participants as an intrinsic asset. In these situations, the user-dealer dyad has sometimes been built up over the years, bringing confidence to the process:

> *'I usually buy the MDMA from one person and the cocaine from another person. I trust them very much. I trust them so much that in two different occasions I returned the product because I was not satisfied (…). Those people from whom I buy are just normal people, they are married, they have children; and they work. We became friends.'* (Participant 5, FG 1)

The majority of participants seem to remain highly attached to traditional offline markets (mainly for cannabis, cocaine, MDMA and amphetamines), while online markets seem especially, but not exclusively, appealing to psychonauts or users interested in specific experiences. Trust, clearly and repeatedly expressed as a basic need for both offline and online communities, posed additional challenges for harm reduction. As one participant effectively summarised it:

> *'The first time you buy; you must trust; it doesn't matter if it is a guy that has sold you [the drugs] or the site you have chosen [for doing so].'* (Participant 4, FG 2).

5   Discussion

The exploratory research presented here illustrates the diversification of drug use patterns and drug user profiles. While patterns demonstrate mostly polydrug use, the profiles of drug users appear to share traits with those described in other studies as non-problematic or socially integrated. This assertion rests on the fact that the participants of this study were neither supported by health services nor involved in legal proceedings related to drug offences, which is arguably a limited criterion. Moreover, the use of NPS, in line with previous research, is limited, except in the case of users who have psychonaut profiles.

Differing motivations for drug use and the range of social meanings ascribed to drug experiences point to a heterogeneity of worldviews among users. In turn, these highlight how drugs (or categories of drugs, i.e. natural versus synthetic) of choice reflect the identities that users construct for themselves. Beyond the symbolic power associated with drugs, the choice of a category and the establishment of certain consumption practices, whether oriented to recreational purposes, self-development, or spiritual ends, contribute to how individuals present themselves within the user community. Drug use experiences are situated in the interplay between the individual, the substance and context. As such, it is the individual's reflection on their relationship with the drug(s) used.

Although in recent years studies have focused on differences between NPS and traditional drug use (Potter & Chatwin, 2018), our study suggests that distinction between drug categories according to substance effect (stimulants, empathogens, depressants, psychedelics, etc.) rather than type (old versus new) is more relevant (see also Rolando et al., 2017).

The habit of using online communities to access information on illegal drugs, including harm reduction strategies, is widespread among users. There is agreement in most studies that the Internet plays a crucial role in how information and experiences are exchanged among a substantial share of the drug-using population (Hearne & Van Hout, 2016; Van Hout & Bringham, 2014). The use of online tools tends to increase when complex information is sought and when certain drug experiences are scarce within offline communities.

Trust is expressed repeatedly as a necessity within both offline communities and online communities. However, it is in online settings that distrust prevents participation (for instance, in forums) or in online business transactions and where more efforts are made to reduce uncertainty. Previous studies (Cruz, 2015) have already revealed how precautionary measures regarding drug supply often lead to a preference for acquiring drugs through face-to-face networks to ensure the quality of a purchased substance.

Final remarks are focused on harm reduction and how these results might assist the design of online interventions, since using a platform constitutes a powerful resource for raising awareness about the possible risks arising from drug use.

Current results reinforce the belief that online communities engage drug users in spontaneous harm reduction strategies (Rolando et al., 2017). Several suggestions provided by online community members demonstrate harm reduction practices (e.g., not mixing different substances, the availability of drug checking services, using in a safe setting and trusted company, careful dosing, the importance of proper eating, drinking water, and taking breaks from drug use. This indicates that many users are well-informed and that online forums are important platforms for awareness-raising among peers, in line with previous studies (e.g. Van Hout & Hearne, 2015; Caudevilla, 2016; Champion et al., 2016).

This engagement of drug users in spontaneous harm reduction strategies also happens in offline communities (e.g. Cruz, 2015). For example, risk awareness has been pointed out as playing a key role in risk reduction insofar as it significantly shapes drug users' choices. Various authors stress that these perceptions are developed mostly within such communities. Interaction of users within offline communities is important not only because it facilitates access to substances (Hunt, Evans, Moloney & Bailey, 2009; Draus, Roddy & Greenwald, 2010), but also because it promotes learning opportunities from people that are trusted (Carvalho, 2007; Velho, 2008; Kubicek, McDavitt, Carpineto, Weiss, Iverson & Kipke, 2007; San Julián & Valenzuela, 2009; Hunt et al., 2009).

The trustworthiness that pervades the online environment reported by some (Van Hout & Bingham, 2014; Tzanetakis, Kamphausen, Werse & von Laufenberg, 2016) is not, however, fully supported by our findings. On the contrary, with some exceptions, cryptomarkets seem to offer little trust to potential clients, as they are mainly focused on commercial ends. Nonetheless, negative experiences within cryptomarkets were not reported by participants in any of the focus groups.

That differences between drug categories (hallucinogens, stimulants, dissociative substances etc.) seemed more meaningful than the distinction between traditional drugs and NPS suggests that preventive and/or harm reduction interventions could benefit from adjusting to the different types of drugs, rather than focusing on traditional drugs versus NPS.

Monitoring of online communities may help professionals identify drug use trends and patterns (Hearne & Van Hout, 2016; Enghoff & Aldridge, 2019), while interventions could target communities by providing credible information, resources and tools. Moreover, our findings support the notion that online communities allow for harm reduction approaches that are similar to those used in offline settings, but with a much broader range (especially when targeting international sites and forums). More Internet-based alcohol and drugs prevention programming (Champion et al., 2016), running threads with drug information and harm reduction counselling services in forums related to cryptomarkets (Caudevilla, 2016), and 'feeding' drug forum discussions with harm reduction guidelines (Vale Pires et al., 2016), are some examples of interventions that could be further developed based on our findings.

Due to the early stage of such initiatives, as well as the relative infancy of online marketplaces and communities, harm reduction attempts via the Internet continue to require further evaluation and systematic empirical investigation (Aldridge & Décary-Hétu, 2016), particularly on how to bridge confidence in such settings. There is consensus that familiarity and routines endow communities with trust (Gambetta, 2000; Luhmann, 2000; Giddens, 2005), which, considering current trends, means considerable potential for harm reduction in online settings.

References

Aldridge, J., & Decary-Hétu, D. (2016). Cryptomarkets and the future of illicit drug markets. In: European Monitoring Centre for Drugs and Drug Addiction (Ed.), *The internet and drug markets: EMCCDA Insights 21* (pp. 23–30). Luxembourg: Publications Office of the European Union.

Aldridge, J., Measham, F., & Williams, L. (2011). *Illegal leisure revisited: changing patterns of alcohol and drug use in adolescents and young adults.* New York: Routledge.

Baptista, L. (2005). Territórios Lúdicos (e o que torna lúdico um território): ensaiando um ponto de partida [Ludic territories (and what makes a territory ludic): rehearsing a starting point]. *Fórum Sociológico, 13/14 (1)*, 47–58.

Barratt, M., Ferris, J., & Winstock, A. (2016). Safer scoring? Cryptomarkets, social supply and drug market violence. *International Journal of Drug Policy, 35 (1)*, 24–31.

Barreto, A. (2000). *A situação social em Portugal 1960–1999 – Indicadores sociais em Portugal e na União Europeia* [The social situation in Portugal 1960–1999 – social indicators in Portugal and in the European Union] (vol. II). Lisbon: Imprensa de Ciências Sociais.

Bartlett, J. (2014). *Dark net markets: the eBay of drug dealing.* Retrieved from https://www.theguardian.com/society/2014/oct/05/dark-net-markets-drugs-dealing-ebay on 14/4/2019

Biernacki, P., & Waldorf, D. (1981). Snowball sampling: problems and techniques of chain referral sampling. *Sociological Methods and Research, 10 (2)*, 141–163.

Boyer, E., Lapen, P., Macalino, G., & Hibberd, P. (2007). Dissemination of psychoactive substance information by innovative drug users. *CyberPsychology & Behavior, 10 (1)*, 1–6.

Boyer, E., Shannon, M., & Hibberd, P. (2005). The Internet and psychoactive substance use among innovative drug users. *Pediatrics, 115 (2)*, 302–305.

Caiata-Zufferey, M. (2012). From danger to risk: categorising and valuing recreational heroin and cocaine use. *Health, Risk & Society, 14 (5)*, 427–443.

Calado, V. (2006). *Drogas sintéticas. Mundos culturais, Música trance e ciberespaço* [Synthetic drugs: cultural worlds, trance music and cyberspace]. Lisboa: Núcleo de Investigação/ODT/IDT.

Calado, V., Lavado, E., & Dias, L. (2017). *Novas Substâncias Psicoativas e outras drogas. Inquérito ao público do festival NOS Alive – 2017* [New Psychoactive Substances and other drugs. NOS Alive festival public inquiry – 2017]. Lisboa: SICAD.

Calafat, A., Gómez, C., Juan, M., & Becoña, E. (2007). Weekend nightlife recreational habits: prominent intrapersonal 'risk factors' for drug use? *Substance Use & Misuse, 42 (9)*, 1443–1454.

Carvalho, M. (2007). *Culturas juvenis e novos usos de drogas em meio festivo. O trance psicadélico como analisador* [Juvenile cultures and new uses of drugs in festive surroundings. The psychedelic trance as an analyzer]. Porto: Campo das Letras.

Caudevilla, F. (2016). The emergence of deep web marketplaces: a health perspective. In: EMCDDA (Ed.), *The internet and drug markets: EMCDDA Insights 21* (pp. 69-75). Luxembourg: Publications Office of the European Union.

Champion, K., Newton, N., & Teesson, M. (2016). Prevention of alcohol and other drug use and related harm in the digital age: what does the evidence tell us? *Current Opinion in Psychiatry, 29 (4),* 242–249.

Chiauzzi, E., DasMahapatra, P., Lobo, K., & Barratt, M. (2013). Participatory research with an online drug forum: a survey of user characteristics, information sharing, and harm reduction views. *Substance Use & Misuse, 48 (8),* 661–670.

Corazza, O., Schifano, F., Simonato, P., Fergus, S., Assi, S., Stair, J., & Blaszko, U. (2012). Phenomenon of new drugs on the Internet: the case of ketamine derivative methoxetamine. *Human Psychopharmacology: Clinical and Experimental, 27 (2),* 145–149.

Cruz, M., Seruya, J., Reis, L., & Schmidt, L. (1984). A condição social da juventude portuguesa [The social condition of Portuguese youth]. *Análise Social, XX,* 285–308.

Cruz, O. (2015). Nonproblematic illegal drug use: drug use management strategies in a Portuguese sample. *Journal of Drug Issues, 45 (2),* 133–150.

Draus, P., Roddy, J., & Greenwald, M. (2010). 'I always kept a job': income generation, heroin use and economic uncertainty in 21st century Detroit. *Journal of Drug Issues, 40 (4),* 841–869.

Duxbury, S. (2018). Information creation on online drug forums: how drug use becomes moral on the margins of science. *Current Sociology, 66 (3),* 431–448.

EMCDDA: European Monitoring Centre for Drugs and Drug Addiction (2011). *Drug policy profiles – Portugal.* Luxembourg: Publications Office of the European Union.

EMCDDA: European Monitoring Centre for Drugs and Drug Addiction (2014). *European drug report 2014: trends and developments.* Luxembourg: Publications Office of the European Union.

EMCDDA: European Monitoring Centre for Drugs and Drug Addiction (2018). *European drug report 2018: trends and developments.* Luxembourg: Publications Office of the European Union.

Enghoff, O., & Aldridge, J. (2019). The value of unsolicited online data in drug policy research. *International Journal of Drug Policy.* doi:10.1016/j.drugpo.

Fernandes, L. (2009). O que a droga fez à norma [What the drugs did to the norm]. *Toxicodependências, 15 (1),* 3–18.

Fernandes, L. (2015). Do fenómeno droga e da perturbação da estabilidade normativa [The drug phenomenon and the disruption of normative stability]. In: M. Cunha (Ed.), *Do crime e do castigo: Temas e debates contemporâneos* [Crime and punishment: contemporary issues and debate] (pp. 45–62). Lisbon: Mundos Sociais.

Gambetta, D. (2000). Can we trust trust? In: D. Gambetta (Ed.), *Trust: making and breaking cooperative relations* (pp. 213–237). Oxford: University of Oxford.

Giddens, A. (1996). *Modernity and self-identity. Self and society in the late modern age.* Cambridge: Polity Press.

Giddens, A. (2005). *As consequências da modernidade* [The consequences of modernity]. Oeiras: Celta.

Girona, J. (2003). Vida (re)decoradas, metáforas biográficas: de la memoria industrial a la (dês)memoria postmoderna [Life (re)decorated, biographical metaphors: from industrial memory to postmodern memory]. *Revista d'Etnologia de Catalunya, 23 (1),* 24–35.

Hearne, E., & Van Hout, M. (2016). 'Trip-sitting' in the black hole: an ethnographic study of dissociation and indigenous harm reduction. *Journal of Psychoactive Drugs, 48 (4),* 233–242.

Hunt, G., Evans, K., Moloney, M., & Bailey, N. (2009). Combining different substances in the dance scene: enhancing pleasure, managing risk and timing effects. *Journal of Drug Issues, 39 (3),* 495–522.

Keene, J. (2001). An international social work perspective on drug misuse problems and solutions: reviewing implications for practice. *Journal of Social Work, 1 (2),* 187–199.

Kubicek, K., McDavitt, B., Carpineto, J., Weiss, G., Iverson, E., & Kipke, M. (2007). Making informed decisions: How attitudes and perceptions affect the use of crystal, cocaine, and ecstasy among young men who have sex with men. *Journal of Drug Issues, 37 (3),* 643–672.

Lopes, J. (1998). Sociabilidade e consumos culturais: contributos para uma sociologia da fruição cultural [Sociability and cultural consumption: contributions to a sociology of cultural fruition]. *Sociologia, 8 (3),* 179–188.

Luhmann, N. (2000). Familiarity, confidence, trust: problems and alternatives. In D. Gambetta (Ed.), Trust: making and breaking cooperative relations (pp. 94–107). Oxford: University of Oxford.

Martin, J. (2014). Lost on the Silk Road: online drug distribution and the 'cryptomarket'. *Criminology & Criminal Justice, 14 (3),* 351–367.

Musselman, M., & Hampton, J. (2014). 'Not for human consumption': a review of emerging designer drugs. *Pharmacotherapy: The Journal of Human Pharmacology and Drug Therapy, 34 (7),* 745–757.

Nicholson, T., Duncan, D., White, J., & Watkins, C. (2012). Focusing on abuse, not use: a proposed new direction for US drug policy. *Drugs: Education, Prevention and Policy, 19 (4),* 303–308.

Nissen, M. (2012). Writing drug cultures. *Culture & Psychology, 18 (2),* 198–218.

Ormsby, E. (2012). *The drug's in the mail. The age.* http://www.theage.com.au/victoria/the-drugs-in-the-mail-20120426-1xnth.html on 12/4/2019.

Pais, J. (1990). A construção sociológica da juventude – alguns contributos [The sociological construction of youth – some contributions]. *Análise Social, XXV,* 139–165.

Pallarés, J. (1996). *El placer del scorpion. Antropología de la heroína y los yonquis (1970–1990)* [Scorpion's pleasure. Heroin and junkies anthropology (1970–1990)]. Lleida: Milenio.

Parker, H., Williams, L., & Aldridge, J. (2002). The normalisation of 'sensible' recreational drug use: further evidence from the North West England longitudinal study. *Sociology, 36 (4),* 941–964.

Pennay, A., & Measham, F. (2016). The normalisation thesis – 20 years later. *Drugs: Education, Prevention and Policy, 23 (3),* 187–189.

Pavarin, R. (2016). First consumers, then socially integrated: results of a study on 100 Italian drug users who had never turned to public or private addiction services. *Substance Use & Misuse, 51 (7),* 892–901.

Potter, G., & Chatwin, C. (2018). Not particularly special: critiquing 'NPS' as a category of drugs. *Drugs: Education, Prevention and Policy, 25 (4),* 329–336.

Quintas, J. (2011). *Regulação legal dos consumos de drogas* [Legal regulation of drug consumption]. Porto: Fronteiras do Caos.

Rolando, S., Beccaria, F., Dovzan, S., Rêgo, X., Pereira, J., Vale Pires, C., & Moura, H. (2017). *Workstream 2 – Web Research Cross-National final report. B.A.O.N.P.S. – Be Aware On Night Pleasure Safety Project.* Italy: Cooperativa Alice Onlus.

San Julián, E., & Valenzuela, E. (2009). El riesgo de las drogas: la percepción de los jóvenes [Drugs risk: perceptions of youth]. *Toxicodependências, 15 (1)*, 43–57.

SICAD (2016). *A situação do país em matéria de drogas e toxicodependências – relatório anual 2016* [The State of the country on drugs and drug addiction – annual report 2016]. Lisboa: SICAD.

SICAD (2017). *A situação do país em matéria de drogas e toxicodependências – relatório anual 2018* [The state of the country on drugs and drug addiction – Annual Report 2018]. Lisboa: SICAD.

Smith, M., & Smith, P. (2005). The problem of drug prohibition for drug users: a Mertonian analysis of everyday experience. *Electronic Journal of Sociology, 7.* http://www.sociology. org/content/2005/tier1/smith.html.

Soussan, C., & Kjellgren, A. (2014). Harm reduction and knowledge exchange – a qualitative analysis of drug-related internet discussion forums. *Harm Reduction Journal, 11 (1)*, 25–34.

Sui, D., Caverlee, J., & Rudesill, D. (2015). *The deep web and the darknet: a look inside the internet's massive black box.* Washington: Woodrow Wilson International Center for Scholars.

Szmigin, I., Griffin, C., Mistral, W., Bengry-Howell, A., Weale, L., & Hackley, C. (2008). Re-framing 'binge drinking' as calculated hedonism: empirical evidence from the UK. *International Journal of Drug Policy, 19 (5)*, 359–366.

Trigueiros, L., & Carvalho, M. (2010). Novos usos de drogas: um estudo qualitativo a partir das trajectórias de vida [New drug use: a qualitative study based on life trajectories]. *Toxicodependências, 16 (3)*, 29–44.

Tzanetakis, M., Kamphausen, G., Werse, B., & von Laufenberg, R. (2016). The transparency paradox. Building trust, resolving disputes and optimising logistics on conventional and online drugs markets. *International Journal of Drug Policy, 35 (1)*, 58–68.

Van Buskirk, J., Griffiths, P., Farrell, M., & Degenhardt, L. (2017). Trends in new psychoactive substances from surface and 'dark' net monitoring. *The Lancet Psychiatry, 4 (1)*, 16–18.

Van Hout, M., & Bingham, T. (2014). Responsible vendors, intelligent consumers: Silk Road, the online revolution in drug trading. *International Journal of Drug Policy, 25 (2)*, 183–189.

Van Hout, M., & Hearne, E. (2015). 'Word of mouse': indigenous harm reduction and on-line consumerism of the synthetic compound methoxphenidine. *Journal of Psychoactive Drugs, 47 (1)*, 30–41.

Vale Pires, C., Caudevilla, F., & Valente, H. (2016). Netreach work: implementing web-based harm reduction interventions with online drug users. *Adiktologie, 2 (16)*, 182–187.

Velho, G. (2008). *Nobres e anjos: Um estudo de tóxicos e hierarquia* [Nobles and angels: A study of toxics and hierarchy] (2nd ed.). Rio de Janeiro: Fundação Getulio Vargas.

Willis, P. (2002). The cultural meaning of drug use. In: S. Hall & T. Jefferson (Eds.), *Resistance through rituals: youth subcultures in post-war Britain* (pp. 106–118). London: Routledge.

Young, J. (1999). *The exclusive society. Social exclusion, crime and difference in late modernity.* London: Sage.

Whiteacre, K., & Pepinsky, H. (2002). Controlling drug use. *Criminal Justice Policy Review, 13 (1)*, 21–31.

10
Medicinal cannabis use: a fuzzy concept?

Frédérique Bawin

The concepts 'medicinal' and 'recreational' cannabis use are commonly used in public discourse and in research. However, multiple studies show that the lines between recreational and medicinal cannabis use are not clear-cut. This chapter aims to unravel the meaning of the concept of medicinal cannabis use by contrasting it to the concept of recreational cannabis use. We draw upon findings from a mixed-methods study that explores the blurred boundaries between recreational and medicinal cannabis use, by studying the narratives of adult self-identified medicinal cannabis users living in Belgium. The analyses are based on data derived from qualitative in-depth interviews (N = 62). Our results show that patterns, experienced effects and purposes of medicinal and recreational use differ on certain aspects but, more often they show a significant overlap. Participants' narratives demonstrate the complexity in which they interpret and contrast the two categories of use. Interestingly, this chapter provides new insights into the existing knowledge on medicinal cannabis use and valuable insights for future policy-making in cannabis regulations. Given the fact that national regulations are still shifting, it is important that the blurred boundaries between medicinal and recreational use are acknowledged when implementing an international framework.

Keywords: medicinal cannabis use, recreational cannabis use, user perspective, qualitative research, interviews

1   Introduction

The concepts 'medicinal' and 'recreational' cannabis use are commonly and unquestioningly used in public discourse and research. However, multiple authors argue that the lines between recreational and medicinal cannabis use are not clear-cut (Bostwick, 2012; Pedersen & Sandberg, 2013; Athey, Boyd & Cohen, 2017) and concepts have been developed to fill in the grey area between the two, such as therapeutic, semi-medicinal and quasi-medical use (Bakalar &

Grinspoon, 1997; Bardhi, Sifaneck, Johnson & Dunlap, 2007; Fischer, Murphy, Kurdyak, Goldner & Rehm, 2015).

Despite findings from previous studies, research exploring the meaning of the concepts recreational and medicinal cannabis use remains scarce. Through a critical lens and based on empirical data, this chapter aims to unravel the meaning of the two concepts by contrasting 'medicinal cannabis use' to 'recreational cannabis use'. Firstly, the way cannabis is consumed as a medicine and as a recreational drug is examined, and secondly the meanings that self-identified medicinal cannabis users ascribe to recreational and medicinal cannabis use are explored.

Multiple studies suggest that a large number of medicinal cannabis users have experience with recreational use (Swift, Gates, Dillon, 2005; Reinarman, Nunberg, Lnthier & Heddleston, 2011; Lucas, 2012). In addition, studies illustrate that there is an overlap between medicinal and recreational users' characteristics (Roy-Byrne, Maynard, Bumgardner, et al., 2015; Lin, Ilgen, Jannausch & Bohnert, 2016). Based on self-reports on motives for use of Canadian self-identified medicinal cannabis users, Athey et al. concluded that 'medicinal motivations for use are wide-ranging and encompass what are traditionally thought of as recreational motivations as well' (2017, p. 218). In qualitative interviews conducted by Pedersen and Sandberg, recreational and medical users in Norway did not distinguish clearly between their recreational and medical patterns of use (Pedersen & Sandberg, 2013). Finally, in the study of Dahl & Frank (2011) Danish cannabis growers described medicinal use as a sliding scale that includes recreational use. On the other hand, previous research has also documented differences between recreational and medicinal cannabis use(rs), with regards to use patterns and self-reported health (Bottorff, Johnson, Moffat & Mulvogue, 2009; Roy-Byrne et al., 2015; Lin et al., 2016; Pacula, Jacobson & Maksabedian, 2016; Hakkarainen, Decorte, Sznitman, et al., 2019).

What currently appears to constitute an important distinction between recreational and drug medical use is the social construction of the 'high' as a desired effect when using recreationally and as an adverse event when using medicinally. While pleasure is considered a typical experience of recreational drug use, it is absent in discourses on medical treatments. (Chapkis, 2007). By referring to the case of the psychoactive medicine Rital (methylphenidate), Keane (2008, p. 401) observes that there are

> *'tensions within medical and drug science about the therapeutic use of psychoactive drugs. Pleasure is central to this anxiety, as medically authorised use of drugs must not be contaminated by the uncontrolled bodily pleasures of illicit drug use.'*

Medicinal cannabis users have identified the high and the associated euphoric feelings as side-effects (Ogborne, Smart, Weber & Birchmore-Timney, 2000;

Clark, Ware, Yazer, Murray & Lynch 2004; Pedersen & Sandberg, 2013). In the study of Coomber, Oliver and Morris (2003), medicinal users claimed that they do not need to feel high to experience therapeutic effects, although what they understood as a high varied. Nevertheless, other research findings show that medicinal cannabis users think that particular mental effects (e.g. cheerfulness) are of therapeutic value (Ogborne et al., 2000; Coomber et al., 2003; Page & Verhoef 2006; Dahl & Frank, 2011).

2 Methods

This chapter draws upon findings from a study that explores the blurred boundaries between recreational and medicinal cannabis use, by studying the narratives of adult self-identified medicinal cannabis users living in Belgium. The majority of these use cannabis illegally and belong to a so-called hidden population. In Belgium, there are no legal sources of cannabis for medical purposes, except for the cannabis-based pharmaceutical medicine Sativex (nabiximols), which is delivered by hospital pharmacies. It is prescribed to patients suffering from multiple sclerosis, under strict conditions, and was made available in hospital pharmacies only shortly before the launch of the study. As a result, the majority of Belgian medical cannabis users are using cannabis illegally.

This is the first study conducted in Belgium to examine self-identified medicinal cannabis users. Respondents were self-selected and recruited through personal networks, social media, online fora, patient organisations, flyers and by snowball referrals. The analyses are based on data derived from qualitative in-depth interviews ($N = 62$) conducted in 2017. The semi-structured interviews lasted between one and 3.5 hours. Interviews were audiotaped and transcribed verbatim. Interview topics focused on participants' medical conditions; cannabis use patterns; (psychoactive) effects; and motives for, and attitudes towards recreational and medicinal cannabis use. The interviews were coded inductively and analysed thematically to uncover trends and emerging themes, using the qualitative data analysis software programme NVivo. The codes were cross-checked by two independent research colleague to confirm the accurateness of the original coding scheme.

3 Results

3.1 Self-identified medicinal cannabis users' profiles

Self-identified medicinal cannabis users' age varied between 21 and 78 years (mean = 46 years). The number of men and women participating in this study were equal. Interviewees suffered from a vast array of conditions, ranging from (self-diagnosed) mental health problems (e.g. insomnia, depression, attention deficit hyperactivity disorder/ADHD, etc.) to life-threatening diseases (e.g. cancer). Most participants' primary conditions for using cannabis were physical (e.g. chronic pain, arthritis, skin disorders, etc.). However, many of them used cannabis for both physical and psychological health purposes.

The majority of the medicinal cannabis users in the present study had experience with recreational cannabis use (35 of 62). Twenty-seven of them reported using recreationally at the time of the interview. However, a couple of participants were unsure about the meaning of recreational cannabis use and their answers were ambivalent on questions on this issue.

3.2 Medicinal versus recreational cannabis use: unravelling the concepts

Interviewees were asked to reflect on the meaning of the concept medical cannabis use. When participants discussed this, they contrasted it many times spontaneously with recreational use to illustrate their dissimilarities.

Motives for use

Most respondents explained recreational and medicinal use in terms of the different motives for use. When participants spoke of medicinal cannabis they referred to treating mostly physical health problems and the necessity of this for their quality of life.

Most participants used cannabis for more than one condition and/or symptom (e.g. inflammations, anxiety, pain, etc.), and cannabis was found beneficial for particular ailments (e.g. stress, wounds, chapped lips, symptoms due to menopause, etc.). The majority noticed that cannabis relieved certain ailments, although they were using it for other health purposes. Many participants noted that cannabis improved sleep and caused mental relaxation, which was reported to be found a positive side-effect, including by those who used cannabis for physical health problems.

Overall, participants' motives for using cannabis encompassed a large variety of different purposes. Cannabis was used to be productive (e.g. working in the garden); for cosmetic use (e.g. night cream); for muscle relaxation after a workout; to focus (e.g. when roller-blading); to cope with boredom; to improve concentration (e.g. translate texts), etc. These motives were also reported by medicinal cannabis users who claimed they were not using it for recreational purposes. Recreational use was primarily referred to as achieving stages of intoxication, i.e. being high or stoned. As one medical cannabis user, who used recreationally and medically recounts:

'What is the climax of recreational use? Getting high.' (Ine, aged 30)

Other frequently reported purposes of recreational use were relaxation, feeling cheerful, having fun, social motives and the intensified enjoyment of certain activities (e.g. attending concerts). A high number of participants explained their own recreational cannabis use by comparing it to drinking alcohol. Many observed that their own alcohol consumption had decreased, including those who claimed to be using cannabis exclusively for medical purposes.

Use patterns

Besides motives for use, differences between the use patterns of medicinal and recreational cannabis use emerged. Certain administration methods were identified as medical ingestion methods, such as medically tested vaporisers, while others were typically referred to as recreational, such as smoking joints. An older man stated that he drunk more cannabis tea instead of smoking joints since he started to use the drug more often medicinally and less often recreationally. Another 70-year-old man, who had no experience with recreational cannabis use, believed that smoking joints could never be considered medical, because 'It is an unhealthy way of consuming cannabis used by people who are addicted and who want to have fun' (Willy 70). Willy drunk low potent cannabis-infused milk to cope with chronic pain. Cannabis oil, orally ingested, was commonly used for medicinal purposes, but rarely for recreational purposes. Smoking pure cannabis without tobacco was considered 'more medical'. Jolien, a 25-year-old living with multiple sclerosis (MS) thought that it was not possible to experience the medical effects of cannabis if she smoked a small amount combined with high amounts of tobacco. She had gradually reduced the amounts of tobacco to zero in stages. This was part of a transition process from using recreationally to using medicinally.

When participants described their own cannabis products, they referred more often to medical cannabis and distinguished this from recreational cannabis. It appeared that participants thought of recreational and medicinal cannabis as two different products. Medical cannabis was characterised by its specific therapeutic effects suitable for particular symptoms. It was often described as containing high levels of CBD (cannabidiol, a non-psychoactive cannabinoid of cannabis), while cannabis destined for recreational use was believed to have higher levels of THC (tetrahydrocannabinol, the main psychoactive cannabinoid of cannabis). Multiple respondents stated that the quantities consumed were higher when using recreationally compared to medicinal use.

While cannabis for medicinal purposes was used alone, recreational use occurred also in group together with friends, and more often when respondents had time off. Respondents' recreational cannabis use patterns were more sporadic, whereas cannabis for medicinal purposes was used daily. Many participants who were former recreational cannabis users noted that their use frequency increased with the transition to medical use.

Multiple participants were using cannabis medically as well as recreationally at the time of the interviews. The majority stated that there were differences between their own recreational and medicinal use patterns. When they used cannabis recreationally it was more often a higher dose, a stronger cannabis product, and in another context and setting. One male respondent noted that when he used cannabis oil as a 'preventive medicine' before he went to sleep. He considered this to be medicinal cannabis use, while when he went to music festivals where he smoked joints, he considered that to be recreational use. He called his use 'integrated cannabis use' (Luc, aged 64). Another man (aged 39) explained that his recreational use patterns from the past were distinct from his current medical use patterns, seven years later. Since he was using cannabis for severe stomach problems his cravings for cannabis had lessened and he no longer enjoy using it at parties as he used to. At the time of the interviews, he used cannabis mostly when sitting in the couch by himself.

Four respondents believed that their medicinal cannabis use was more controlled than their recreational use (see also Bottorff et al., 2009), which meant that they had to pay more attention to the dose, the type of cannabis product and ingestion method. On the other hand, few other participants said that their medicinal and recreational use were intertwined. Using cannabis relieved their symptoms, they said, but at the same time it also made them feel happy.

Mental effects

The mental effects of cannabis were interpreted variously by our participants. They believed that recreational users experienced more (intense) mental effects, while medical use was mostly characterised by therapeutic physical effects. One female interviewee (aged 37), who used cannabis exclusively for medical purposes, thought that she did not experience the same effects as recreational cannabis users, because the potency of her cannabis products was lower. She and another participant thought that the overall experience between the two types of use must be different because of medicinal cannabis users' poor (er) health. Two male interviewees who had used cannabis recreationally in the past said they did not have the 'stoned' experience like they used to have, but rather cannabis only relieved their symptoms.

During the interviews, participants, reported the presence of particular motives for their use and the absence of other motives as arguments to illustrate that their own cannabis use was medical. For instance, a 64-year-old man argued that he used cannabis only right before he went to sleep, and as a consequence he was not able to experience cannabis' psychoactive effects. The impossibility of experiencing psychoactive effects was, for him, the main proof that his use was not recreational. Many participants stated that the purpose of their use was not to get high or stoned, to indicate that their use was not for recreational purposes.

Whether someone experiences and/or enjoys psychoactive effects appeared to be an important way to differentiate medicinal from recreational cannabis use. Participants mentioned a large variety of mental effects caused by cannabis. While most physical effects were considered to be therapeutic by our respondents, far more of the mental effects were considered not (as) important for therapeutic purposes. Multiple respondents who used cannabis exclusively for medical purposes noted that they never experienced any (or only very mild) psychoactive effects, because of the small doses and/or low potency of their cannabis products. More often, the drug's psychoactive or euphoric effects were mentioned as side-effects. On the other hand, many other participants could enjoy cannabis' psychoactive effects. These were mainly individuals who used for recreational purposes as well as medicinally:

'CBD oil … that might help against pain, but I also like using recreationally. To feel a bit mellow, I think that's nice. I've never tried it, but I think if I would try CBD oil, then I don't have that buzz, and I don't want to have to miss this, because I like it in a way.' (Maarten, aged 37)

Whether respondents liked or disliked the mental effects of cannabis depended on the context in which the substance was used. During leisure time, they enjoyed the euphoric effects, but at other times they preferred their symptoms to be relieved, while having a clear state of mind, in order to be able to function. One participant stated that she enjoyed smoking cannabis when she went for a walk, and she used cannabis to focus when cooking. She believed this was not equal to recreational use because she 'could not live without cannabis due to my ADHD' (Sandra, aged 42). Another participant, who took cannabis oil exclusively for severe neuropathic pain in her jaw due to cancer, observed:

'My daughter asked me "did you take your drops already, because you're all in a sudden happy again?" It is true that I tend to be depressive at times. I can honestly tell you that the relationship with my husband is over. At times this is difficult, so I don't take cannabis oil for this, but it does help.' (Liesbeth, aged 56)

These effects of cannabis can be considered therapeutic or as welcome side-effects (Chapkis, 2007). Two other female participants also claimed that they were not using recreationally, while at the same time they believed that cannabis stimulated their creativity when painting. One of them thought of these mental effects more as (pleasant) side-effects, since she needed cannabis for pain relief. She argued that she would not be using cannabis if she was still healthy:

'I do think it has a recreational result, but it's not my intention to use it recreationally. I notice that I become more creative when I use it medically.' (Sabine, aged 51)

Sabine's comment might be an adequate summary of all the previous examples. Most participants used cannabis for health purposes in the first place, but experienced positive non-medical results that improved their quality of life overall.

The value of mental effects

The fact that cannabis has a mental influence was most valuable to participants who used the substance as a treatment for their mental health problems (e.g. Tourette's syndrome, post-traumatic stress disorder/PTSD). Cannabis helped tackle those psychological problems in different ways (e.g. relaxation, sedation, anxiolysis). The psychotropic effects of cannabis were perceived beneficial for relieving physical complaints as well (e.g. pain), this time through mental distraction. Cannabis made it possible for participants to distance themselves mentally from their symptoms and to refocus on other things instead of their discomforts (see also Chapkis, 2007). A few respondents who dealt with physical conditions which impacted their mental health negatively, said that, due to cannabis use they were able to cope with both physical as well as mental health problems. A man suffering from prostate cancer described this as follows:

'The first proof of cannabis efficacy was when I could eat again, the second proof when I could dance again. The next was my mind... It is incredible, you have to have it tried yourself, especially when you are severely ill. It helps you, I think of it as a person that helps me. You know what the worst thing is you go through in life? The moment that you know you are mortal. Oh boy that hit me hard. Then I cried and had to smoke joints.' (Bruno, aged 55)

3.3 Clear boundaries?

Many of the self-identified medicinal cannabis users had broad interpretations of the concept of medicinal cannabis use. They thought that medical indications valid for use were wide-ranging and that cannabis benefited health in general:

*'When I think in the weekend: "I want to be fully relaxed and absorbed
in a movie", that's recreational. But then again, recreationally ... medicinally... Because what isn't better for healing? Actually relaxing. You can't
say it is only recreational. No, when you are completely relaxed, you forget your worries and then, it also works on your body.'* (Vivian, aged 53)

Few self-identified medicinal cannabis users believed that there were no significant differences between medicinal and recreational cannabis use. Other
participants thought that the distinction was unclear. They argued that the lines
between the two were thin, blurred, and it was hard to know where to draw
them. A young woman aged 21 and living with scoliosis stated that her friends
used cannabis to cope with stress and she was wondering if this could be still
called recreational use.

Multiple respondents experienced difficulties in explaining and distinguish-
ing recreational from medical cannabis use with regards to their own and others' use. It was clear from their narratives that cannabis use did not always fit in
one or the other term, but that that there is more nuance:

*'Recreational users, I think those people use cannabis for relaxation. Of
course there are ADHD patients and so on ... well ... actually that is
also medical. I think the dividing line is very thin. I know someone with
ADHD who smokes too and that is the only way for that person to have
a normal life. But those people might use it from morning until night.
Recreational use [sighs] ... what is that? Is it sitting around a campfire
and smoking? I don't know...'* (Sabine, aged 51)

More often, when respondents had multiple motives for using cannabis, it was
not always clear which were considered as health motives by the respondent
and which were not. The following participant used a non-psychoactive cannabis oil at the time of the interviews for trying to prevent cancer, while she had
smoked joints in the past for mental health purposes:

*'The joints ... that was really to numb myself. I know and admit that too.
But my sister's child died and that was really ... [takes a deep breath].
And cannabis helped me a lot. Back then, for me it was medicinally. But
actually that is not true, if you do it because you cannot handle real-
ity... But yeah is this medicinal or recreational? From both a bit right...?'*
(Marie, aged 43)

Other respondents' narratives contained more narrow interpretations of the
concept of medical cannabis use, as they believed only certain medical conditions qualified and merited the term 'medical use'. A few of them knew other
medicinal cannabis users, but were not sure if those people genuinely needed

cannabis for health reasons (see Pedersen & Sandberg, 2013). As Chris (aged 37) said: 'I have a comrade who says he uses it for medical reasons, he has ADHD, but it is more recreational though'. He continued by using the following argument to support this: 'He takes a lot more drops in the evening, that is just to watch TV all night long.' A 55-year-old lung cancer patient argued that three palliative patients he knew used cannabis more recreationally than he did. He believed that they smoked cannabis recreationally, because they coped with pain through mental distraction, while his own pain was relieved physically. This narrative suggests that there are perceived gradations in the types of use, and illustrates the perceived superiority of physical therapeutic effects above mental therapeutic effects.

Several self-identified medicinal cannabis users were convinced that recreational and medical cannabis use were completely different. Most of these participants did not use cannabis for recreational purposes, and emphasised the benefits of medicinal use and the risks of recreational use:

'I think there is an immense difference between medicinal and recreational cannabis use. Smoking a joint has absolutely nothing to do with medical use. To me recreational use is feeling stoned. The purpose of medicinal use is to have medicinal effects and not a stoned effect. It has nothing to do with drugs, with the misery caused by drugs to addicts and junkies.' (Isabelle, aged 46)

3.4 The medicinal cannabis user identity

A couple of respondents mentioned that they were not real or typical medical cannabis patients compared to other medical cannabis users, and they doubted the eligibility of their participation in the study because of their purposes of use. By other 'medical cannabis users', they meant those using to deal with more severe medical indications:

'In a way I fall outside of the research goal, because I'm not really 100 percent a medicinal user. I'm a person who has discovered during the years that there are also medicinal parts and who uses it now as a kind of preventive therapeutic substance, like others who drink tea to maintain their health. In that way I'm not representative for a medicinal user, because I consider it as an investment in my health.' (Luc, aged 64)

However, the majority of the respondents in this study thought of themselves as medicinal cannabis users. Most of the participants who considered themselves recreational users as well thought they were primarily medicinal cannabis users, as the medical purpose was their most important motive for use:

'I consider myself a medicinal user, because it is really necessary. I really have to use it every day, because otherwise I can't even talk because it is so tiring, painful and I have slurred speech. Because of this I am really a medical user. And recreational... I do love the plant and I enjoy smoking joints and to taste new strains. I like that, but I am a medical cannabis user.' (Jolien, aged 25)

One interviewee (Armand, aged 54) stated he was somewhere in between medical and recreational cannabis use because he was self-medicating with cannabis for bowel, sleep and pain problems. Another man (aged 50), suffering from comorbid psychiatric conditions, spoke of being first a recreational cannabis user and slowly becoming a medicinal cannabis user. While the transit from recreational to medicinal use happened spontaneously for most self-identified medicinal cannabis users, Armand noted that he had needed to learn how to use cannabis medically, similar to the learning process described by Athey et al. (2017):

'If I would have had the chance to use cannabis as a medicine, then I had learned to use it as medication a long time ago. I really had to learn how to use cannabis. I've abused cannabis for a long time. Walking around high... I had to learn that cannabis also can help without having to use this much.' (Armand, aged 54)

4   Discussion

Self-identified medicinal cannabis users' attitudes regarding the meaning of the concepts 'recreational' and 'medicinal' cannabis use were mixed. While some had a clear understanding of the two concepts, and thought there was an obvious distinction, others experienced difficulties when defining the two types of use. Lancaster, Seear and Ritter (2017) argue that medicinal and recreational cannabis are mutually co-constitutive in medical cannabis policy. Our data show that on the individual level too, medicinal cannabis use is construed on the basis of the absence of the presence of recreational use.

While most participants had experience with recreational cannabis use ($n = 35$), it is important to note there were novice users among the self-identified medicinal cannabis users ($n = 27$). Our explorative findings suggest that they were less likely to be male, to use cannabis for mental health problems and to smoke joints. Further research is required to improve our understanding of the experiences and attitudes of these naïve medicinal cannabis users, and to identify possible differences between them and experienced users.

Motives for use were the most important determinants for cannabis use to be defined medical by self-identified medicinal cannabis users. Other points of difference which distinguished medical use from recreational use included use patterns and perceived effects. Participants believed that recreational users experienced more intense psychoactive effects, while medical use was mainly characterised by therapeutic physical effects. It is plausible that medicinal cannabis users experience less psychoactive effects due to administration methods, dose and the levels of psychoactive cannabinoids of their cannabis products. However, since cannabis is the same substance whether used for recreational or medicinal purposes, effects and experiences are also likely shaped by the beliefs and expectations of the users as well as the setting (Zinberg, 1984; Chapkis, 2007; Dahl & Frank, 2011). This became clear in the cases of self-identified medicinal cannabis users who had used cannabis recreationally in the past, and reported different experiences since they became ill.

While participants' discourses on recreational cannabis use were loaded with stereotypes, their attitudes were ambivalent. Self-identified medicinal cannabis users thought of (other) recreational cannabis users mostly as people who want to get high. This would be the same as claiming that consuming alcohol is inseparable from being drunk. Furthermore, the meaning of the concept 'high' is far from clear. This stereotyping might be a way for self-identified medicinal cannabis users to disassociate themselves from the types of users who are more stigmatised (Pedersen & Sandberg, 2013), in order to gain acceptance of their own use.

When looking at previous studies into recreational and medicinal cannabis use, a difference between the two types of use seems to be that recreational cannabis use is a social and group phenomenon, especially among youth (Järvinen & Demant, 2011) and medicinal cannabis use is not (Roy-Byrne et al., 2015; Sznitman, 2017). However, this image of recreational cannabis users, that was also portrayed by our interviewees, matches better with adolescents' recreational users' profiles, while medicinal cannabis users' own profiles and attitudes appear to correspond more with adult recreational users (Rossi, 2019). The function of cannabis appears to diverge depending on the user's stage of life (Järvinen & Demant, 2011). It is likely that self-identified medicinal cannabis users' own perceptions of recreational use are influenced by the dominant discourses on recreational use.

In public discourses, recreational cannabis use is a catch all-term for many types of cannabis use. At the same time, it brings stereotypical images to mind, such as languid youth at social events. This chapter therefore identifies the need for more studies on cannabis use in adult populations, as other researchers have argued that cannabis users are aging and have different profiles (Rossi, 2019). Since motives for cannabis use are interwoven, it is important to perform research starting without predefined concepts. This will teach us more about the needs and preferences of cannabis users. The next step is to acknowledge the existence of the various purposes for using cannabis, depending on the context, including instrumental, creative, spiritual, therapeutic, religious, etc., which do not fit in the currently employed dichotomy.

Policy makers argue it is important to consider recreational and approved medicinal cannabis use as two separate categories when regulating cannabis products. A recent draft motion for a resolution from one of the committees in the European parliament reads:

> *'Calls on the Commission and national authorities [...] to draw a clear distinction between cannabis-based medicines approved by the EMA or other regulatory agencies, medical cannabis not supported by clinical trials, and other applications of cannabis (e.g. recreational or industrial)'* (Committee on the Environment, Public Health and Food Safety, 2019, p. 4).

Other researchers claim that without a clear distinction between recreational and therapeutic use it is impossible to develop two distinct strategies to approach the two phenomena (Growing, Ali, Christie & White, 1998). Duff argues that the term 'cannabis' can no longer be used as if we are talking about one single coherent object (see Duff, 2017).

In practice, it is possible to make a clear distinction between recreational and medicinal cannabis regarding approved cannabis products, for instance, by only considering cannabinoid pharmaceuticals prescribed by physicians as legitimate for medical use. However, our interviews illustrate that self-identified medicinal cannabis users value the natural and holistic aspect of cannabis in contrast to chemical conventional medicines (see also Pedersen & Sandberg, 2013). In addition, people growing their own plants and taking care of their own health can be empowering. Making a clear distinction between therapeutic and recreational use could be in contrast with the reality and incompatible with human needs (Grinspoon, 1999).

5   Conclusion

By contrasting the concepts 'recreational' versus 'medicinal' cannabis use, we might create an artificial dichotomy. Participants' narratives show that the concept of medicinal cannabis use is subjective, personal and not easily defined. This chapter shows that using this psychoactive substance for health purposes goes beyond the strict medical definition. The recognition of pleasure and holistic approaches are less common in western medicine, whereas fragmentation and dualism is standard. Medicinal cannabis moves beyond targeting one specific symptom, as it affects various aspects of patients' lives. The results show that cannabis can be used differently and adjusted depending on the context. Our findings indicate that motives for recreational and medicinal cannabis use are intertwined and not mutually exclusive. While the relief of symptoms was their main self-reported reason for using cannabis, self-claimed medicinal cannabis users reported motives for using cannabis moving beyond strictly medical purposes. This group of participants included those who claimed they had never used cannabis recreationally, or had done so only in the past.

Language, categorisations and simplifications make everyday life and society easier to organise and to structure. Concepts are constructed through social experience and power relations, and have real-life consequences. Therefore, it is important to look critically at existing concepts and to allow nuance to break through existing categorisations. Pulling the medicinal side away as much as possible from the recreational side, in medicine as well as in policy, might be unbeneficial for both types, as we would be ignoring certain realities. As noted by Lancaster and colleagues (2017), we found overlaps between the types of pleasurable effects experienced by medicinal cannabis users. (Medical) cannabis research and policy debates should acknowledge pleasurable and desirable effects, by which we might look differently at the concepts of 'medical' and other types of drug use (Lancaster et al., 2017). A limitation of the present study is that it relies on self-reports: more objective data is necessary on the use patterns of cannabis users. However, our findings provide new insights into the existing knowledge on medicinal cannabis use and valuable insights for future policy-making in cannabis regulations. Given that national regulations are still shifting, it is important that the blurred boundaries between medicinal and recreational use are acknowledged when implementing an international framework.

References

Athey, N., Boyd, N., & Cohen, E. (2017). Becoming a medical marijuana user: reflections on Becker's trilogy – learning techniques, experiencing effects, and perceiving those effects as enjoyable. *Contemporary Drug Problems, 44 (3),* 212–231.

Bakalar, J.B., & Grinspoon, L. (1997). *Marihuana, the forbidden medicine.* New Haven: Yale University Press.

Bardhi, F., Sifaneck, S.J., Johnson, B.D., & Dunlap, E. (2007). Pills, thrills and bellyaches: case studies of prescription pill use and misuse among marijuana/blunt smoking middle class young women. *Contemporary Drug Problems, 34 (1),* 53–101.

Bostwick, J.M. (2012). Blurred boundaries: the therapeutics and politics of medical marijuana. *Mayo Clinic Proceedings, 87 (2),* 172–186.

Bottorff, J.L., Johnson, J.L., Moffat, B.M., & Mulvogue, T. (2009). Relief-oriented use of marijuana by teens. *Substance Abuse Treatment, Prevention, and Policy, 4 (1),* 1.

Chapkis, W. (2007). Cannabis, consciousness, and healing. *Contemporary Justice Review, 10 (4),* 443–460.

Clark, A.J., Ware, M.A., Yazer, E., Murray, T.J., & Lynch, M.E. (2004). Patterns of cannabis use among patients with multiple sclerosis. *Neurology, 62 (11),* 2098–2100.

Committee on the Environment, Public Health and Food Safety (2019). *Motion for a resolution further to Question for Oral Answer B8-0001/2019 pursuant to Rule 128 (5) of the Rules of Procedure on use of cannabis for medicinal purposes (2018/2775 [RSP]).*

Coomber, R., Oliver, M., & Morris, C. (2003). Using cannabis therapeutically in the UK: a qualitative analysis. *Journal of Drug Issues, 33 (2)*, 325–356.

Dahl, H.V., & Frank, V.A. (2011). Medical marijuana – exploring the concept in relation to small scale cannabis growers in Denmark. In: T. Decorte, G.R. Potter, & M. Bouchard (Eds.), *World wide weed. Global trends in cannabis cultivation and its control* (pp. 116–141). Farnham: Ashgate.

Duff, C. (2017). Natures, cultures and bodies of cannabis. In: T. Kolind, G. Hunt, & B. Thom (Eds.), *The SAGE handbook of drug and alcohol studies* (pp. 679–693). London: SAGE.

Fischer, B., Murphy, Y., Kurdyak, P., Goldner, E., & Rehm, J. (2015). Medical marijuana programs – why might they matter for public health and why should we better understand their impacts? *Preventive Medicine Reports, 2*, 53–56.

Grinspoon, L. (1999). Medical marihuana in a time of prohibition. *International Journal of Drug Policy, 10 (2)*, 145–156.

Growing, L.R., Ali, R.L., Christie, P., & White, J.M. (1998). Therapeutic use of cannabis: clarifying the debate. *Drug and Alcohol Review, 17 (4)*, 445–452.

Hakkarainen, P., Decorte, T., Sznitman, S., Karjalainen, K., Barratt, M.J., Frank, V.A., Lenton, S., Potter, G., Werse, B., & Wilkins, C. (2019). Examining the blurred boundaries between medical and recreational cannabis – results from an international study of small-scale cannabis cultivators. *Drugs: Education, Prevention and Policy, 26 (3)*, 250–258.

Keane, H. (2008). Pleasure and discipline in the uses of Ritalin. *International Journal of Drug Policy, 19 (5)*, 401–409.

Lancaster, K., Seear, K., & Ritter, A. (2017). Making medicine; producing pleasure: a critical examination of medicinal cannabis policy and law in Victoria, Australia. *International Journal of Drug Policy, 49*, 117–125.

Järvinen, M., & Demant, J. (2011). The normalization of cannabis use among young people. Symbolic boundary work in focus groups. *Health Risk and Society, 13 (2)*, 165–182.

Lin, L.A., Ilgen, M.A., Jannausch, M., & Bohnert, K.M. (2016). Comparing adults who use cannabis medically with those who use recreationally: results from a national sample. *Addictive Behaviors, 61*, 99–103.

Lucas, P. (2012). It can't hurt to ask: a patient-centered quality of service assessment of health canada's medical cannabis policy and program. *Harm Reduction Journal, 9 (1)*, 2.

Ogborne, A.C., Smart, R.G., Weber, T., & Birchmore-Timney, C. (2000). Who is using cannabis as a medicine and why: an exploratory study. *Journal of Psychoactive Drugs, 32 (4)*, 435-443.

Pacula, R.L., Jacobson, M., & Maksabedian, E.J. (2016). In the weeds: a baseline view of cannabis use among legalizing states and their neighbours. *Addiction, 111 (6)*, 973–980.

Page, S.A., & Verhoef, M.J. (2006). Medicinal marijuana use: experiences of people with multiple sclerosis. *Canadian Family Physician, 52 (1)*, 64–65.

Pedersen, W., & Sandberg, S. (2013). The medicalisation of revolt: a sociological analysis of medical cannabis users. *Sociology of Health & Illness, 35 (1)*, 17–32.

Reinarman, C., Nunberg, H., Lanthier, F., & Heddleston, T. (2011). Who are medical marijuana patients? Population characteristics from nine California assessment clinics. *Journal of Psychoactive Drugs, 43 (2)*, 129–135.

Rossi, M. (2019; in press). On aging cannabis users: a welfare economics analysis. In: Z. Kaló, J. Tieberghien, & D.J. Korf (Eds.), *Why? Explanations for drug use and drug dealing in social drug research.* Lengerich: Pabst Science Publishers.

Roy-Byrne, P., Maynard, C., Bumgardner, K., Krupski, A., Dunn, C., West, I.I., Donovan, D., Atkins D. C., & Ries, R. (2015). Are medical marijuana users different from recreational users? The view from primary care. *The American Journal on Addictions, 24 (7),* 599–606.

Sznitman, S. R. (2017). Do recreational cannabis users, unlicensed and licensed medical cannabis users form distinct groups? *International Journal of Drug Policy, 42,* 15–21.

Swift, W., Gates, P., & Dillon, P. (2005). Survey of Australians using cannabis for medical purposes. *Harm Reduction Journal, 2 (1),* 18.

Zinberg, N. E. (1984). *Drug, set, and setting.* New York: Human Sciences Press.

11
In search of the ideal drug

Alfred Springer

The search for an ideal drug, a traditional topic of drug folklore, has continued for centuries, reflecting changing socio-cultural attitudes to drug use. The concept of the 'ideal drug' is varied and serves different needs and conceptions in different layers of society at different times. Historically, medical visions of the ideal drug have repercussions on motivation for social drug use. Accordingly, the individual, seemingly transgressive search for the ideal social drug is bound up with the search for the ideal drug in medicine. The handling of mental disorders and the associated development of psychoactive drugs stimulate consumption needs in the area of social drug use, and the searches for the ideal psychotherapeutic substance and the ideal social drug merge. The actual definition of an ideal drug reflects the general need for individual enhancement and therefore complies with the requirements of the architects of the enhancement philosophy. Public debate on the use of enhancement technologies is overdue and must be stimulated by new analysis and research. Both the licit and illicit use of chemically identical psychoactive substances is increasing, and in both settings is based on similar interpretations, requirements and desires. There is a need to put prohibitive drug policies concerning social, non-medical use of these substances into perspective and to open a discourse about legalisation of production and distribution of 'sensual drugs' with known low risk profiles to counter the dangers of experimental use of illicit compounds.

Keywords: cultural history, psychopharmacology, enhancement, enhancement technologies, legal considerations

1   Introduction

Why is the need for drug experience a constant phenomenon in all cultures and at all levels of civilisation? The answer seems simple enough: drugs are taken because they are available, because individuals and social groups want to take them, and because drugs are given cultural significance. The justification of the individual need also seems relatively simple. People take drugs because they expect them to improve their condition. In traditional discourse, therefore, great importance is attached to the hedonistic domain. Even a complex thinker like Sigmund Freud made this simple connection, attaching great importance to drugs and their efficacy while reflecting on 'Civilisation and its discontents':

'But the most interesting methods of averting suffering are those which seek to influence our own organism. All suffering is nothing else than sensation; it only exists in so far as we feel it, and we only feel it in consequence of certain ways in which our organism is regulated. The crudest, but also the most effective among these methods of influence is the chemical one – intoxication. ... The service rendered by intoxicating media in the struggle for happiness and in keeping misery at a distance is so highly prized as a benefit that individuals and peoples alike have given them an established place in the economics of their libido. ... The man who sees his pursuit of happiness come to nothing in later years can still find consolation in the yield of pleasure of chronic intoxication; or he can embark on the desperate attempt at rebellion seen in a psychosis' (Freud, 1989b, p. 14).

In 'The Future of an Illusion' Freud assigned a quasi-religious efficiency to the soothing effect of drugs:

'That the effect of religious consolations may be likened to that of a narcotic is well illustrated by what is happening in America. There they are now trying... to deprive people of all stimulants, intoxicants, and other pleasure-producing substances (Reiz-, Rausch- und Genussmittel), *and instead; by way of compensation, are surfeiting them with piety'* (Freud, 1989a, pp. 49–50).

Freud commented ironically on this development: 'This is another experiment as to whose outcome we need not feel curious' (Freud, 1989b, p. 50). However, the great thinker was mistaken in his assessment of the power of the prohibition movement to assert itself. Since the mid-20th century, prohibitive drug policy has restrictively regulated social use of psychoactive substances. Among the changes that prohibitive order produced is the fact that simple answers to the question of why people take drugs have become obsolete.

The simple interpretation mentioned above is based on the assumption that there is a fundamental need for drug use, that consumption behaviour is considered a normal activity and that the underlying desire is understood as a normal variant within the human need structure. These attitudes are based on the cultural acceptance of drugs as more-or-less 'normal' commodities. Prohibitive drug policies cannot allow a comparable understanding of drug use and of drugs themselves. In their view, the only legal use of psychoactive substances is medically justified use. Any non-medical use is labelled 'abuse' and considered illicit. Therefore, the human tendency to integrate the use of such substances into everyday life becomes an abnormality. New, highly complex explanatory patterns have become necessary to make the appetite for drugs comprehensible. It is no longer just about understanding why people take psychoactive substances, but why they long for certain prohibited substances and are willing to go beyond the law to fulfil their desire.

There is no doubt that prohibitive drug policies have influenced addiction and drug research, and that in this scientific-political interconnectedness the search for the cause of non-medical drug use has formed a large part of the research agenda.

2   Theories about use motives revised

Over the years, one of the more striking aspects of drug research became the relative upsurge of various models and theories explaining, wholly or in part, the problems of drug use and drug abuse. This rapid growth signalled the need for a broader understanding of the phenomenon, since research activities also showed the diversity, convergence, and complexity of the array of existent explanatory perspectives.

Research interest remarkably increased in the times of particular lifestyle changes of young populations, including new patterns of drug use. When these lifestyle changes became part of youthful unrest and subversive political positions, non-medical drug use became transformed into the major symbol of opposing youth and consequently an issue of growing concern.

We know that motives for drug use are diverse and complex. Any interpretation of the motives that steer drug-taking behaviour has first to consider what drugs mean to the people who use them. Qualitative research in separate defined groups can provide insight concerning drug use related attitudes and behaviours in those social units. Otherwise, because of the highly diverse meanings attached to drugs and drug use, the results of such research cannot easily be transferred onto other groups nor explain the overall desire for drug use in a complex and diversified socio-cultural space.

Exhaustive research has shown how the meaning attached to a drug differs considerably within different social groups and influences the experience of the drug itself. That meaning is not derived from rational knowledge and rational considerations. It represents a construction based on expectations, feelings and subjective experiences and interpretations that are again influenced by the frame of a given society undergoing a particular historical process. Motivations for drug use and the resulting use patterns therefore emerge from complex interactions between pharmacological, physiological, psychological, behavioural and sociocultural variables. Although linked to the current cultural situation, the new notions seem to express needs that were once satisfied by the traditional tonic, Vin Mariani. They suggest that, within the ideological framework of neuroculture and transhumanist considerations, there is a persistent need to eliminate the boundaries between medical and social use and to make room for various forms of social use of psychoactive, stimulating substances.

The Canadian project on non-medical use of drugs conducted in the early 1970s provides an excellent example of early research into our problem. The research questions raised at that time and the interpretations found have not lost any of their relevance (Canadian Government Commission of Enquiry, 1971). The authors of that report suggested that sociological or environmental factors are far more important than psychological ones for understanding drug use.

However, improving understanding of the complex motivational structure of drug use requires a comprehensive approach that considers as many causes and their interactional diversity as possible. Several interactive theories have been developed and much research conducted to pave the way for such a broader understanding. A single essay does not leave enough space to reconsider all these research activities and their results. However, particularly valuable to our topic is an interactionist concept that focuses on the impact of socio-cultural systems of influence (Huba, Wingard & Bentler, 1980).

Socio-cultural influence systems are a series of more distal cultural influences, including subcultural norms, models and impersonal socialisation influences such as advertising and popular culture artefacts, which together produce a 'drug-related folklore'. This folklore contains messages about the meanings and importance of drug use. Although they regularly depend on the current historical framework, they are also rooted in the past and transfer traditions (Springer, 2001).

3 The 'ideal drug'

One traditional 'folkloristic' topic is the somewhat utopian search for an 'ideal drug'. That search has continued for centuries and reflects changes in socio-cultural attitudes to drugs. The concept of the ideal drug is varied and serves different needs and conceptions in different layers of society and within different historical contexts. On one hand, it represents wishful thinking of consumers, partly based on experience. On the other, it serves specific interests of pharmacology, drug producers, the treatment community and other stakeholders. The search for the ideal drug runs on parallel tracks through the cultural space. It is a theme within mainstream culture, that is paralleled by a continuing reckless search in diverse subcultural settings (Springer, 2001). In general, it corresponds to the search for pleasure and to the meanings that are attached to functional drug use in diverse cultural settings.

In mainstream culture, the search is mainly bound to actual wishes and necessities, but also to the historical framework. As we explore the historical development of mainstream drug use, we can define time periods that provide leitmotifs that correspond to specific characteristics and needs at a given time.

3.1 The first age of modernity: Vin Mariani and the ideal drug

In the late 19th century, drugs became a prominent topic. The awareness of the dangers related to the use of alcohol and opium/morphine led to the establishment of the temperance and abstinence movements. Otherwise, the separation of pharmacology and medicine and social drugs was not as strict as it is today. The boundaries were blurred, as we can learn from pharmacological terminology. Baron von Bibra (1855/1995), an early ethnobotanist, labelled drugs such as opium, coca and cannabis as 'Narkotische Genussmittel'. The correct English translation of this term would be 'Narcotic Substances of Enjoyment'. The most recent translation of his book uses a rather shy vocabulary: 'Plant intoxicants'.

The fact that there were no boundaries between the medical and social use of certain drugs may be because substances from different regions of the world were introduced into European society and became common goods before structured research into their medical benefits began. Of course, it was known that they were considered traditional remedies in their own countries. But this aspect of drug-related folklore had to be demonstrated through systematic research.

In particular, coca, when newly imported, aroused broad interest in the generally positive potential of drug use. The research devoted to the plant and its alkaloids led to insights into the medical benefits of cocaine, which were in some ways revolutionary. The fact that the medical value of coca and cocaine could be demonstrated did not result in coca preparations no longer being marketed as common goods. On the contrary, knowledge of the drug's medical efficacy was used to expand the market for the non-medical social use of consumer-friendly formulations of the drug.

Among the many coca products that took advantage of the lack of a line between medicine and social drugs for their marketing, Vin Mariani, a composition of red wine from the Bordeaux region and coca extracts, gained particular importance. Angelo Mariani, the pharmacist who designed and marketed this product from 1863, conducted a special type of consumer research and published the positive assessment of the quality of his coca-wine. More than 8000 knowledgeable and famous personalities responded and praised the quality of the product. The contributing personalities came from different social backgrounds. These included: inventors such as Branly, Edison and the Lumiere brothers; 153 artists; 23 composers; 85 actors; 220 writers; 32 members of medical academies; 50 lecturers in medicine; 24 selected representatives of medical disciplines; five military doctors; close to 10,000 written contributions from medical experts (Mariani, 1910); 40 representatives of high-ranking clergy:

three popes and the Chief Rabbi of France; 24 representatives of the military; and 35 members of the French academy, as well as high-ranking politicians and representatives of the nobility. The answers of this selected group of people were published between 1894 and 1925 in 14 volumes of beautifully produced yearbooks (entitled *'Figures Contemporaines'*). It is noteworthy that some initial utopian considerations have been made in this context regarding the possibility of positive effects of drug use on human development (Bouchor, 1901).

Of course, this source is rather biased. We do not know how many of the personalities invited by Mariani to assess the quality of his product did not respond, we do not know whether Mariani suppressed negative reactions, and we do not even know whether all the respondents really used the wine or responded just because they wanted to join the elite represented in the Mariani yearbooks. Nevertheless, analysis of these publications allows us to design the concept of an ideal drug that is medically, professionally and socially beneficial in equal measure (Springer, 2009).

The consumers' presentation of their experience with the product reveals a multitude of effects, qualities and applications of that special coca-wine preparation. The product was described as:

* a medication that can also improve quality of life and prolong life;
* an euphoriant drug that produces a 'high' state, as well as;
* a generally enhancing substance (increases performance, creativity, athletic ability, erotic feelings, sexual function and reproduction).

It was also pointed out that it was designed to benefit both sexes and all generations from early childhood to very old life. From the military environment, the product was found to be capable of increasing military efficiency. All-in-all, the answers can be read as a blueprint for the formulation of a substance that can take the role of an 'ideal drug'.

3.2 The age of anxiety and the ideal psychotherapeutic drug

After the Second World War, there was a great need to come to terms with fear. The fear that resulted from the post-war situation, the experience with the technologies of destruction and the continuing threat of the Cold War shaped individual and group behaviour as well as the artefacts of popular culture. This socio-cultural situation was aptly referred to as 'bomb culture' (Nuttall, 1970). Nuttall described how the disappointment that the protest against the general threat proved ineffective led to a cultural attitude among youth and young adults that included the need for quick kicks and thus irresponsible drug use.

'That they could be addictive or fatal was comparatively irrelevant, because such dangers were part of the future, and the future was, to say
the least, not a sure thing, too unlikely to be taken seriously' (Nuttall,
1970, p. 106).

Efforts to address the general problem included pathologising and confront-
ing medicine and psychiatry with the task of developing efficient therapies for
'anxiety states'. The responses to this problem included pathologisation and
confronted medicine and psychiatry with the task of developing therapeutic
possibilities against 'anxiety disorders'. The rise of psychopharmacology and its
focus on the development of anti-anxiety drugs at this time can be interpreted
as a reaction to the general cultural situation. The new anxiety-relieving drugs
were advertised as relatively harmless and were soon used for non-medical
purposes, often in combination with alcohol. This crossing of the line between
medical and social use, as well as increasing knowledge about the addictive
qualities of the substances, raised concerns for several reasons, which ultimately led to tighter prescription rules and restrictions on the accessibility of these
drugs.

Strangely enough, the search for an ideal drug also took on a new form in
this context. The American scientist Leo Hollister coined the term 'ideal psychotherapeutic drug'. Such a drug would:

1) cure or alleviate the pathogenetic mechanisms of the symptom or disorder;
2) be rapidly effective;
3) benefit most or all patients for whom it is indicated;
4) be non-habituating and lack potential for creating dependence;
5) not allow tolerance to develop;
6) have minimum toxicity on the therapeutic range;
7) have a low incidence of secondary side-effects;
8) not be lethal in overdoses;
9) be adaptable both to inpatients and outpatients; and
10) not impair any cognitive, perceptual, or motor functions (Hollister, 1975).

This was also the first period of the therapeutic use of psychedelics, substances
that were idealised a little later.

3.3 The age of playpower: neo-modernism, liberation and oppression

Although in the two international conventions regulating the production, trafficking and proper use of narcotics (1961) and psychotropic substances (1971),
a strict distinction was made between (licit) medical-therapeutic and (illicit)
social use, the 1960s and 1970s saw an increased blurring of the boundaries
between these two modes of use. This development contributed to fragmentation in the search for the ideal drug. The search for the 'ideal therapeutic drug'

continued to take place within the industry-science-treatment nexus, while the search for the 'ideal social drug' spread in modernist 'neophilic' youth cultures (Booker, 1969). The motives were complicated: the importance of drug use was created by practitioners in youth cultures and varied in terms of users. A thorough review of the literature on the diversity of motives and meanings among drug users during this period is not possible here. It suffices to point out that in the 1960s and early 1970s it was possible to distinguish between three primary drug orientations: recreational, creative and transcendental (Springer, 2012). Drug use was increasingly interpreted as a means of counteracting the performance principle and paving the way for a future under the rule of the pleasure principle (Neville, 1970). At the same time, it was regarded as a determining component of a protesting and subversive lifestyle. Experience showed that the possible orientations towards drugs were not mutually exclusive and that they may overlap for a particular user. If there were drugs at that time that were idealised and regarded as magical potions, it was hallucinogens that were attributed high transformative potency for individuals as well as for society (Blum, 1964; Stafford & Golightly, 1967).

On the control level, this cultural climate led to a tightening of prohibition policies and to an increased division between social and medical consumption. Drug users became folk devils and a different kind of drug folklore emerged. Non-medical, hedonistic drug use became increasingly presented as problem behaviour, which, according to critics, would have serious individual and social consequences. A landmark publication in which this position was represented was the book 'Sensuous drugs' by Jones & Jones, published in 1977. According to their definition, sensuous drugs are substances that 'the body does not need, but which give the user a strong sense of pleasure' (Jones & Jones, 1977, p. 2). The authors explained that such drugs initially stimulate erotic sensations, but eventually cause numb feelings and ultimately lead to total sensory deprivation for users. Jones & Jones were convinced that cannabis was the prototype of all sensuous drugs, with insidious and long-lasting effects and therefore strongly opposed the liberalisation of marijuana use.

3.4 The 'plague years' – AIDS and the body high

The 1980s were overshadowed by the rapid spread of AIDS. As a blood-borne disease, it particularly affected intravenous drug users and people who were engaged in risky sexual practices. This, and the fact that well-known representatives of popular culture quickly fell victim to the disease, influenced the features of hedonist subcultures and the patterns of hedonist drug use.

In this context, Michel Foucault expressed a vision of an ideal drug adapted to this tragic situation. In one of his last interviews, he ruminated on the necessity to detach pleasure from desire and to develop the body's ability to procure pleasure outside the usual circle of food intake and sex. Drugs seemed to him to be useful tools for this purpose:

'I think drugs should become an element of our culture... as source of pleasure. We must study drugs. We must experiment with drugs. We must produce good drugs which are able to provoke extreme intense pleasure' (Foucault, 1984, in Rabinow, 2003, pp. 165–166).

The early days of rave seemed to render Foucault's vision possible. Perhaps the right music and the right drugs came together to produce a space where it was possible to cling to the vision of bodily pleasure in an age in which the main traditional strategy, 'normal' performative sex, had become outdated because of HIV-related risks. The pleasure of the drug-induced high depends on set and setting but also on drug specific dimensions. Some drugs act more on the mind and on perception, while others, like MDMA and similar compounds, procure the feeling of a 'body high' together with a stimulation of erotic needs and a reduction of sexual desire and sexual potency. During the early days of dance culture, the use of such drugs probably initially helped to create a 'pleasure dome' where the realms of bodily pleasure could be explored without engaging in (dangerous) sexual behaviour. The protective function of that special high was most prominent during the first years of the rave phenomenon and diminished in the ongoing transformation of the dance scene.

3.5. The 'decades of the brain' – the age of neuroculture and transhumanism

The remarkable development of the use of psychoactive substances, which has taken place since the 1980s within and outside the medical care system, correlates with changes in the cultural framework. From the end of the 1980s, 'decades of the brain' were declared. What began as a requirement to focus research on the function of the brain and the significance of the brain for human life evolved into a broad concept encompassing various research activities, eventually leading to a radical reassessment of the significance of the brain for all manifestations of human individual and social life. New approaches to the medical and non-medical use of psychoactive substances and to changing patterns of use are part of this cultural change. Interest in the treatment of pathological conditions such as attention deficit hyperactivity disorder (ADHD) and dementia has led to increased medical use of so-called 'brain drugs', mainly in the amphetamine-type stimulants (ATS) category. This re-evaluation of such substances regarding their safe medical use also influenced non-medical patterns of use. As a result, there is a continuous and increasing demand for stimulants in the field of strategic (aim-oriented) social drug use. This demand is partly met by prescriptions for treatment, but even more so by new supply routes for illicit drug trafficking.

Once again, the boundaries between medical and non-medical use are blurring. Certain positions of medical experts, who postulate a non-medical, but nevertheless medically controlled delivery of certain psychoactive drugs, contribute to the dissolution of these borders. This expression of cultural change in health policy manifests itself in a multitude of approaches:

a) Cosmetic psychopharmacology, also known as enhancement therapy, uses psychiatric drugs to support more or less normal functioning people according to their wishes and ideas and to make them even more attractive to society. According to this concept, the substances can be prescribed to people who are not ill, but who express the desire to 'feel better than good' and expect the drug effect to improve their social competence. The concept was first formulated by psychiatrist Peter Kramer in his book 'Listening to Prozac' (Kramer, 1993, pp. 246, 247).

b) Psychedelic psychiatry: the research projects on the enhancing effect of LSD microdosage carried out as part of the psychedelics research at Kings College London form a bridge between the psychedelic revival (Oberhaus, 2017; Springer, 2018; Beckley Foundation, 2019) and the new philosophy of enhancement.

c) Neuroenhancement: while psycho-enhancement (cosmetic psychopharmacology) remains a domain of psychiatry and regularly involves psychiatrists who transcend their professional boundaries, neuro-enhancement is a concept that both regulates medical interventions (especially in ADHD and/or Alzheimer's) and increasingly becomes a non-medical practice of healthy people who want to improve their cognitive abilities (DeSantis & Hane, 2010; Ragan, Bard & Singh, 2012; Battleday & Brem, 2015; Schwartz, 2016; Lucke, Jensen, Dunn, et al., 2018). Already in the late 1990s, the WHO observed an increasing demand for ATS outside the medical treatment system. Originally, this phenomenon was interpreted as a US specialty. However, according to the Global Drug Survey, 2018, very high growth rates can also be observed in European countries. Between 2015 and 2017, prevalence increased in France from three percent to 16 percent and in Great Britain from five percent to 23 percent (Maier, Ferris & Winstock, 2018). In terms of motivation for drug use, this development shows a radical departure from the motives of the playpower era. The extra-medical use of stimulants is no longer a practice of hedonistic subcultures, but has entered schools and academic circles. The new usage patterns aimed not at pleasure, but were motivated by a desire to improve performance, cognitive functions and memory processes. An informal reader questionnaire conducted by Nature in 2008 (Maher, 2008) found that 20 percent of 1,400 responders from 60 countries had used central nervous system stimulants (methylphenidate (Ritalin), modafinil (Provigil), adderall, dexedrine, pirazetam or beta blockers or some alternative medicines) to increase concentration and memory. The development of such lifestyle patterns has raised some criticism (Sahakian & Morahin-Zamir, 2007). Ethical concerns were raised because the use of lifestyle-related stimulants among healthy academics seemed comparable to doping practices in competitive sports.

4   The cultural framework of neuroenhancement

In neuroculture, the brain became a defining symbol of contemporary culture. Inspired by new technologies of brain imaging, the brain has increasingly become the organ with which a human is identified: the thesis of the 'cerebral subject' has emerged. This development and the rise of a multitude of new fields of research shows that originally purely-neuroscientific knowledge has begun to penetrate further areas of society, life and culture, influencing areas such as law, ethics, artistic expression and advertising (Ehrenberg, 2010).

One effect of the central importance attached to the brain, its functions and its performance is a redefinition of autonomy, social skills, performance and competitiveness of the individual as defining characteristics. This reorientation brought with it both new possibilities and new tasks, which take the individual to their limits in a culture that is no longer controllable anyway. The current need for psychoactive substances, especially central nervous system stimulants, can also be understood from this point of view. It corresponds to the socio-political orientation of the new modern age under the influence of the ideology of neuroculture. The desire for stimulants can be understood as a reaction of the self that is 'exhausted' by the new challenges (Ehrenberg, 2009).

In the bioethical discourse triggered by Kramer's (1993) concept of cosmetic psychopharmacology, non-medical use of psychotherapeutic drugs was classified as enhancement technology. This attribution enables consumers to understand the use of such drugs as a useful tool for personality development, authenticity and self-realisation. Furthermore, ethical and philosophical considerations on the non-medical use of the antidepressants selective serotonin reuptake inhibitors (SSRIs) maintain utopian speculations about the transformative significance of drug effects for human, social and cultural conditions. It seems that the justifications of drug use, which were accepted and widely disseminated around the early 1900s, have regained their importance in mainstream culture after having been assigned to subcultural discourses under the influence of prohibitive drug policies.

In this respect, the new demand for improvement corresponds to the situation of the late 19th century, with the difference that in the earlier epoch access to drugs was not equally restricted and 'exhaustion' was interpreted as a general cultural situation and not only as a problem of the performance and competitiveness of the individual. However, both epochs are characterised by the use of psychoactive stimulant substances, which are intended to cause 'enhancement' in the broadest sense, and by the emergence of utility models that dissolve the boundaries between medical and social use of psychoactive substances. The ideal social drug and the ideal psychotherapeutic medication coalesce in this process.

This process cannot only be observed in the current situation. In all the periods we have studied, the medical vision of the ideal drug does not remain without repercussions on motivation for social drug use. Accordingly, the individual, seemingly transgressive search for the ideal drug is bound up with the search for the ideal drug in the general cultural context. The handling of mental disorders and the associated development of psychoactive drugs stimulate consumption needs in the area of social drug use: the search for the ideal psychotherapeutic substance and the ideal social drug merge into each other.

Since the stimulants they use are controlled substances, the adepts of neuroenhancement – unlike the clients of cosmetic psychiatry – are banished to a legal twilight zone. At the same time, the pharmaceutical industry is trying to make a profit by openly promoting certain drugs as lifestyle agents (Healy, 2001). Based on neuroethical considerations, initiatives have been launched to alleviate this situation. Greely, Campbell, Sahakian and colleagues (2008) argued that the responsible use of cognitive stimulants by healthy people should be reconsidered. Society should adapt to the new situation and turn away from understanding improvement as a 'dirty practice'. The authors further argued that it makes no sense to treat students like delinquents who use, buy and sell substances such as Adderall or Ritalin, not to intoxicate themselves, but to increase their learning skills in order to compete with other students and achieve better study results. Amended drug laws should pave the way for better use of technology to improve.

5   The future of the ideal drug: discussion, conclusions and recommendations

A special feature of the new shape of the discourse on the meaning of drug use is its insistence on human rights aspects of drug use and drug users. This position contributes to a renewed loosening of the boundaries between medical and social use. A discourse has been opened that contains visions of responsible use of drugs, the liberalisation of self-medication (Fainzang, 2017) and self-enhancing pharmaceutical technologies. At the same time, initiatives concerning the liberation of responsible use of cognitive-enhancing drugs by the healthy have been started from a neuroethic perspective. This new discursive frame prepares the possibility of new and improved motivations for non-medical drug use. In such cases, users really have the chance to decide about the safe use of known and well-researched drugs for self-defined aims within their search for their private ideal drug.

Nevertheless, such a situation implies some challenges for the control framework. Like all new technologies, cognitive enhancement can be used well or poorly. One must think about the problems that such use of drugs could create or exacerbate. With this, as with other technologies, we need to think and work hard to maximise its benefits and minimise its harms. Probably the ideas of control that are generated in that context could help to move on from the impasse of prohibition and to develop a general realistic and rational control system for the implementation of the concept of responsible use.

The positioning of our problem in the neurocultural discourse opens a new perspective. It allows the understanding that user, controller, dealer, doctor, prevention worker, researcher and scientist are all characters within a common space, on the neurocultural stage, in need of an understanding and integrating director.

The expectations of the modern performance society and the requirements of the individual functioning in it lead to the fact that apparently healthy people do not feel able to cope with the socially generated and expected normal state and that their individuality is seen as a deficiency (Ehrenberg, 2010).

Although linked to the current cultural situation, the new notions seem to express needs that were once satisfied by the traditional tonic, Vin Mariani. They suggest that, within the ideological framework of neuroculture and transhumanist considerations, there is a persistent need to eliminate the boundaries between medical and social use and to make room for various forms of social use of psychoactive, stimulating substances.

Neuro-enhancement can thus also be seen as a restoration of socially expected 'normal states' in the modern performance society. In a neurocultural landscape in which the licit as well as the illicit use of chemically identical psychoactive substances is increasing, and in both settings is based on similar interpretations, requirements and desires. There is the need to put prohibitive drug policies concerning social, non-medical use of these substances into perspective and to open a discourse about legalisation of production and distribution of 'sensual drugs' with known low-risk profiles, to counter the dangers of experimental use of illicit, produced compounds. If sensual drugs could be produced in a controlled way, it would be possible to transfer the model of consumer information from medical onto social use and to inform the users about safe use conditions. We are faced with the question of whether such marketing should only be available for cognitive (i.e. competitive) enhancement, and not also as a solution for other spaces of non-medical use – mood, drive, spirituality, sexuality, lust, creativity.

The lifting of the ban on extra-medicinal use would create the possibility for the pharmaceutical industry to contribute to the development and marketing of psychoactive drugs ('psychotherapeutic drugs') for their social use. Individual medicines could be tested for their suitability in terms of risks and side-effects and, if appropriate, consumer-friendly and dose-adapted formulations could be developed, which could be taken in normal social settings. It may turn out that the 'ideal social drug' and the 'ideal psychotherapeutic drug' are not so different. Why should a substance, which can be assigned desired effects from the spectrum of activity of Vin Mariani, be withheld from persons who cannot be assigned to a psychiatric diagnosis, but who strive for pharmacological enhancement, if it, according to Leo Hollister's ideal conception, does not lead to pharmacological tolerance, hardly brings about undesired side-effects, does not impair cognitive, perceptual or motor functions, exhibits minimal toxicity, and does not lead to fatal incidents even in the case of overdose?

If such a change in control policy could take place, users would really be able to decide on the safe use of known and well-researched drugs for self-defined purposes in the search for their private ideal drug.

In addition, it appears that such a move would only normalise the given situation, as pharmaceutical company executives and others openly refer to certain medicines as lifestyle agents (Healy, 2001), neglecting that their non-medical use could endanger consumers. In a society where the non-medical use of psychoactive substances is illegal and generally rejected, users are ipso facto engaged in non-conforming behaviour and therefore, despite their original intention, run the risk of being paradoxically stigmatised and marginalised (Teter, McCabe, LaGrande, Cranford & Boyd, 2006; Bogle & Smith, 2009; Varga, 2012; Schwartz, 2016). Normalised production would help to avoid such harmful social processes. Similarly, 'responsible use' requires a controlled and regulated supply. Finally, normalised production is a basic prerequisite for balancing inequalities regarding the accessibility of enhancement technologies (Beyer, Staunton & Moodley, 2014).

References

Battleday, R.M., & Brem, A.K. (2015). Modafinil for cognitive neuroenhancement in healthy non-sleep-deprived subjects: a systematic review. *Eur Neuropsychopharmacol, 25 (11),* 1865–81.

Beckley Foundation (2019). *Microdosing.* Retrieved from https://beckleyfoundation.org/microdosing-lsd/.

Beyer, C., Staunton, C., & Moodley, K. (2014). The implications of methylphenidate use by healthy medical students and doctors in South Africa. *BMC Medical Ethics, 15 (1),* 20.

Bibra, E. (1995). *Plant intoxicants: a classic text on the use of mind-altering plants* (Hedwig Schleiffer, tansl.) Rochester, Vermont: Healing Arts.

Blum, R. (1964). *Utopiates. The use and users of LSD-25.* New York: Atherton.

Bogle, K.E., & Smith, B.H. (2009). Illicit methylphenidate use: a review of prevalence, availability, pharmacology, and consequences. *Current Drug Abuse Reviews, 2 (2),* 157–76.

Booker, C. (1969) *The neophiliacs: the revolution in English life in the fifties and sixties.* London: Fontana Books.

Bouchor, M. (1901). *Causerie preliminaire.* Album Mariani, vol. 6. Paris: Floury.

Canadian Government Commission of Enquiry (1971). *Interim Report of the Canadian Government Commission of Enquiry. The non-medical use of drugs.* Ottawa, ON: Health Canada.

DeSantis A.D., & Hane, A.C. (2010). 'Adderall is definitely not a drug': justifications for the illegal use of ADHD stimulants. *Substance Use Misuse, 45 (1-2),* 31–46.

Ehrenberg, A. (2009). *The weariness of the self.* Harrogate, UK: Combined Academic Publishers.

Ehrenberg, A. (2010). The 'social' brain. An epistemological chimera and a sociological fact. In: F. Ortega, & F. Vidal (Eds.), *Neurocultures. Glimpses into an expanding universe* (pp. 117–140). New York, Frankfurt, Berlin: Lang.

Fainzang, S. (2017). *Self-medication and society.* New York: Routledge.

Freud, S. (1989a). *The future of an illusion (The Standard Edition) (Complete psychological works of Sigmund Freud).* New York: Norton & Co.

Freud, S. (1989b). *Civilization and its discontents (The Standard Edition) (Complete psychological works of Sigmund Freud).* New York: Norton & Co.

Greely, H., Campbell, P., Sahakian, B., Harris, J., Kessler, R., Gazzaniga, M., & Farah, M. J. (2008). Towards responsible use of cognitive-enhancing drugs by the healthy. *Nature, 456 (1),* 702–705.

Healy, D. (2001). *Psychopharmacology & the government of the self.* https://davidhealy.org/articles/

Hollister, L.A. (1975). Drugs for emotional disorders. Current problems. *JAMA 234 (9),* 942–947.

Huba, G.J., Wingard, J.A., & Bentler, P.M. (1980). Framework for an interactive theory of drug use. In: D.J. Lettieri, M. Sayers, M., & H. Wallenstein-Pearson (Eds.), *Theories on drug abuse. Selected contemporary perspectives. NIDA Research Monograph 30* (pp. 95–101). North Beseda, MD: NIDA.

Jones, H.B., & Jones, H.C. (1977). *Sensual drugs.* Cambridge: Cambridge University Press.

Kramer, P. (1993). *Listening to Prozac.* New York: Penguin.

Lucke, J., Jensen, C., Dunn, M., Chan, G. Forlini, C., Kaye, S., Partridge,B., Farrall, M., Racine, E., & Hall, W. (2018). Non-medical prescription stimulant use to improve academic performance among Australian university students: prevalence and correlates of use. *BMC Public Health, 18 (1),* 1270.

Maher, B. (2008). Poll results: look who's doping. *Nature, 452 (1),* 674–675.

Maier, L.J., Ferris, J.A., & Winstock, A.R. (2018). Pharmacological cognitive enhancement among non-ADHD individuals-A cross-sectional study in 15 countries. *International Journal of Drug Policy, 58 (3),* 104–112.

Mariani, A. (1910). *Figures contemporaines tirees de l'Album Mariani* (douzieme volume) [Contemporary figures from the Mariani album (12th volume)]. Paris: Floury.

Neville, R. (1970). *Play power.* London: Paladin.

Nuttall, J. (1970). *Bomb culture.* London: Paladin.

Oberhaus, D. (2017). First-ever LSD microdosing study will pit the human brain against AI. *Motherboard.* https://motherboard.vice.com/en_us/article/gvzvex/first-ever-lsd-microdosing-study-will-pit-the-human-brain-against-ai.

Rabinow, P. (2003). *The essential Foucault: Selections from essential works of Foucault, 1954–1984*. Harmondworth: Penguin.

Ragan, C.I., Bard, I., & Singh I. (2012). What should we do about student use of cognitive enhancers? An analysis of current evidence. *Neuropharmacology, 64 (3)*, 588–595.

Sahakian, B., & Morein-Zamir, S. (2007). Professor's little helper. *Nature, 450 (7173)*, 1157–1159.

Schwartz, C. (2016). Generation Adderall. *NY Times Magazine*, Oct 12 2016. https://www.nytimes.com/2016/10/16/magazine/generation-adderall-addiction.html.

Springer, A. (2001). Lifestyles and drug abuse: implications for prevention. In: O.C. Sociás, & M. Cerdá (Eds.), *The 9th Annual Conference on Drug and Drug Policy, Palma 2000*. Universitat de les Illes Balears, Palma.

Springer, A. (2009). Die Moderne und die Droge [Modernity and drugs]. In: D. Sollberger, F. Müller-Spahn, E. Boehlke, & M.P. Heuser (Eds.), *Geist der Moderne* [Spirit of modernity] (pp. 128–139). Berlin: DGPA.

Springer, A. (2012). High strategies. In: M. Wouters, J. Fountain, & D.J. Korf (Eds.), *The meaning of high. Variations according to drug, set, setting and time* (pp. 23–39). Lengerich: Pabst Science Publishers.

Springer, A. (2018). The 'psychedelic renaissance' – will there be a change in control attitudes? In: G.R. Potter, J. Fountain, & D.J. Korf (Eds.), *Place, space and time in European drug use, markets and policy* (pp. 139–162). Lengerich: Pabst Science Publishers.

Stafford, P.G., & Golightly, B.H. (1967). *LSD – the problem-solving psychedelic*. New York: Award Books.

Teter, C.J., McCabe, S.E., LaGrange, K., Cranford, J.A., & Boyd, C.J. (2006). Illicit use of specific prescription stimulants among college students: prevalence, motives, and routes of administration. *Pharmacotherapy, 26 (10)*, 1501–1510.

Varga, M.D. (2012). Adderall abuse on college campuses: a comprehensive literature review. *Journal Evidence Based Social Work, 9 (3)*, 293–313.

Contributors

Frédérique Bawin
Institute for Social Drug Research
Ghent University
Belgium
frederique.bawin@ugent.be

Olga S. Cruz
ISMAI I JusGov
Portugal
ocruz@ismai.pt

Zsolt Demetrovics
Institute of Psychology
ELTE Eötvös Loránd University
Hungary
demetrovics.zsolt@ppk.elte.hu

Katalin Felvinczi
Institute of Psychology
ELTE Eötvös Loránd University
Hungary
felvinczi.katalin@ppk.elte.hu

Mélina Germes
CNRS PASSAGES
France
melina.germes@cnrs.fr

Jakub Greń
Institute of Psychiatry and Neurology (IPiN)
Poland
jgren@ipin.edu.pl

Zsuzsa Kaló
Institute of Psychology
ELTE Eötvös Loránd University
Hungary
kalo.zsuzsa@ppk.elte.hu

Luise Klaus
Goethe-Universität
Germany
klaus@em.uni-frankfurt.de

Dirk J. Korf
Bonger Institute of Criminology
University of Amsterdam
The Netherlands
d.j.korf@uva.nl

Ximene Rêgo
APDES I RECI
Portugal
ximene.rego@apdes.pt

Rafaela de Quadros Rigoni
Department of History and Art History
Utrecht University
The Netherlands
r.dequadrosrigoni@uu.nl

Marco Rossi
Dipartimento di Scienze Sociali ed Economiche (DISSE)
Università di Roma "La Sapienza"
Italy
marcosabatino.rossi@uniroma1.it

Lukas Sarvari
Centre for Drug Research
Goethe-Universität
Germany
lukas.sarvari@live.de

Thomas Friis Søgaard
Centre for Alcohol and Drug Research
Aarhus University
Denmark
tfs.crf@psy.au.dk

Alfred Springer
Medical University of Vienna
Austria
alfred.springer@meduniwien.ac.at

Julie Tieberghien
Centre for Research and Expertise in Social Innovation
VIVES University College
Belgium
julie.tieberghien@vives.be

Michelle Van Impe
Institute for International Research on Criminal Policy
Ghent University
Belgium
michelle.vanimpe@ugent.be

Bernd Werse
Centre for Drug Research
Goethe-Universität
Germany
werse@em.uni-frankfurt.de